Ground Rules for
Humanitarian
Design

READER

Ground Rules for Humanitarian Design

Edited by
**Alice Min Soo Chun
and Irene E Brisson**

WILEY

Registered office
John Wiley & Sons Ltd, The Atrium, Southern Gate, Chichester, West Sussex, PO19 8SQ, United Kingdom

For details of our global editorial offices, for customer services and for information about how to apply for permission to reuse the copyright material in this book please see our website at www.wiley.com.

ISBN 978-1-118-36159-7 (paperback)
ISBN 978-1-118-36144-3 (ebk)
ISBN 978-1-118-36143-6 (ebk)

Executive Commissioning Editor: Helen Castle
Project Editor: David Sassian
Assistant Editor: Calver Lezama

Design by Artmedia, London
Printed in Italy by Printer Trento

Front cover image: Port-au-Prince, Haiti, 2013. Rebuilt and remaining structures in informal settlements three years after the earthquake. © Damian Fitzsimmons.

To Quinn Arnold Lewis

Acknowledgements
Ground Rules for Humanitarian Design began as a discussion with students and faculty
at Columbia University and became a much larger dialogue with students and faculty at
Parsons The New School for Design. The global disasters caused by the 2010 earthquake in
Haiti, the 2012 Kamaishi earthquake and tsunami in Japan and the 2013 Typhoon Haiyan in
the Philippines had struck a cord in all of us. We could no longer stand by and watch what
was happening to the environment, we had to take action. The tides, rifts and storms that
had moved oceans and earth had also motivated in us a desire to create ways of deciphering
such a complex and multifaceted problem.

We would like to thank Brian McGrath for his mentorship and support for this book and for
proposing it on our behalf. He is dedicated to new research in urban ecosystems and is a
leader in this field. Many thanks to Cameron Sinclair for the discussion we had about the
lessons he had learned while at Architecture for Humanity. Kenneth Frampton was also a
great inspiration, and we thank him for taking the time to be interviewed. We are indebted
to the authors who contributed to this book and thank them not only for their essays but
also for the many hours of work spent writing each essay. This project has taken two years
to complete; we are very grateful to Helen Castle and Calver Lezama for their perseverance
and patience over the past two years and their commitment to this publication.

Editorial Note
With the exception of one essay (pp 142–4), this book is an anthology of texts created
specifically for this publication.

Contents

Charcoal seller in Haiti. Because of
extensive poverty and the cultural
tradition of using charcoal for
cooking, trees have been cut down
to make charcoal. The effect this has
had is extreme land degradation.
© Damian Fitzsimmons.

Introduction

Ground Rules for Humanitarian Design

Ground Rules or basic rules about what should be done in a particular situation or event[1] is predicated on the notion that there is a playing field on which team members are united in the adherence to specific principles. In the case of this book, the playing field refers to the ground on which we build and the environment in which we live. There have been a series of events that, like dots, have been connecting for centuries; these events, in hindsight, unveil the interconnectedness of the choices we make every day. These small and sometimes mundane choices, in multiplicity of billions, have affected the environmental and social context of our lives in the most catastrophic ways imaginable. From the elimination of hundreds of species of animals within the last century,[2] to the degradation of our ecosystem, to extreme hunger from poverty, to outbreaks of terrorism, we are all compromised. This book is conceived as a response to witnessing the catastrophic events in the past decade, in order to reconcile these ruptured grounds and start with design thinking[3] as a tool for levelling the playing field.

Humanitarian designers and anyone ambitious enough to effect a difference within the context of climate change, extreme poverty and ecological or political upheaval, may collectively play this field with a set of principles that are interconnected with regard to all of the above. This pioneering generation of architects and designers are participating in a global vision of a world where the design and the aggregate choices we make as individuals have the power to transform it dramatically. Design is always influenced by individual preferences. The design thinking method shares a common set of traits, namely, creativity and ambidextrous thinking,[4] which requires teamwork, empathy, curiosity and optimism. Hopefully we are professionals who believe that human dignity begins with an appreciation and inclusion of wonder and art, and take creative steps towards making things better because, however small to however vast, we can do so. Historically, the conventional ways of coping with complexity in human settlements are not satisfactory. Much of the difficulty comes about because hubris, population growth and technological advancement interact in a vicious cycle.[5] Architects and designers in developing and developed regions are, in a sense, problematising the past solutions, highlighting good design as a critical and necessary human right. They are instigating and inventing an active voice to lead better practices of conservation, mitigation and recovery.

overleaf. The hillsides of Port-au-Prince, Haiti, are a collage of shelters. The colours act as a codification for the nongovernmental organisations that built them. These plywood structures are called 'transitional' homes, although none have running water, sanitation or electricity. © Damian Fitzsimmons.

An orphaned girl reading with a SolarPuff, an inflatable solar light invented by Alice Min Soo Chun, designed to replace kerosene lanterns. Two million children die each year because of poor indoor air quality caused by kerosene lanterns. In areas of extreme poverty people spend up to 30 per cent of their income on kerosene to light their world at night.
© Damian Fitzsimmons.

Rules of Measure

The purpose of this text is to provide a survey of salient issues that will face any designer initiating work with communities in crisis. Each topic that serves as a structural section is incredibly large and broad; we hope that these parts may serve as devices for further research and reference tools by which to check one's design process. Have you considered, at minimum, each of these fields of impact within this situation? Two voices are paired in each part through essays, which are intended to elucidate disparate issues within these expansive categorisations. The issues raised and projects discussed are by no means exhaustive; rather, they barely scratch the surface and each part dovetails, contradicts and incorporates issues raised in the other parts of the text. The chapters in this publication are codified and organised to identify the primary and principal issues, which are a system of parts that should be referenced as an organic network, greater than the whole. What the contributors demonstrate is that there is a need for basic yet less linear systems that allow for creative adaptation. For instance, land and property rights are interrelated to issues of economy as well as environment. This anthology of contributed essays is specifically structured to enhance the developments that are already in place from nongovernmental organisations, such as Médicins Sans Frontière/Doctors Without Borders, to the burgeoning '*For Profit and Purpose*'[6] model that is accelerating humanitarian design movement through entrepreneurial channels.

Across socioeconomic spectrums, designers and architects take risks because of a belief in something bigger than ourselves. In Part 6: Local Materials and Local Skills, we see how the importance of shifting away from petrol-based plastics, such as polystyrene, has given birth to entrepreneurial ventures that collaborate across disciplines, inventing and investing on economic returns while resolving pressing problems. New companies such as Ecovative Design[7] are picking up momentum for this very reason. Designers are trained to understand that they have the capability to make something better, be it a policy, a structure, components made of paper, plastic bottles, grass and so on.

What Matters

Architects and designers are not only challenged but also provoked by a dehumanising environment or object — be it a plywood temporary shelter in Haiti, a cup of kerosene set on fire for light or a barren brown landscape marking hunger — to make the unimaginable come to pass. In a conversation about the themes of this book, Cameron Sinclair, cofounder of the former Architecture for Humanity, discussed the process of working for social change through design:

> cultural sustainability should be more important than environmental sustainability. If people don't feel comfortable and they don't love the places they live, they'll trash it anyway. Stick a solar panel on every one of those cookie-cutter cardboard homes and people are going to trash the environment. So it's counterintuitive to focus on a 'carbon-neutral slum'. The most perfect architect is someone who

is a secret anthropologist. Someone who has an inherent curiosity and respect for the community they work in, and a willingness to learn from them. Part of the role of the architect is not to come in with an aesthetic focal point, but actually to understand — what does beauty mean, what does space mean for that community? It's even more nuanced than critical regionalism.[8]

Sinclair reminisced about Sam Mockbee, a significant architect and activist who left a huge legacy, with Rural Studio:

Sam had a saying: "Work as if no one's listening." This means that the reason for actually doing this work is not because you want people telling you how great you are … you're doing it because the work needs to get done. The attention should always be focused on the work. When you start doing it because, "everyone thinks I'm cool because I'm helping others", it's no longer about actually helping or implementing. The rule should be about what the questions should be: "What is your objective?" Having a heart is not enough. Just because you care, it is not enough. You have to have the confidence that the skills that you can bring to the table will have a dramatic effect on the community in which you are serving.[9]

Architecture, more than any other art form, is a social art and must rest on the social and cultural base of its time and place. For those of us who design and build, we must do so with an awareness of a more socially responsive architecture. The practice of architecture not only requires participation in the profession, but also it requires civic engagement. As a social art, architecture must be made where it is, and out of what exists there. The dilemma for every architect is how to advance our profession and our community with our talents, rather than our talents being used to compromise them.[10]

Another key voice providing intellectual underpinnings for this project, through his early writings on critical regionalism to a current perspective is architectural historian, Kenneth Frampton. While discussing with him his thoughts on critical regionalism he said:

I am committed to the idea of critical regionalism. Although it is not something that I speak about much these days, I'm committed to this way of looking at the world. There is a really impressive global phenomenon taking place right now, everywhere you find exceptional creativity, people are doing sensitive work in relation to a certain kind of economy. It is this concept of an architecture of resistance you know, and the fact that you can find it all over the world in a way, is something that I still believe is the case … It's very responsive to the place in which it's in — the topography, the site, the materials of the place, the light and the climate — as opposed to being driven by fashion.[11]

Haiti, aerial view of land degradation. Owing to the lack of agriculture, the brown area to the left indicates no ecology. Firewood is used for cooking food and so the poor have cut down all the trees. This leaves the bare land prone to extremely dangerous mudslides and flash flooding. © Alice Min Soo Chun.

MASS Design Group,
Housing for Doctors, Butaro,
Burera District, Rwanda,
2012. This construction for
permanent housing has
basic amenities, such as
running water, electricity
and sanitation. Yet beauty,
wonder and design are the
principles for Ground Rules.
© Iwan Baan.

Parameters of Engagement

Today, the ambition of reducing the world's ecological and sociopolitical vulnerability, and producing a more humanitarian architecture, is driving design innovation among professionals and enlightened schools of architecture across the world. While still at college, many North American and European students are now being given the opportunity to participate directly in programmes that provide vital facilities for impoverished or disaster-stricken communities. As well as showcasing traditional knowledge and new technologies, which are leading design in a socially active direction, this text seeks to lay parameters for engagement at a time when these international initiatives remain largely ad hoc. The integration of culture, art, architecture, economy, ecology, health and education, are absolute necessities for design and architecture. In each section, essays speak on key issues surrounding humanitarian or social design, touching on the political, the social and the technical.

We do not design buildings as products optimised to serve one need, but rather we create platforms through our buildings to address the complex ecological, economic and social force facing all the underserved – most pressingly the poorest, most marginalised and most vulnerable of our population. Humanitarian design is about commonality and an endgame of resilience; regardless of race, economy or religion, we are all interconnected and must be united in the pursuit of a designed alternative promoting human dignity. Once you see what is possible, once you experience the power of it, you become not only an advocate but also an addict of good design and a member of a global design ethic. And thus we are motivated to begin, to establish Ground Rules from which to operate.

Notes

1   Merriam Webster Dictionary online, www.merriam-webster.com/dictionary/ground%20rule (accessed 10 January 2015).
2   This timeline of extinctions shows more species were made extinct in the past two centuries than there were since the Ice age, http://en.wikipedia.org/wiki/Timeline_of_extinctions (accessed 10 January 2015).
3   Design Thinking, http://en.wikipedia.org/wiki/Design_thinking (accessed 10 January 2015).
4   Rolf A Faste, 'Ambidextrous Thinking', *Innovations in Mechanical Engineering Curricula for the 1990s*, American Society of Mechanical Engineers, November 1994, p 1.
5   Willem van Vliet, *Cities in a Globalizing World: Global Report on Human Settlements 2001*, United Nations Center for Human Settlements, Earthscan Publications (London; Sterling, VA), 2001, p 27.
6   'Profit with Purpose', *The Economist*, 26 January 2013, www.economist.com/news/business/21570763-how-profit-firm-fosters-protest-profit-purpose (accessed 10 January 2015).
7   The factories are truly revolutionary, they harness the power of nature – the cleanest technology on Earth – eliminating pollution generated across the petroleum-based plastics supply chain, www.ecovativedesign.com (accessed 10 January 2015).
8   Cameron Sinclair, interview by the author, New York, New York, July 2012.
9   Ibid.
10 Sam Mockbee, Rural Studio, 1998, www.samuelmockbee.net/work/writings/the-rural-studio (accessed 10 January 2015).
11 Kenneth Frampton, interview by the author, New York, New York, September 2012.

Histories of Humanitarian Design and Aid

1

The essence of humanitarian design, which may be shifting to the label of public interest design, is long and deep in our professions, but has moved in and out of different identities, and been carried forward by proponents of varying moral impulses. In 'Notes for Definition' the authors begin to sketch out the forking and reconverging histories of the idea. What we can claim is that fundamentally, building has always focused on the provision of comfort and utility and providing for people's 'life and safety'. In some sense, all design is humanitarian design because it is expected to provide all of these things; but time and again shelter available to different populations fails to live up to the same standards of comfort and care. Humanitarian design is, unfortunately, a necessary genre of architecture that takes as its focus the marginalised, underserved, crisis-threatened people of the world, because mainstream practices and industries have failed them.

The history of humanitarian design is in some sense challenging to trace, as in various utopian or idealistic guises it tends towards an ahistorical point of view. Given our current struggles, the argument may be made that historical methods have failed to sustainably open a space for the current problem solver. As any historian – or engineer for that matter – will tell you, prior failures are the beginnings of a solution. And more radically, it is possible that prior strategies were not flawed but their implementation, context or simple lack of interest from necessary parties at past moments may have doomed them. We must understand why and where humanitarian design, by many names, has improved people's situations, harmed natural ecosystems, caused relief, conflict and so forth in order to move forward in heady and enthusiastic times.

Dilapidated
tower block.
© Imageplus/
Corbis.

Humanitarian Design
Notes for a Definition

Christian Hubert and Ioanna Theocharopoulou

Christian Hubert and Ioanna Theocharopoulou both ground and destabilise the basic definition and history of what this volume discusses at great length as 'humanitarian design'. Looking at the historical genealogies of appropriate technologies and 'good' design, as well as the contemporary discourse and emerging practices of participatory citizenship, Hubert and Theocharopoulou position humanitarian design within a broader social movement, rooted in late 19th- and 20th-century experimentation but once again emerging at the forefront of professional exploration, and argue it is important to substantively acknowledge the human component of its current manifestation.

We must elevate 'design for the greater good' beyond charity and toward a socially sustainable and economically viable model taught in design schools and executed in design firms, one that defines the ways in which we prototype, relate to clients, distribute, measure, and understand. We must be designers of empowerment and rewrite our own job descriptions. We must design with communities, rather than for clients, and rethink *what* we're designing in the first place, not just *how* we design the same old things. We must constantly find ways to do things better, through both our designs themselves and the ways in which we operate as designers.

Emily Pilloton[1]

Is there such a thing as *humanitarian design*? Can design thinking that typically only responds to crises help provide new models of more equitable and socially responsible living? To think through these questions, it is important to uncouple the phrase *humanitarian design* from too close an identification with benevolent or charitable interventions on behalf of the poorest and most vulnerable, even if those dimensions must remain a crucial part of the humanitarian project. Instead, we will focus on those features of the humanitarian impulse that extend to all humans qua human beings. If we do in fact live in the geological era of the Anthropocene, in which humans have become the dominant influence on the planet, those humane qualities and universal values must extend not only to humans as a whole, but to all living species and to the environment at large.

By exploring the outlines of a humanitarian design project, our purpose is not to promote a catchphrase or even to define a particular theory of practice. Instead, we hope to indicate some features that any effective definition of this project would require. Even in its broadest sense, design can be only one small part of the humanitarian project, but as it is currently practised, design serves primarily to promote consumption, to materialise status and to manipulate desire. The humanitarian design project must address the just allocation of wealth and resources, not only in the present but also in the future. It must make plans for rapid global urbanisation and the very real possibilities of massive dislocations of urban populations, particularly in coastal areas. It must be informed by an ethos of sustainability. Most of all, it must be broad enough to address all humanity.

We see two main paths or features, emerging as characteristics of this larger conceptual project that sees design as a humanist activity. The first requires a fresh look at the history of the idea of 'intermediate' or 'appropriate' technology, as it was articulated in the early 1970s, to create a richer background against which to view today's efforts. The second needs 'humanitarian' design to be seen within a broad movement towards participatory citizenship, which is emerging from many different quarters worldwide. In combination, these two paths can inform a concept of humanitarian design that bridges both ethics and aesthetics — a 21st-century definition of *Good Design*.

Appropriate Technology and Design for the Other 90 Per Cent

What are these machines? … various solar devices, almost all hand tools, bio-gas digesters, wind machines, greenhouses, various pedal-powered machines (including, of course, bicycles), composting toilets, and so on. The origin of these devices is largely either from less developed countries (what used to be called 'village technology') or from the youth culture. The categories are not hard and fast; hand tools are preferred over machines, but small machines are preferred over big machines, and even big machines are viewed more favorably than very large plants.

Witold Rybczynski[2]

The 'Appropriate Technology' movement emerged as a popular cause in the late 1960s and early 1970s. As the first moment when designers and other thinkers self-consciously tried to figure out ways to bridge social inequality through design, the Appropriate Technology movement is a crucial precursor to today's *humanitarian design*. We could say that humanitarian design, as we are trying to define it here, is not so much a radical departure but a re-engagement with some of the same issues that have been lost since the 1970s, with a different emphasis and new contexts.

The political events of the late 1960s acted as a trigger for seeing a link between design and society more clearly. Opposition to the Vietnam War, the student protests of 1968, and particularly the 1973 to 1974 energy crisis, were the backdrop to the emergence of an American 'counterculture' that rejected conventional society and uncritical technological 'progress'. Publications such as Rachel Carson's *Silent Spring* (Houghton Mifflin, 1962), EF Schumacher's *Small Is Beautiful* (Blond & Briggs, 1973) and Buckminster Fuller's extensive writings, were formative influences on what we now think of as early instances of environmentally conscious design; the most well-known examples of which include the first 'intentional communities', Paolo Soleri's Arcology, the 'droppers' of Drop City, Trinidad, Colorado, and Michael Reynolds's Earthships.[3]

While American counterculture did not invent appropriate technology, its 'environmental pragmatism' promoted 'tinkering' and improvising solutions to design problems. The best illustration of this approach to technology was the *Whole Earth Catalog*, published between 1968 and 1972. Its founder, Stewart Brand, 'hoped to create a service that would blend the liberal social values and technological enthusiasm of the counterculture with the emerging ecological worldview he cultivated as a Stanford University biology student'.[4] Brand provided information on emerging ideas about appropriate technologies, along with common-sense advice for those who wanted to participate in what he saw as a new environmental culture. His innovative idea to provide *access* through a new information system, the *Whole Earth Catalog*, aimed to empower individuals about alternative paths and tools to achieve them:

> By reclaiming an amateur tradition of invention and technological development and celebrating an ecological focus to technological research, the *Whole Earth Catalog* provided moral support for young optimists working to map a brighter future free from flaws of technocratic thinking but not free from technology. These appropriate technologists believed a survivable future was still a possibility if technological development could be wedded to insights emerging from ecology and environmentalism while avoiding the political entanglements of Right/Left ideologies...
>
> Andrew G Kirk[5]

Whereas the ideas of the Appropriate Technology movement were varied and diffuse, they shared an approach to technology that was low-tech, inexpensive, simple and ecologically safe. Rather than identifying with either of the two poles of 'tradition' and 'modernisation', the appropriate technology pioneers were interested in establishing an 'intermediate' zone that could use and modify existing technology in simple and inexpensive ways, in order to help human society more broadly. One of these pioneers, British economist Ernst Friedrich Schumacher (1911–1977), had spent a great deal of time in poor parts of Southeast Asia. He saw 'intermediate' technology as a step towards the alleviation of poverty in the so-called developing world. Borrowing from the Buddhist concept of the 'Right Livelihood', in a highly influential essay entitled 'Buddhist Economics', written in 1966, Schumacher argued that appropriate technology can be a third way, a better path *between* tradition and rapid modernisation. Schumacher, who had also been influenced by the writings of Mahatma Gandhi, believed that appropriate technology ought to be small- rather than large-scale, people-centric, labour intensive, environmentally sound and locally controlled.[6]

Another important thinker from the 1970s who deserves attention today is Victor Papanek (1923–1998). A Viennese-born designer, teacher and prolific author, Papanek called for design to take a radically different approach, away from the goal of aesthetically pleasing objects. Papanek's first book, *Design for the Real World: Human Ecology and Social Change*, was published in 1971. It included an Introduction by Buckminster

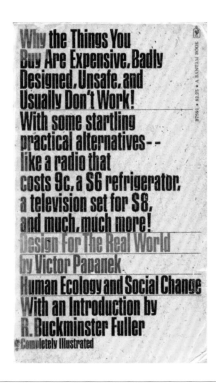

The cover of the seminal work by Victor Papanek, first published in 1971, inspired a generation of designers and activists.
© Random House LLC.

Fuller and extensive references to Fuller's work. To underscore Papanek's critique of mainstream design practice, on the cover of the first edition, in large fonts, we read that the book is about '*Why the Things You Buy Are Expensive, Badly Designed, Unsafe, and Usually Don't Work! With Some Startling Practical Alternatives – like a radio that costs 9c, a $6 refrigerator, a television set for $8, and much, much more!*'[7]

Design historian Victor Margolin notes that Papanek's book, 'came hard on the heels of the student movement of the 1960s and embodied the simultaneous rage and hope of that period'.[8] His design thinking was closely informed by local knowledge and techniques from which he actively sought to learn. In the early 1970s, Papanek suggested working closely with people in developing countries to invent and construct products using simple technology, and he called on designers to counter the growing environmental problems of his time.

Despite the ongoing allure of 'living off the grid', contemporary interests are not so concerned with extolling 'self-sufficiency' or creating a counterculture. They are more resolutely global in intent and local in implementation. New terms, such as 'leapfrogging' and 'crowdsourcing', and a new emphasis on advanced communication networks are enabling these shifts to happen. While a sense of impending crisis and an ethical discomfort in the face of unfair distribution of wealth continues to inform humanitarian design impulses, these are also coloured by a sense of possibility – that there are real possibilities for social, technological and political change.

There have been a plethora of recent initiatives, exhibitions and publications that make a case for such humanitarian design impulses. Examples include the publications by Architecture for Humanity (a United States-based charitable organisation launched in 1999 and closed in January 2015), *Design Like You Give a Damn* (2006) and *Design Like You Give a Damn II* (2012); the exhibition *Design for the Other 90%* (Cooper-Hewitt, National Design Museum, New York, 2007); Katie Wakeford's *Expanding Architecture: Design As Activism* (2008); Emily Pilloton's *Design Revolution: 100 Products that Empower People* (2009) and the exhibition *Small Scale Big Change: New Architectures of Social Engagement* (MoMA, New York, 2010). These initiatives are rooted in the history of 'social' design as already mentioned[9] but with a sidelong glance to the history of the appropriate technology pioneers from the 1970s. At the core of the projects documented in these collections is a renewed shared sense that design must be for the greater good of all human society.[10]

But human society is created through community, and this new hopeful emphasis promotes community, not only in terms of ways of life, but also through scale, means of production and materials. Examples of these community-oriented projects range from immediate responses to crisis like the earthquake emergency housing projects by Shigeru Ban from the early 1990s, using recycled paper tubes; to a variety of projects that deployed unused shipping containers to create housing for earthquake victims in Haiti in 2010; to longer-lasting design solutions that help communities in the daily struggle for existence and cover aspects or sectors, such as health and education.

Some of the most notable examples of the latter may include the Emergency Paediatric Clinic in Darfur by the firm TAMassociati (Massimo Lepore, Raul Pantaleo and Simone Sfriso) from 2011, and the ongoing work of Diébédo Francis Kéré in Gando, Burkina Faso. The Darfur clinic is built around an enormous baobab tree (*tabaldi*), adopting principles of Mediterranean and Arab architecture, such as shading the building facades from the sun, and creating a large courtyard with smaller pavilions. The building combines traditional and modern techniques and technology in new ways.[11]

Diébédo Francis Kéré was awarded the Gold Global Holcim Award in 2012 for the secondary school in Gando, Burkina Faso. Going back to Burkina Faso and working with the local community, Kéré used traditional forms that work with the local climate, using local materials and techniques. Another notable aspect of Kéré's work is his involvement with the whole community: we may think of him more as a master builder than an architect, teaching and disseminating skills to a younger generation.[12]

The Danish-based INDEX Design Awards, created to award 'design to improve life' are another forum for the support and dissemination of design solutions that help whole communities. Looking through the list of INDEX Design Award finalists since 2005, one sees some of the best socially conscious, technically advanced designs, ranging in scale from a city to a small object. Recent examples include Sanergy (2013), a model for viable sanitation infrastructure in the slums of Nairobi,[13] and Mexico City's 'Plan Verde', a 15-year strategy 'to develop new transport, water, waste, land conservation and alternative energy programmes for the city'.[14]

below: DHK Architects and Two Think
Architecture, Ahmed Baba Centre,
Timbuktu, Mali, 2009. © Iwan Baan.

overleaf: DHK Architects and Two Think
Architecture, Ahmed Baba Centre,
Timbuktu, Mali, 2009. Timbuktu's
association with 'a place at the end of the
world' is ironic considering that the city
was once the main intellectual centre of
Islam in Africa. Timbuktu is a city in Mali,
born in proximity to the Niger River, at
the intersection of 10th-century trans-
Saharan trade routes. © Iwan Baan.

above and overleaf: Peter Rich Architects. Mapungubwe
Interpretation Centre, Mapungubwe National Park,
Limpopo, South Africa, 2008–10. Mapungubwe, located
on South Africa's northern border with Botswana and
Zimbabwe, prospered between AD 1200 and 1300 by
being one of the first places to produce gold. After its
fall it remained uninhabited for over 700 years, until its
rediscovery in 1933. The society living in what today is a
UNESCO World Heritage Site, is thought to have been the
most complex in the region, implementing the first class-
based social system in southern Africa. © Iwan Baan.

At the scale of the small object, some notable projects have aimed to provide clean drinking water to areas in need, both in the so-called developing world and in regions that have experienced large-scale environmental crises. Today, appropriate technology requires not only technical simplicity, but also economic viability, best served by local production and distribution networks. These are potential points of intersection between economic and social benefits.

Design and Participatory Citizenship

> The environmental crisis is a crisis of society in the fullest sense: It signals the fact that a one-sided development of human productive powers without a commensurate change in the social relations by which we govern society spells social and ecological disaster. … At issue is the possibility of a radical transformation of society: the creation of a society of equals dedicated to social justice and environmental sustainability.
>
> John Bellamy Foster[15]

The best practices of contemporary design are based on cooperation between rich and poor, north and south, coming together to define and address problems by utilising knowledge and expertise from both educated professionals and local knowledge sources. The quality of these relationships is key.

In a fairly recent shift that gives us great hope and optimism, one can look today to areas of culture as diverse as political science, the production and consumption of food, discussions of copyright, crowdsourcing and the World Wide Web, to see common projects for the development of a global public sphere. One that is democratic in the best sense of the word, where individual freedom, open discussion, dissemination of information and consensual action are achieved both on local and global scales. There is a groundswell of optimistic forward thinking today about the potential for new forms of citizenship, unmoored from nation-states, enabled by global networks and capable of effective scalar organisation through peer production and new forms of communal action.

Optimists point to new spaces of noncommercial discourse, to nonmarket and nonproprietary production, to the global impact of environmentalism (despite some significant hemispheric divisions), to the growing interest in the 'other 90 per cent' of the global populace, and to the proliferation of political 'Springs' as evidence that new spaces of freedom are possible today. The subtitles of three important references for this discussion, Elinor Ostrom's *Governing the Commons* (1990), Yochai Benkler's *The Wealth of Networks* (2006) and Tina Rosenberg's *Join the Club* (2011), identify some of the basic issues: *The Evolution of Institutions for Collective Action, How Social Production Transforms Markets and Freedom* and *How Peer Pressure can Transform the World*.

The latent energies of these movements can be 'crowdsourced' in every sense of the word. The emerging understanding of the power of peer pressure has provided insights into recent developments of the 'citizen sector'. Tina Rosenberg's evocations of 'the social

cure', from the Comprehensive Rural Health Project (CRHP), Jamkhed, India, which trains poor rural women to provide local health care, to her descriptions of OTPOR's nonviolent resistance to Slobodan Milošević in Serbia — which served as a direct lesson for mass action in the Arabic countries of North Africa — illustrate some of the capacities of 'join the club' social movements as enabling social transformation.

An example of a successful crowdsourced project that has now grown to a remarkable organisation is the *Ushahidi* Platform. Swahili for 'testimony', *Ushahidi* began as a website mapping incidents of violence and peace efforts, based on citizens' reports submitted via the web and mobile phones, during the 2008 Kenyan elections. This platform, initially made up of volunteers, has now grown to a large team of individuals with a wide span of experience ranging from human rights work to software development. Together they form a not-for-profit technology company that develops free and open-source software for information collection, visualisation and interactive mapping.[16]

Yochai Benkler's explications of social production in the 'networked information economy' point to the power of collaborative models where the means of cultural production and communication are widely distributed instead of concentrated in a small number of corporate entities, and where cultural production takes place within a 'commons' rather than a proprietary system. The success of the 'Slow Food' movement has shown how a networked organisation that articulates its core values can function as an effective network of local organisations.

This shift has led to the rise of 'public interest design', serving the needs of the billions of people on the planet living in unsafe and unhealthy conditions. Promoting 'the emerging practice of designing for social impact', the Social Economic Environmental Design Network (SEED Network) has become a clearinghouse for community-based design projects around the globe. SEED is one of myriad efforts engaged in a public-health version of architectural practice, focused not on the wealthy of the world who can pay design fees, but on the rest of the world who cannot — and yet who need designers' services as much or more than the top one per cent.

Humanitarian Design as *Good Design*

Although the expression 'good design' is of fairly recent vintage and carries its own historical baggage, questions regarding both the aesthetic and the social values of design have been asked repeatedly, at least since the second half of the 19th century, with the rise of industrially made objects and goods. The first design reform movements originated in England, where the Industrial Revolution began as a reaction to what was deemed the poor quality of manufacturing, along with the devaluation of craft and craftsmen. Negative reactions towards the 'arts manufacturers' gained strength following *The Great Exhibition of the Works of Industry of All Nations* at the Crystal Palace, London, popularly known as *The Great Exhibition* of 1851.

A great cultural polemic swirled around the question of what ought to be considered appropriate design for the modern age, led by figures such as Henry Cole (1808–1882), Owen Jones (1809–1874) and Richard Redgrave (1804–1888). These reformers tried to create formal guidelines, not only for manufacturing but also for design education, in the hope of imbuing the nation with a sense of design principles that would in turn bolster the British economy. They founded government schools of design, published a journal and helped to form what later became the Victoria and Albert Museum.

But the critique of manufactured objects also served as a starting point for an altogether more fundamental questioning of modern industrial society and its values. The Arts and Crafts movement, founded by the British designer William Morris (1834–1896), explicitly addressed these issues, and was already underway by the 1860s. Rooted in the writings of architect August Welby Northmore Pugin (1812–1852) and art historian John Ruskin (1819–1900), the Arts and Crafts movement rejected the early reformers' more progressive approach and tried to recreate a preindustrial ethos with the emphasis on the relationship between the individual worker and the work produced. The movement advocated that good, moral design could only come from a good and moral society.

Urban industrial society did not qualify exactly. In the late 19th- and early 20th centuries, the injustices of industrial nations towards their workers were highlighted by the early documentary work of photographers Jacob Riis (1849–1914) in New York and Thomas Annan (1829–1887) in Glasgow, who showed the world the squalid living conditions of 'the other half'. These images nourished the growing movement to reform housing conditions for the working class and the poor. We might think of the efforts to reform inner-city tenement housing as the first instance of humanitarian design, at least in aspiration. Later, particularly post-First World War, and continuing through the post-Second World War period, architects and designers tried to implement methods of industrial production, applying innovative lessons in prefabrication, learned during the wars, to low-cost housing.

From the 1920s *Existenzminimum* housing projects in Germany, to attempts at devising inexpensive prefabricated homes throughout the postwar period, some of the most notable examples of modern architecture were the result of socially conscious architects striving to use design to address society's problems and crises. In the postwar American context, the notion of 'good design' was explicitly articulated via a number of important competitions and exhibitions organised by the Museum of Modern Art (MoMA), New York, literally entitled 'What is Good Design?' (1950–5). The exhibitions were organised by Edgar Kaufmann Jr, working under the very title of *Director of Good Design*.

But this postwar project had lost the critical and social dimension of reform. It served primarily to reconcile modern style with the expansive consumer culture that would produce a 'good life' domestic modernism filled with tasteful and labour-saving objects. As a recent MoMA exhibition revisiting that moment claimed, the values of 'good design' were 'promoted (and disputed) by museums, design councils and department stores'[17] These would later come to define the 'lifestyle' design project that has achieved global hegemony through branding and consumer products.

Today the 'good' in Good Design needs to be redefined. We need to broaden our concerns, perhaps drawing closer to the aspirations of early 20th-century housing reform than to the later, more commercially minded iterations of Good Design, in order to address 21st-century issues. The subjects of design can no longer be thought of as consuming individuals, responsible only for themselves, but as citizens actively shaping a good society or at least as would-be citizens, since citizenship lacks effective institutions that can scale up from local communities to global issues.

Rather than promoting an essentially hedonistic conception of individual pleasure, the shared or communal benefits of the 'good' need to be design's primary source of satisfaction. For design to be good, it must *do* good. It must address questions of justice, including environmental justice. These goals and values cannot be left to marketeers and their corporate 'messages'. Nor can one expect much from politicians, most of whom – at least in the United States – are too beholden to corporate interests, or too enamoured of pandering to their 'base' to consider the ethical politics of the 'good', especially in long-term or global considerations.

But social good is not just a desirable result or benefit, such as an increase in distributive or environmental justice, as vitally important as this might be. Instead, it is inseparable from particular forms of social activity: those that strengthen the bonds of social solidarity through cooperative work. The strengthening of social solidarity itself enacts a crucial social good at a time when individualistic consumerism and state-sanctioned forms of political activity are clearly inadequate to the tasks of social and environmental change.

In concluding our 'notes towards a definition' of humanitarian design, if new forms of Good Design are to develop, or if they are in fact already emerging, it will be through a new conjunction of social and environmental goals with cooperative social methods. The prime question for the present moment is whether the new networks of civil societies, those 'movements' that are outside the market or state spheres, and which make creative use of both new communication technologies and the strengthening of communities based on civic values, can establish a new and global public sphere, whose values are first and foremost 'humanitarian'.

Notes

1   Emily Pilloton, *Design Revolution: 100 Products That Empower People*, Metropolis Books (New York), 2009, p 10.

2   Witold Rybczynski, *Paper Heroes: Appropriate Technology: Panacea or Pipe Dream?* Penguin Books (London), 1980, reprint edition 1991, p 212. The very title of Rybczynski's book speaks to how the debate has shifted since the 1970s. Contemporary discussion is no longer about 'panacea' or failure, nor either 'modernisation' or 'tradition' or 'anti-modernisation' – all terms from the 1970s – but anticipates a new and updated spectrum of possibilities as we try to argue here.

3   Arcosanti, Arizona, a self-contained experimental town begun in 1970 by architect Paolo Soleri (1919–2013), used a concept he called 'arcology' – from 'architecture' and 'ecology' – designed to explore how urban conditions could be improved with a minimal amount of destruction caused to the Earth. For Soleri, an arcology was a hyperdense city designed to maximise human interaction; 'Drop City' in Trinidad, Colorado, was a fluid group of 14 to 20 artists, and functioned from 1965 to 1969, before it was abandoned in 1973. For an analysis of Drop City, see Bill Voyd's essay 'Drop City' in Paul Oliver's *Shelter and Society*, FA Praeger (London), 1969; Simon Sadler's 'Drop City Revisited', in the *Journal of Architectural Education*, 2006, and Felicity Scott's 'Acid Visions' in *Grey Room* no 23, spring 2008. Lastly, since the 1970s architect Michael Reynolds has been experimenting with various forms of building with mud and recycled materials, such as glass bottles, in what he calls 'Earthship Biotecture'. More recently, he has been involved

in global relief projects, helping to build housing in areas that have suffered environmental disasters, such as the Andaman Islands in India, after the 2004 tsunami, http://earthship.com/india-andaman-islands-disaster-relief (accessed 10 January 2015).

4   Andrew G Kirk, *Counterculture Green, The Whole Earth Catalog and American Environmentalism*, University Press of Kansas (Lawrence, KS) reprint edition, 2011, p 1.

5   Kirk, *Counterculture Green*, p 9.

6   Ernst Friedrich Schumacher: 'The keynote of Buddhist Economics, is simplicity and nonviolence. From an economist's point of view, the marvel of the Buddhist way of life is the utter rationality of its pattern – amazingly small means leading to extraordinarily satisfactory results … the aim should be to obtain the maximum of wellbeing with the minimum of consumption. [...] Buddhist economics is the systematic study of how to attain given ends with the minimum means.' 'Small is Beautiful', essay reprinted in Michael Allaby (ed), *Thinking Green: An Anthology of Ecological Writing*, Barrie & Jenkins (London), 1989, pp 184–5.

7   Victor Papanek, *Design for the Real World: Human Ecology and Social Change*, c 1971, Academy Chicago Publishers, 2nd revised edition, 2005. Other books by Papanek include *Nomadic Furniture: How to Build and Where to Buy Lightweight Furniture That Folds* (1973); *How Things Don't Work* (1977), both co-written with Jim Hennessey; *Design For Human Scale* (1983) and *The Green Imperative: Natural Design for the Real World* (1995).

8   Victor Margolin, 'Design for A Sustainable World', *Design Issues*, vol 14, no 2, summer 1998, pp 83–4. This is an excellent article, still extremely valuable to any thinking about 'sustainability' today.

9   See, for example, the very thoughtful and well-presented timeline of socially informed design by Kate Stohr in *Design Like You Give A Damn*, Metropolis Books (New York), 1st edition 2006.

10 In 2005 the Danish non-profit, *Index*, began handing out €100,000 cash awards to 'designs that improve life'.

11 For a full description, photographs and credits for this project, please see the publication of this project in *Domus* 949, July 2011, www.domusweb.it/en/architecture/emergency-pediatric-clinic-darfur (accessed 10 January 2015).

12 See Kéré's excellent website for a full list of projects, awards and credits, www.kerearchitecture.com (accessed 10 January 2015).

13 'Worldwide, 2.6 billion people do not have access to adequate sanitation and the resulting diseases and water pollution cause 1.7 million deaths and a loss of US $84 billion in worker productivity each year. In Kenya's slums, a staggering 8 million people lack access to adequate sanitation, and therefore INDEX Award 2013 finalist, Sanergy has developed a sustainable sanitation cycle to terminate this massive problem in Nairobi', http://designtoimprovelife.dk/sanergy (accessed 10 January 2015).

14 'Mexico City gets a huge environmental makeover: Plan Verde', INDEX Award 2013 finalist, http://designtoimprovelife.dk/plan-verde (accessed 10 January 2015).

15 John Bellamy Foster, *The Vulnerable Planet: A Short Economic History of the Environment*, Cornerstone Books (New York), 1994, reprint edition, 1999, p 148.

16 See also the 'Open Source Appropriate Technology' (OSAT) that, according to *Wikipedia*, 'refers to technologies that are designed in the same fashion as free and open-source software. These technologies must be 'appropriate technology' – meaning technology that is designed with special consideration to the environmental, ethical, cultural, social, political and economical aspects of the community it is intended for', www.appropedia.org/Open_Source_Appropriate_Technology (accessed 10 January 2015).

17 *What Was Good Design? MoMA's Message, 1944–56* (2009–11), http://moma.org/visit/calendar/exhibitions/958 (accessed 10 January 2015).

Fifty Years of the Community-Led Incremental Development
Paradigm for Urban Housing and Place-Making

John FC Turner and Patrick Wakely

This new essay from John FC Turner and Patrick Wakely is a response, almost 50 years later, to the concepts and principles of community-led incremental development, then referred to as 'progressive development', which Turner first articulated in the paper, 'Uncontrolled Urban Settlements', published by the United Nations in 1968. In this review and contemporary response, Turner reflects on the development of the informal settlement story that began at the time of his initial publication and continues today as an incredibly popular field of inquiry, both within and without academic architecture. Patrick Wakely examines the durational history of incremental housing and contributes further support to the case made for incremental development in relationship to four sites, initially developed in the 1970s and tracked through to the present day. The observation of these sites over the past 40 years supports their conclusions regarding community land trusts and suggest an alternative to the immediate analysis of the success or failure of urban settlements.

A Lima *barriada* as
seen by Turner and
visitors in 1961.
© John FC Turner.

Part 1 Rediscovering Incremental Housing Development

Background

Half a century ago *AD* published evidence that governments of rich and poor countries alike saw no value in what we now call 'incremental housing development'. During John FC Turner's years working in Peru (1957–1965) with Peruvian colleagues assisting squatters building their urban settlements, *barriadas*, he learned how difficult it was to share his enthusiasm with opinion and policy-makers.

In 1961 and 1962 Turner was asked to take influential individuals to typical *barriadas* on the desert outskirts of Lima. On the first visit with Pedro Beltrán, owner-director of *La Prensa*, the principal national newspaper, Turner remembers: 'standing together on a hillside overlooking a typical *barriada* at an early stage of squatter-building permanent houses: a classic example of informal incremental development. Beltrán was close to tears of pity for those people; I was silenced by my failure to impress him with the extraordinary capability of low-income Peruvians.' The next visitor – a British minister of state – was appalled, shocked and speechless, asking to return to the British Embassy where Ambassador Sir Berkeley Gage had suggested the distressing visit. Gage was aware of, and sympathetic to, Turner's and his Peruvian colleagues' view of the *barriadas*, shared with the codirector of the United States Peace Corps in Peru, Frank Mankiewicz, and anthropologist William Mangin. Sir Berkeley Gage wanted to see a *Sunday Times* centre-page spread on a 'bleeding heart' view of Lima's *barriadas* by James Morris, slated and corrected.

The third visit, an extended tour with Monica Pidgeon, then editor of *Architectural Design*, resulted in the special issue, *Dwelling Resources in South America*, published in August 1963. It was probably the first international publication presenting informal incremental housing development as a solution rather than a problem.[1] The *AD* publication caused turmoil in at least one Latin American faculty of architecture. It also led to the production of the controversial UNTV film, 'A Roof of My Own'.[2] The film included a reconstruction of a squatter committee organising the invasion of a site for a new *barriada*. On film, a Peruvian housing agency director clearly explained a 'sites and services' project, a successful adaptation of informal community-based incremental development as illustrated in the above-mentioned special *AD* issue. The film was followed by the *International Seminar on Development Policies and Planning in Relation to Urbanization* at the University of Pittsburgh in 1966. The working paper prepared at the Harvard-MIT Joint Center for Urban Studies for the seminar (with the essential but unacknowledged assistance of PhD candidate Rolf Goetze) was edited and published by the United Nations in 1967.[3]

The Pioneers

Some antecedents should be better known. Years before Turner's reports from Peru, middle-class misconceptions of urban squatter settlements had been challenged by Peruvian professionals, notably architect Eduardo Neira Alva, anthropologist José Matos

Mar and the British geographer John P Cole. In 1955, Neira, a senior official in the National Ministry of Public Works, set up the *Oficina de Asistencia Técnica en Arequipa* (OATA) in Arequipa, the second city of Peru. It was probably the first government initiative anywhere to assist local communities with planning and developing 'informal' urban settlements. In 1962 the *Corporación Nacional de Vivienda* demonstrated an effective form of 'sites and services' projects based on the informal, community-organised incremental housing format. Illustrated in the *AD* special issue of 1963,[4] they were simpler and more economic than those later funded by the World Bank in 1971.[5]

Turner says that through his friendship and work with anthropologists William Mangin, Eduardo Soler and Marcia Koth de Paredes, he was a messenger; the role that he insists was his contribution. Too often he is seen to be an innovator. The essential message is that *barriadas* solve more problems than they create and that 'uncontrolled urban settlement is a manifestation of normal urban growth under historically unprecedented conditions', as stated on the first page of the published version of the above-mentioned working paper. There is more than enough evidence proving that, as Dr Tony Gibson puts it in his famous nutshell: 'Local commitment and professional expertise plus government support equals towns and cities that work',[6] and that all such initiatives depend on institutional reforms is discussed in Part 3.

A Key Principle

The key principle underlying the cases made by Patrick Wakely in Part 2 are the Law of Requisite Variety applied to both Form and Function, or use. Applied to Form alone, the charitable belief that better houses make better people lingers and the lopsided focus on Form continues. The issue became clear to Turner after a game he and a Peruvian colleague devised. The games were played in the half-built home of *barriada* chairman, Manuel, his wife Maria, with another neighbour and a resident Belgian priest. Each player held a set of cards representing approximate costs of material components for the house: from the plot, all stages of home building, domestic connections to utilities and commercial and public facilities; and stages, from setting up a provisional shack to the anticipated completion of their house in a modern residential neighbourhood. Like everyone at different stages of personal, family and social life, Manuel and his family members had widely changing priorities based on or including their locations, their material dwelling standards and forms of tenure. When Manuel arrived in the relatively vast city from his provincial home village or, more likely home town, with little money or urban experience, his priority would have been for a location in a dense area of economic activity, for the cheapest form of shelter – even a bed space shared with a friend working nights or vice versa – that would give him and his friend freedom to leave at short or no notice.

This was the exact opposite of any priorities he and his family shared at the time of the game. Their highest priority would have been the security of ownership of their plot, even without the house, followed by the anticipated completion of a fully serviced modern house and a primarily residential neighbourhood anywhere within an affordable distance of their sources of livelihood.

top: Permanent squatter self-building two to five years after site occupation. © John FC Turner.

middle: A workshop fronting a completed ground-floor dwelling with a second floor for the extended family being built 10 to 15 years after site occupation. © John FC Turner.

bottom: Carabayllo, Lima, Peru in 2010 is now a fully serviced city district. A main street in the same area of Lima as above, 50 years after the original *barriada* was established. © Kathrin Golda-Pongratz.

The criteria that people really have, and demonstrate freely, to choose between a sufficient number of options at any particular time and situation in their lives proves the importance of real values, ie in the relationship between form and function or the relative importance of the basic requirements of a dwelling. These include location, shelter and tenure that it must provide to be a habitable, three-dimensional place in time – one with boundaries of use and privacy, physical and service networks providing access to the essentials of life and livelihood and minimal space at least. The great advantage of incremental development is its resilience to changing circumstances and therefore priorities, especially for those who give a high priority to the security and transferability of a home of their own.

Part 2 The Implementation of Incremental Housing Strategies[7]

The Context

The 1971 round of national population censuses revealed more than 50 per cent of city populations in many rapidly urbanising countries, lived and worked in 'self-built' informal settlements that were 'unsightly', often unhealthy and in some cases physically unsafe. But these settlements were flexible, responsive, affordable and planned and built by processes that enabled households to extend and improve their dwellings incrementally over time, as their resources allowed. However, they were usually insecure in terms of their legal status and generally underserviced, making them prone to endemic health hazards

that could impact upon all parts of the city. So governments set out to assist low-income groups who could not afford to join the regular private-sector housing market by building highly subsidised, fully completed and serviced social housing. In no rapidly growing cities in market-economy countries, however, were such programmes able to meet more than a very small proportion of the targets set for construction. Consequently, the 1970s and 1980s saw a change in approach promoted by several international aid agencies, notably the World Bank, which, building upon the observations and principles set out by John FC Turner and others (see Part 1), sought to improve the successful aspects of informal housing processes by providing appropriate legal and technical support to households' and communities' own efforts. This took two forms: 1) the environmental upgrading of existing informal settlements with safe water, sanitation, drainage, electricity and access ways – slum upgrading – and 2) providing recognised title, at affordable prices, to new plots of serviced land – sites and services (S&S) – on which low-income households could build their own dwellings.

The initial motive behind these programmes was to reduce the cost of housing both to the state and to households. The social and economic benefits of engaging the users – families and communities – in all stages of the procurement process were not well understood, neither was the time that it takes poor householders to develop finished high-quality buildings. Many governments and international agencies, fearing that they would be accused of condoning the creation of new slums, imposed stringent (and

opposite: Carabayllo, Lima, Peru. The weekend that the squatters invaded and occupied the *barriada* site. © John FC Turner.

left: A typical slum of rented rooms, originally on land squatted by self-builders in the mid- to late 1940s, photographed in 1960. They represent settlements that have little or no prospects of improvement but are still used by the otherwise homeless, including young migrants, as the only affordable accommodation accessible to unskilled workers. © John FC Turner.

unaffordable) controls on the speed and standard of construction. Many such projects were 'evaluated' only one or two years after their start and were (erroneously) judged to have failed and governments and international aid agencies, alike, abandoned such strategies. However, revisiting them a decade or two later, after they have had time to 'mature', attests to their success. Over time the social and economic benefits of engaging communities and the realistic time needed for poor households to build better quality dwellings has become clearer. This learning and a better understanding of urban poverty, and new approaches to urban planning and management provide the basis for remaking the case for incremental housing.

The Case for Incremental Housing

The case for governments to support participatory incremental urban housing strategies for low-income groups rests on a set of six interrelated arguments:

1 *The numbers case*

   The numbers case rests on the adage: 'if you can't beat them, join them'. Governments do not have the financial, technical or managerial resources to build subsidised completed dwellings for all low-income households in the rapidly growing cities of the developing world. However, every day people demonstrate their own ability to house themselves even if they cannot afford to do so legally in the formal sector. By engaging in, and improving, the production and management of people's own strategies for the development of their dwellings and neighbourhoods, a far greater number of legal, safe and healthy dwellings, affordable to low-income groups, can be procured than by conventional approaches. By switching from a 'supply approach' to a 'support approach' to housing policy in the 1980s, the Government of Sri Lanka's 'Million Houses Programme' achieved a tenfold increase in the number of low-income families reached.

2 *The financial case*

   By providing security of tenure and access to services, even poor households are able to raise significant sums through family savings and informal borrowing to invest in housing and neighbourhood development, thereby liberating unproductive wealth and sharing the cost of urban development with government. It is estimated that for every dollar of government input to the Parcelles Assainies S&S project in Dakar, Senegal, in the 1970s, US$8.2 million of private funds were subsequently invested in housing and local facilities.

3 *The urban management case*

   By recognising the most effective levels of participatory decision-making (national, municipal, community, household), and delegating authority to the most appropriate level and actor (the principle of Subsidiarity), partnerships can be built between government, the private sector, civil society and community groups, which enhance the efficiency of urban management, and the administration of urban service delivery and delegating authority accordingly. Partnerships can be built that enhance the efficiency of urban management and the administration of urban service delivery. In the citywide Favela Bairro upgrading programme in Rio de Janeiro, Brazil, in the 1990s, authority for the administration of urban services was devolved to local partnerships of residents' associations and the field offices of state and private utility companies. This improved the delivery, maintenance and management of water, sewerage and electricity at the same time as reducing the administrative overheads of meeting the changing needs and demands of the incremental settlement upgrading process.

4   *The urban development case*
Governments' engagement with incremental housing strategies provides an opportunity to regulate ongoing informal (illegal) urban development processes, ensure an adequate and relatively efficient provision of infrastructure and service delivery and the rational use of urban land. It has the ability therefore to shape the development of towns and cities in accordance with strategic priorities developed for an entire urban area, rather than just engaging in small-scale firefighting. Supported incremental housing can be a means to reduce uncontrolled, low-density urban sprawl in favour of high-density, compact and efficient development. In the context of a citywide development strategy (CDS), the Municipality of Aleppo in Syria established an Informal Settlements Development Department to integrate the 'formalisation' of existing informal settlements, which account for some 45 per cent of the city's population, and new illegal housing areas that are growing on the urban fringes, in a development policy and plan for the city as a whole.

5   *The governance case*
By engaging households and community leaders in the incremental development of their housing and neighbourhoods, a system of good governance can be created that helps ensure transparency and accountability in decision-making and the allocation of resources. The Busti Baseer Odhikar Surakha Committee (BOSC) structure, set up in Dhaka, Bangladesh, in the late 1990s by a coalition of nongovernmental organisations (NGOs), has established a citywide network of 'accountability mechanisms' to incorporate the urban poor in urban governance working with the city's Ward Commissioners, the lowest level of public administration. The BOSC structure is a hierarchy of elected committees. The ward commissioner, also elected by his/her constituents, provides the link to Dhaka City Corporation and other service providers. This interface between government and organised representative nongovernmental bodies has become widely accepted and works well in many of the city's 90 wards, reducing corruption and giving voice (and confidence) to low-income communities.

6   *The social and economic development case*

Incremental housing processes can be an important and effective catalyst to the social and economic development of poor households and communities. Organising themselves (or being organised) to engage in developing their housing and local environment inevitably brings people together in a 'common cause'. This presents an opportunity to develop and consolidate social solidarity and to introduce and support local enterprise initiatives and employment, notably in the infrastructure and house construction activities of the projects themselves. But they can also build social capital around issues that are not related to the immediate urban environment, developing wider networks and involving other groups, for example, sporting or cultural activities that specifically engage the youth and/or women. By encouraging cooperation through incremental development local communities are built and strengthened, and by creating job opportunities through the provision of training and technical supports household incomes can be increased, thereby reducing the likelihood of social conflict and anti-social behaviour — building community. In Phnom Penh, Cambodia, the nongovernmental Urban Poor Development Fund supports a growing number of community-based savings groups, largely run by women community leaders, and provides loans and grants for land acquisition and for upgrading, house building, income generation and food production.

Components of Incremental Housing Strategies

Many early S&S and upgrading projects confined their support to the provision of land and infrastructure. However, subsequent experience has shown that in order to make incremental housing strategies sustainable and 'to take them to scale' national or citywide incremental housing strategies entail new approaches to public sector support in five key areas of intervention:

1   *Land and location*

The selection of land for the incremental development of low-income housing is difficult though crucial to the success of any incremental housing policy or project. Peri-urban land has often been acquired because of its relatively low price, only to find that the cost of extending infrastructure to it renders it unaffordable to the target groups. With no provision for affordable transport links to employment centres, commerce and community facilities, a poor location was one of the keys to the unpopularity of many S&S schemes in the 1980s. The identification of land on which to develop S&S for low-income housing requires a much more rigorous analysis of its costs and benefits than merely its initial price and the cost of servicing it.

2 *Finance*

In early S&S projects the provision of finance to enable the construction process was not generally considered to be the government's responsibility. Indeed, in many slum-upgrading programmes it is still not included in the package of supports to householders. Yet one of the criticisms was the slow progress of construction, most often because households did not have the resources to build in addition to paying their contributions to the cost of land and infrastructure. However, as pointed out above, in other projects the opposite was often true: households were able to raise considerable amounts of funding independently. Therefore access to appropriate and affordable credit as part of a support package needs to be considered seriously, preferably in terms of small incremental short-term loans.

3 *Infrastructure and services*

The timing, standard and level of infrastructure and service provision is a key component of support to incremental housing initiatives. Where projects have provided infrastructure and services at too high a level, costs have proved unaffordable for low-income households and middle-income groups have bought them out. Where infrastructure and service standards have been too low, or their installation delayed, plots have remained empty, making such projects unattractive to all income groups. So a careful balance has to be struck. Returning to the principle of subsidiarity best does this. In theory decisions concerning the level of infrastructure provision can only equitably and effectively be made at the level of the community of users, provided that they fully understand the implications of the trade-offs between initial capital cost, cost in use, and the tenets of environmental health, safety and amenity. However, this may not always be practicable in situations where new communities are being formed. Community Action Planning (CAP), pioneered in Sri Lanka in the 1980s, is one of a series of techniques to engage low-income communities in establishing priorities and setting standards for infrastructure and service provision based on a thorough understanding of the costs and benefits of their decisions.

4 *Site planning and building controls and supports*

Site planning is invariably undertaken as a centrally controlled technical service, though on a micro level it has occasionally been done with the participation of the project beneficiaries. The distribution of land uses, plot sizes and access layouts will normally be determined by prevailing norms and regulations. However, incremental housing projects, which tend to be treated as 'experimental' exercises, have often been used to test and/or demonstrate the rationalisation of excessively generous planning standards, while maintaining adequate conditions of health, safety and amenity — learning-by-doing. The Sri Lanka Million Houses Programme, mentioned earlier, provides an excellent example of this.

Allowing for mixed land use, both at the outset of incremental housing projects and in their future development is an important principle that applies to all low-income settlements. The extent to which low-income groups depend on home-based industries and enterprises for their livelihoods and for their integration into the urban economy at large is becoming well understood.

Planning and building standards also tend to present problems. Unable to breakaway, either psychologically or legally, from long-established and unrealistic prescriptive planning and building codes, government officers, on occasions, have sought to impose unrealistically (and unaffordably) high standards on S&S and upgrading projects, for example, large plot sizes, mandatory standard house designs, high-cost construction materials and low densities.

5   *Community organisation and asset management*
The importance of a sense of 'ownership' of local community facilities that engenders a degree of collective responsibility for their maintenance and management by the community is now well understood. What is often less clear is the link between 'ownership' and the participation of households in all stages of the project planning process. Few of the upgrading and resettlement projects of the 1970s and 1980s engaged with people, least of all at the appraisal and planning stages of project implementation. User needs and demands for land and services were assumed by the responsible authorities with little or no consultation. In new 'open access' S&S projects where the beneficiaries are not identified until after the site-planning stage, such participation is obviously not possible, so support to community building with an emphasis on the new and developing environment should be a high priority right from the first days of occupation. The administration of the successful Dandora S&S project in Nairobi, Kenya, in the 1980s was centred on a Community Development Department especially established by the city government for the project. Over time, community-based management organisations may develop to cater for local collective needs. In Dakar, Senegal, for instance, insufficient infrastructure was installed and there was inadequate planning for the future growth of the settlement. Cultural and religious organisations that developed within the community gradually built the capacities required to deal with the area's deficits in education, healthcare, solid waste and sewage collection. But this was a slow process that, with more support in the initial stages of the project, would probably have been more effective.

In short, the capacity to support local organisations with the management and maintenance of community assets is essential right from the start of the incremental development process. In most cases this entails careful educative processes that in the long run lead to permanent local governance and management structures.

Operational Lessons Learnt and the Need to Build Capacity

As indicated at the beginning of this section, sufficient operational experience of government support to incremental housing processes has been gained over the last four decades to ensure a good understanding of the processes outlined above. It has also revealed a wide range of gaps and inadequacies, and the continuing need to build the capacity of many of the (potential) actors in a wide range of levels and fields of operation of support to incremental housing production, maintenance and management, by urban low-income households and communities.

In most countries and cities organisational and institutional capacity needs to be built with even greater urgency than the development of professional and technical skills at the level of individual human resources.

Organisational development is the process by which things get done collectively within an organisation, be it a central government ministry, a local authority department, a private sector enterprise, a nongovernmental organisation or community group.

Institutional development encompasses the legal and regulatory changes that have to be made in order to enable organisations and agencies to enhance their capacities. It embraces such issues as regulations controlling the financial management and the borrowing and trading capacity of government agencies and municipal authorities; the ability of local government to negotiate contracts and form partnerships with private enterprises and community organisations; land management and regulations; statutory building standards and other development controls and democratic legislation that allows, enables and encourages communities to take responsibility for the management of their own neighbourhoods and services. Such institutional and legal issues generally need the political and legislative authority of national government to bring about effective changes.

These pragmatic, strategic and operational issues concerning the efficiency and efficacy of public sector support to community-based incremental housing and neighbourhood development, maintenance and management raise more fundamental questions that are discussed in Part 3 of this essay.

Part 3 Challenges and Opportunities

The six cases for incremental housing development raise three challenging issues that confront all actions promoting cooperative transitions to a steady-state economy. First, *Authority*, who decides and who commits to actions, rather like players on a playing field? Second, *Rules*, who decides and referees the game, or life in society? Third, *Money*, how are goals scored or how is it used? These basic institutional issues are raised by incremental housing development or any procedures that are currently innovative, however ancient their form and tradition. These paragraphs summarise the principles reflected by the unchallengeable cases for updated incremental development described in this essay, namely, the principles of *Subsidiarity, Proscriptive Rules and Regulations* and *Interest-free Money*. The final paragraph brings all three issues together with the issue of *Land*, common to all human activities on Earth.

Ciudad Bachue, Bogotá, Colombia

Begun in 1977 by the government housing agency, Instituto de Credito Territorial (ICT), the low-rise component of the project, illustrated here, provided terraced housing of concrete post-and-beam construction with precast wall and floor. Householders could extend it by building a second floor themselves.

opposite: 1981. Owner-builders have replaced many of the prefabricated panels with conventional block and brick construction – technology familiar to local builders.
© Patrick Wakely.

top: 1979. Prefabricated core houses. Already households are assembling building materials for extensions, replacing doors and installing security grilles. © Patrick Wakely.

middle and bottom: 2008. Roof terrace and third-floor extensions are being added.
© John FC Turner (middle),
© Patrick Wakely (bottom).

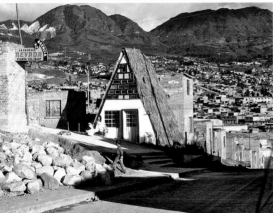

Chinagudili, Visakhapatnum, Andhra Pradesh, India

A sites and services project on the urban fringes to resettle squatters from the centre of Visakhapatnum. Only communal water points and individual pit latrines were provided for each plot.

opposite top: 1988. Informal private sector building materials suppliers arrived at the site on the first day of occupation. © Patrick Wakely.

opposite middle: 1989. Pour-flush pit latrines were supplied on each plot. Construction was still largely of temporary materials. © Patrick Wakely.

opposite bottom: 2009. Chinagudili has developed into a thriving suburb of Visakhapatnam. Photo courtesy of P Rambabu.

Las Guacamayas, Bogotá, Colombia

A sites and services project started in 1976 by the Caja de Vivienda Popular, on the city fringes but with good access to the city centre and industrial areas.

top: 1976. Core service units with one room on each plot were provided. Many households moved onto the site with second-hand building materials and components to start extending their dwellings immediately. © Patrick Wakely.

middle: 1977. Within one year several families had extended their houses to include a second floor. © Patrick Wakely.

bottom: 2009. Barrio Guacamayas has become fully urbanised, with traffic confined to the perimeter roads and pedestrian precincts in the interiors of the blocks. Houses continue to be extended and improved. Guacamayas has its own community website, http//www. barrioguacamayas.com. Photo courtesy of Maria Victoria Echeverri.

Nawagampura, Colombo, Sri Lanka

A sites and services project initiated by the National Housing Development Authority (NHDA), on an inner-city site, as part of the 1985 Sri Lanka Million Houses Programme.

below: 1985. The project was laid out as terraced housing with shared 'party walls' between each dwelling – an innovation in Sri Lanka, where people were used to detached houses on individual plots. © Patrick Wakely.

bottom: 1986. The uniform roof level was spontaneously maintained in the initial construction stages. © Patrick Wakely.

opposite: 2009. Nawagampura has become a regular part of the urban fabric of Colombo and is still being developed by its residents. Photo courtesy Kumudu Jayaratne.

Subsidiarity is the current buzzword for decision-making and control structures of Authority, whether statutory or customary, 'formal' or 'informal' or through the interdependent powers of governance, rules or finance. Discussion is often confused by the two basic meanings of 'power' in society. According to the Oxford English Dictionary, the widely neglected first meaning is *capacity*, the ability to do, while it is usually assumed that 'power', the second meaning, is *power over* others. As Václav Havel pointed out so sharply in 'The Power of the Powerless', 'power over' people does not necessarily mean a state's 'capacity to do' what it pretends.[8] Whichever way it is intended, the classic definition of 'subsidiarity' condemns frustration of people's capacities:

> It is an injustice and, at the same time a grave evil and disturbance of right order to assign to a greater and higher association what lesser and subordinate organisations can do. For every social activity ought of its very nature to furnish help to the members of the body social and never destroy and absorb them.
>
> *Encyclical Quadragesimo*, Pope Pius XI, Anno 1931[9]

This initially surprising declaration quoted by Ernst Friedrich Schumacher in *Small is Beautiful* (Blond & Briggs, 1973) can be understood paternalistically, assuming a superior level of responsibility is to delegate as well as to support responsibilities made at subsidiary levels – a top-down interpretation. It can also be understood as decision and control from the bottom up in a directly democratic system or, more likely, as a subsystem. In open societies, both top-down and bottom-up controls operate, as in incremental development of housing incorporated in regulated development. Government policies for 'informal' settlement continue to oscillate between violent evictions and laissez-faire, ignoring the incremental alternative and the principle of subsidiarity.

Proscriptive rules and regulations that limit what *may* be done are positive and liberating, as long as they allow for enough space and time for the users' constructive capacities. Prescriptive rules and regulations that specify what or how things *must* be done frustrate or pervert potential capacities and intentions, especially at personal and local community levels. Deep knowledge of the elements of development and their relationships in space and time (or scale and duration) is required for the codification of planning and building standards. Owing perhaps as much to muddled categories as to technical knowledge, the understanding of processes is inadequate to that task. The temptations of cutting Gordian Knots with standardised prescriptions can be overcome by attention to patterns providing precedents that work – the principal source of understanding and the modelling of proscriptive rules that regulations of more general laws often demand.

The abuse of money by making money from money through compound interest inflates the costs of goods and services. For Germany, it is estimated that 'the average per cent increase of the cost of essential goods and services due to compound interest is 35 per cent; 12 per cent for the provision of rubbish collection to a whopping 70 per cent for the provision of public rental housing'. No wonder that incremental home and neighbourhood builders cannot afford commercial credit or that their low per capita tax-base governments cannot afford public housing on a significant scale. The challenge for programmes promoting incremental housing and local development is the search for interest-free money of fee-based financing: a problem solved by squatting and renouncing commercial credit, and suffering discomfort, to say the least, for a decade or more. Michael Lewis and Pat Conaty report a growing number of diverse precedents for all the above modern standard investments, both in higher- and lower-income contexts (eg Brazil) in all the above, in their footnoted publication and a paper by Patrick Wakely.[10]

An issue common to all activities dependent on land tenure is the relationship between tenure and rights over use of the land and of the 'improvements' on the land. Traditionally they were always separate, whether the land was regarded as a commons, like the air we breathe and water from streams, rivers or the ground. The king may claim to usurp the land from nature (or God) for his own interests, irrespective of the community using it, stewarding it on their behalf. A likely claim perhaps but a false one unless the land is a commons ie there is extensive community participation in land management and the king respects and takes responsibility for its members.[11] That excludes of course, all who are 'enclosed' in undifferentiated tenures, usually mortgaged to levels that inflate the costs of property transfer as well as acquisition. Housing cooperatives with zero equity shares can imprison members who cannot use any equity earned from the investments they make when they need to move. So, sooner or later, they fail. Updated versions of the traditional principle I, such as Community Land Trusts (CLTs), for example, avoid the dominant rigid and inflationary property systems absurdly labelled 'public' or, ironically for many if not most in the modern world, 'private'.

Cooperative alternatives, such as CLTs, with shared cooperative ownership of housing, enable tenants to become co-owners with shares to sell as well as earning equity in their own dwelling. Additionally, this mutual home ownership approach reduces costs because the land is removed from the market to ensure perpetual affordability, and the mortgage is corporate and collective. Members thereby gain the initial reduction of capital costs (on the land and on the finance) and share the benefit of any future valuation of the property as a whole. When the comparative development is large enough to rent plots for nonresidential uses, public or commercial, the cooperators can reinvest the earnings in improvements that may also reduce charges or services taken over from former providers. Adding the great advantages of incremental development potential to that of recovering the traditional separation of land and improvement costs could eliminate the need for 'beneficiaries' and all that word implies.

Notes

1   William Mangin, 'Urbanisation Case History in Peru', *Dwelling Resources in South America, Architectural Design,* no 8, 1963, pp 365–370. See also William Mangin, 'Latin American Squatter Settlements: A Problem and a Solution', *Latin American Research Review*, vol 2, no 3, 1967, pp 65–98; and William Mangin, 'Squatter Settlements', *Scientific American*, vol 217, no 4, 1967, pp 21–30.
2   Directed and filmed by David Myers with a commentary by Alastair Cooke. Ironically, Fernando Belaúnde, then President of Peru, demanded that his congratulatory concluding remarks be cut from the film. After initial telecasting, less surprisingly, much more serious cuts were demanded by the Brazilian military junta.
3   John FC Turner, 'Uncontrolled Urban Settlement: Problems and Policies Urbanization: Development Policies and Planning', *International Social Development Review*, no 1, United Nations, New York, 1968, http://communityplanning.net/JohnTurnerArchive (accessed 10 January 2015).
4   John FC Turner, 'Minimal Government-Aided Settlement' in *Dwelling Resources in South America, AD* August 1963, http://communityplanning.net/JohnTurnerArchive (accessed 10 January 2015).
5   Turner's experience with the World Bank is not discussed in this article. It is covered by Ana María Fernández-Maldonado, 'Fifty Years of Barriadas in Lima: Revisiting Turner and De Soto' in *Habitat International*, 2010, p 24. See also Ana María Fernández-Maldonado and Jan Bredenoord, 'Progressive Housing Approaches in the Current Peruvian Policies', *Habitat International*, vol 34, no 3, 2010, pp 342–50.
6   Tony Gibson, *The Power in Our Hands: Neighbourhood Based, World Shaking,* Jon Carpenter Publishing (Charlbury), 1996; and Tony Gibson, *Streetwide Worldwide: Where People Power Begins,* Jon Carpenter Publishing (Charlbury), 2008.
7   This part draws upon, P Wakely and E Riley, *The Case for Incremental Housing*, Cities Alliance Policy Research and Working Paper Series, no 1 (Washington, DC), June 2011.
8   Václav Havel, 'The Power of the Powerless' in Jan Vladislav (ed), *Vaclav Havel: Living in Truth*, Faber and Faber (London), 1989, pp 22–122.
9   Quoted in Ernst Friedrich Schumacher, *Small is Beautiful*, Blond & Briggs (London), 1973, p 36.
10 Patrick Wakely and Elizabeth Riley, *The Case for Incremental Housing*, 2011, see note 7; Michael Lewis and Pat Conaty, *The Resilience Imperative: Cooperative Transitions to a Steady-State Economy*, New Society (Gabriola Island BC, Canada), 2012; Pat Conaty, *Co-operative Money as a Commons: Convivial Technology for Economic Democracy,* Paper prepared for the First International Social Transformation Conference, University of Split, Faculty of Economics (Split, Croatia), July 2012, pp 10–12.
11 Herman E Daly and John B Cobb Jr, *For the Common Good: Redirecting the Economy Towards Community, the Environment, and a Sustainable Future*, Green Print (London), 1990.

Land | 2

The issue of land in humanitarian design, or any design for that matter, may seem too obvious to even require a statement. It is the matter that literally underlays our buildings, agriculture, transportation networks and so forth. The composition, stability, ownership and distribution of land contribute in ways subtle and profound to the built environment.

The relationship between the ecology of the ground and property or modes of ownership is integral. In fact, we begin not with the material fact of land and soil but with a discussion of the legal issues around land tenure and property rights. While this may seem separate from the technical and ecological concerns of engineering and managing stable, sustainable treatments of the land, it hardly ever is. In case after case, the poorest, most vulnerable populations are pushed into the most fragile landscapes – on to earth that is least desired for its environmental safety, comfort or economic potential. Abandoned industrial sites or brownfields, are common scars on the landscape and are often the legacy of a toxic and polluted history. Design and management of these particular sites are crucial to land recycling and reformation in order to catalyse agricultural, ecological and community reform.

In areas of extreme poverty land degradation occurs at catastrophic rates. People resort to cutting down trees for fuel and the result is barren brown, naked hillsides. Further erosion occurs when the rainy season activates serial mudslides, resulting in rampant destruction. © Alice Min Soo Chun.

Miami Beach, Florida
USA. Perceptible and
imperceptible layers of
use and privacy rights,
formal and informal.
© Jesse M Keenan.

Real Estate and Property Rights in Humanitarian Design

Jesse M Keenan

In the practice of humanitarian architecture, designers must often expand their professional responsibilities to address the real property concerns of formal and informal, permanent and temporary land tenure. The architect working in a humanitarian or disaster context must consider property not just as structures to be built, but the very ground on which they are acting and planning.

In this new essay, Jesse M Keenan, research director at the Center for Urban Real Estate, Columbia University, brings scholarship in real estate, architecture and law into conversation, to discuss emergent practices in land tenure and property rights as utilised by humanitarian organisations. He examines the transition of humanitarian policies, from implicit imperialism to emerging corporate structures, and tracks the interrelationships between monetary flow and capital values, to design actions and build artefacts. Keenan presents basic theories of property systems and contemporary logistical and practical considerations that underpin the actions of those in reconstruction and development. Building on humanist traditions, this article highlights the capacity of designers to increase their awareness of these embedded relationships to affect meaningful change.

There is no architecture without action, no architecture without events, no architecture without program. By extension, there is no architecture without violence.

Bernard Tschumi[1]

Humanitarian design is the act of architectural design wherein the actor is principally driven to contribute expertise and capital to advance the design and construction of architecture, which is a consequence of the violence engendered by human and natural disasters. This essay examines a variety of formal and informal real property constructs, which impact design decisions for the provision of architecture in times of need. Humanitarian design is bounded by a series of emerging rules, codified as operational protocol and/or international laws, which are driving the strategic actions of the world's leading humanitarian organisations. These professional practices are framed in the context of a critical examination of the relationships between the actors, beneficiaries and the property. This essay attempts to identify generalisable concepts, which may provide the designer with some sensitivity to the timing, content and implications of his or her design decisions.

The Humanitarian Designer as Critical Actor

The imposition of a universal set of natural law constructs, or humanist orders, to rationalise a design, a programme or a master plan is perhaps one of the most dangerous facets of humanitarian design and development. Inverse to the notion of natural law, the historical application of formal real property rights, in the humanitarian context, has more often than not been a subterfuge for market commodification as an instrument of socioeconomic control. In more indirect terms, the retrospective impact of humanitarian design is often framed within a deeper set of intentions referenced to the neocolonial discourse of well-intentioned but fatally flawed actors and actions.[2] The more immediate critiques follow in the rhetorical footsteps of cultural relativists who reject the universality of western codifications of law in the name of civilised progress. To this end, the historical distinction between humanitarian intervention and outright conquest is often blurred.[3] More acutely, this relativism intersects in law and design, as noted by Sousa Santos who argued that:

> The pillar of emancipation is constituted by three logics of rationality as identified by [Max] Weber: the aesthetic-expressive rationality of the arts and literature, the cognitive-instrumental rationality of science and technology, and the moral-practical rationality of ethics and the rule of law. These three logics ... destabilise the horizon of possible expectations by expanding the possibilities of social transformation beyond a given regulatory boundary. [4]

opposite: Brasilia, Brazil. An aerial view of the National Congress building and surrounding urban context in Brasilia, planned and developed by Lúcio Costa and Oscar Niemeyer in the 1950s. © Ueslei Marcelino/ Reuters/Corbis.

left: Rio de Janeiro, Brazil. View of the Barcellos neighbourhood and the Rocinha *favela*, one of the largest in the country. © Carlos Cazalis/Corbis.

Unfortunately, rationality is not the exclusive emancipatory agent when contextualised to the *realpolitik*. Since the emergence of the humanitarian governance and third sector economics in the 20th century, the track record for the execution of a principled design rationalised by law and order has been marred by the global politics of the nation-state.[5] With the postwar era, the humanitarian movement was defined by an implicit imperialism of the developed nation-states. In the post-Cold War era, humanitarian soft power has been shaped by an emerging corporatism of nongovernmental organisations (NGOs) that utilise instruments of the rhetorical 'free' market to empower consumers and liberate governments. In terms of real estate, these instruments are defined by concepts such as: (i) titled ownership and leasehold estates; (ii) land registration systems; (iii) estate administration; (iv) property tax and valuation systems; (v) notarial execution and, most importantly, (vi) equity and mortgage debt financing. This corporatism arguably reinforces a neoliberal economic world order (ie property rights), which has done much to contribute to the subjugation and manipulation of the developing world.[6] That is not to say that all property rights are instruments of a neoliberalism. By example, the codifications of the 'Right to the City' in countries like Brazil have institutionalised a new set of property rights, which balance obligations, investments and autonomy of residents in determining the fate of – and recouping their investment in – their city of the future.[7]

The current policy of humanitarian institutions is increasingly being driven by mass media-influenced public awareness and corporate public relations strategies – both of which are antecedents to the power of the purse. As Cedric Johnson noted, '[w]ithin the

humanitarian-corporate complexes, the global poor are constructed as objects of elite benevolence and non-profit largesse, rather than as historical subjects possessing their own world views, interests, and passions'.[8] This trend has exacerbated a misalignment of interests between donors, providers and beneficiaries to the extent that providers feel the pressure for immediate results, which are often defined by the aggregate amount of money allocated to 'solve' a particular problem – a particular problem that still resonates in the public's limited attention span.[9]

This immediacy reinforces a certain radicalism of process, which is often socially disruptive and aesthetically shortsighted. In very real terms, the monotony of the architecture and the resulting left-over urban condition is a by-product of the cost-effective production of prototypes. As a consequence, the sterility of the environment reinforces an institutional paternalism, which is confused for replacing existing systems of authority and power. With a disproportionate amount of resources focused on short-term housing with short-term reporting results, the momentum of long-term reconstruction is often compromised, especially when one considers that a short-term housing unit costs as much as one-third of a permanent unit.[10] This cycle of radical short-term interventions utilising long-term funding allocations very often reinforces existing population displacement by virtue of the infusion of large amounts of money within a specific geography. This has the negative consequence of inflating property values and reinforcing speculative transactions.

Port-au-Prince, Haiti.
Housing built in the
two years following
the 2010 earthquake in
Zoranger, a rural area
north of Port-au-Prince,
for the resettlement of
displaced persons.
© Imani Dixon.

The counterpoint to the corporate humanitarian mission is the emergence of a professional ethic in design, which promotes well-intentioned, autonomous and independent action. Actors are autonomous to the extent that they are guided by their own moral framework and independent by virtue of their decentralised, organisational and logistical operations. While professional ethics have historically served a self-regulating function, the ethics of humanitarian design are oriented towards a subjective moral obligation, which is loosely defined as an objective and absolute good. The reality of disasters is not so clear cut, wherein absolutes must be mediated, and local interests have little regard for the same or similar paternalism, which has often failed in their own nation-state.[11] In an attempt to curate objectivity through design, the applications of open-source architecture, design workshops and other transparent processes are too often a screen for pre-editorialised platforms, which reinforce an ideological identity of the 'do-gooders' themselves. Likewise, transparency and participation are illusory concepts in the name of empowerment when language, culture and education are the barriers to progress.

With the recent emergence of the United Nations-led cluster system, made up of a diverse group of NGOs who collectively respond to global disasters, the ability of the international community to police its own humanitarian providers has been compromised in the name of pluralistic management models operating, more or less, as dysfunctional forums.[12] The clusters provide an operational umbrella for both individual and corporate actors. As yet, there is no peer review or horizontal governance. Legitimacy is often misapplied to those who cloak themselves in a transparency that has a variable degree of ideological import. As such, the cluster system has provided an alignment of self-perpetuating foreign interests, which have given rise to a 'Republic of NGOs' phenomenon that further disconnects personal and civic autonomy in determining priorities for redevelopment.[13] However, not all humanitarian actors work in inherent contradiction to the will of the people to rebuild. As the global disaster response system has increasingly lost the ability to self-regulate its own subjectivity (ie cluster system), the onus is on individual actors to undertake a critical examination of their own subjectivities and overt impositions of a moral order, which may or may not be aligned with the subject beneficiaries.

From one perspective, the very idea of a humanitarian designer is arguably inconsistent with the phenomenological and humanist traditions so prevalent in historical and contemporary architectural discourses; many would argue that all architects are humanitarian designers. The denotation of a humanitarian designer also raises a deeper set of questions as to whether designers should be designers, facilitators, enablers, technicians or simply observers. The reality is that humanitarian designers should, and do, operate in all of these capacities. In a perfect world, technologies should be transferred; construction and asset management practices should be facilitated; education should be enabled and behaviour and culture should be observed.

For as much as organisations are subject to unaccountable corporate behaviour, there is a new generation of culturally sensitive and ambitious designers who do have the capacity to effectuate meaningful contributions and positive change. The necessary predicate to these actions requires a certain reflexive state of awareness as to one's professional actions. Managing the complexities surrounding the construction, management, capitalisation and ownership of real estate requires a variety of skill sets, which may very well define the specialisation of a humanitarian designer in the future. In this sense, the designer is as much a manager, technician and educator as he or she is an artist or an architect.

Property Systems

Property systems are made of the processes, which memorialise as rule of law the transfer, securing, recording, financing and termination of interests, which vest in favour of the ownership and/or the use of real property. The first skill set a humanitarian designer should develop is a facility in the language of the laws and customs of real property. These laws and customs are very often 'subject to complex layers of changing [and conflicting] land tenure systems introduced during feudal, colonial and independence phases of [the] political and economic development [of the subject territories]'.[14] Separating property from its historical genesis often reveals intricate layers of customs and rights: legal and extralegal, written and oral and, public and private. Some rights are future or contingent interests, which have yet to vest. Others rights are mediated and enforced within a family or a community. Some rights relate to the physical land while others are measured in increments of time or natural life. Some rights are incidental to natural order while others are products of discrimination. The dynamic relationship of people and property is nearly infinite in its manifestations as only the notions of memory and the mathematics of ecological diversity and resource economics bind it.

With the acceleration of global urbanisation there has come greater stress on formal and informal property systems, which often work with a lack of administrative and legal synchronicity that may result in the frictions of exploitation and social disruption. In the 1970s, the percentage of the world's urban population was 35 per cent and there were an average of 74 million people a year impacted by disasters.[15] In the late 2000s, the world's urban population hit 50 per cent and accounted for an average annual impacted population of 258 million.[16] With a greater demand on humanitarian resources comes a greater responsibility to rebuild human settlements in a way that breaks the cycle of casualty. While breaking this cycle often amplifies existing displacement in the short term, it mitigates displacement in the long run.

Property systems are critical determinants in all phases of a redevelopment process. For instance, when humanitarian organisations site a refugee camp, very often they 'must first evict squatters and post-displacement occupants, some of whom may have unknowingly acquired title to [the] property on the basis of fraudulent and forged sales transactions. Others must contend with having sold or transferred title to their property under circumstances of extreme duress or coercion.'[17] The siting of camps is just one of several drivers of displacement in the face of reactionary economic and social orders. The international protocol for protecting displaced persons is referenced to a restatement of external conventions and international treaties known as the United National Principles on Housing and Property Restitution for Refugees and Displaced Persons (2006).[18] While these principles do not independently hold the rule of law, they are widely regarded as a fundamental standard for the physical and economic protection of persons who have been physically dislocated by disasters.

To reinforce these principles, the protocol has been for response organisations to sign a Memorandum of Understanding (MOU) with federal jurisdictions as early as possible in the disaster assessment phase.[19] These MOUs recite the authority of various parties to transact, as well as to waiver certain legal liabilities arising from their actions. In some cases, the MOUs have been utilised to cause the government to temporarily or permanently implement seizure of property that is critical for life-safety and redevelopment functions. MOUs with local and state governments are often advisable as the idea of 'home rule' perpetuates a parallel local system of regulation. While these MOUs have the potential to reinforce a constitutional foundation of the 'Republic of NGOs', they can be effective at preventing future conflicts between NGOs and subject jurisdictions. By example, NGOs were unable to execute any type of meaningful MOU following the 2010 earthquake in Haiti. As a result, the organisations themselves became the *précariat* as they were held hostage on month-to-month leases with rapidly inflating rents.

Contextual Orientation of Designer to Property Rights & Actions

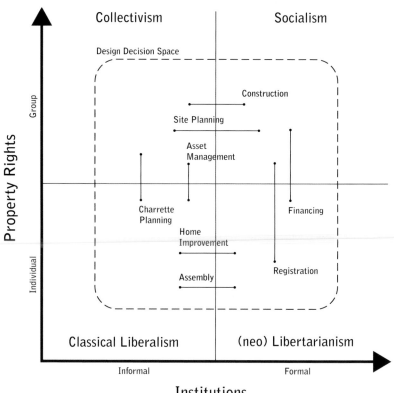

Contextual Orientation
of Designer to Property
Rights and Actions.
© Jesse M Keenan and
Mingsze Amanda Chan.

Logistics and Practical Considerations

The radicalism manifested by corporatised and unregulated response organisations, the uncertainty of property rights, and the resulting socioeconomic dislocation, all contribute to undermine the ability of collective action to promote responsible and sustainable long-term redevelopment. The friction between short-term response and long-term planning is called the 'Gap', and there is little academic consensus on the best way to fill the void.[20] There is, however, an emerging professional consensus that returning the design, planning and construction tasks back to a local level is the first step in mitigating the Gap.[21] While not widely utilised at present, the Sphere Standards promulgated by the Red Cross, among others, is increasingly gaining traction as a means of maintaining quality control in the project management of redevelopment.[22]

The emerging subfield of Community Asset Management (CAM) represents a practical model with pragmatic implications for advancing the notion of social, economic and environmental sustainability.[23] Community Asset Management offers a process that can be flexible, to account for cultural and legal variability for the engagement of stakeholders and end users. It perpetuates the idea of transferring knowledge and technology for a broader economic empowerment of a subject community. Community Asset Management advocates a perspective that engages local expertise and materials from a bottom-up approach, which works to not only maintain the long-term physical integrity of a building stock but also to advance social entrepreneurship for a new class of technicians and designers. Whether it is design, project or asset management, these processes reflect the architectural re-emergence of local incrementalism first championed in the 1960s and 1970s.[24] The distinguishing feature of the second generation of incrementalism is a more attuned notion of consumer wealth management and a greater acceptance of standardisation – albeit not standardisation that is a product of external central authority.

An additional distinction should be made between project management, the administrative process and the necessity to adjudicate property rights. Following disasters, land registration records, personal estate planning, personal identification records and judicial records are often damaged and subject to fraud. As a consequence, adjudication of property and/or estate interests can be a significant deterrent to redevelopment. Given the preponderance of international protocol to promote the compensation of displaced persons who are subject to seizure and/or discrimination, there is a necessity to also organise a system that can accurately and equitably value a variety of interests whose instrumental complexity and cash-value equivalency may be meaningless in the face of homelessness. To this end, the development of Alternative Dispute Resolution (ADR) protocol, which attaches to existing power structures, is critical for maintaining continuity of place and community.[25]

In more immediate terms, the securing of property rights is just the first step in advancing redevelopment—assuming that a given geography should be redeveloped in the first place given its underlying risk for future disasters. The implications for design and development reach every stage of the response. Disaster debris represents a source of materials and pollution. Maintaining security requires adherence to design security protocol. Property transactions require corporate, tax, procurement and audit planning. The implications and contradictions of territoriality and law are numerous in the immediate aftermath of disasters. Yet the management of risk and process in real estate development is a well-developed science, which offers yet another avenue for skill development for the emerging humanitarian design professional.

Professionalisation

The proliferation of the scale and frequency of global disasters is forcing humanitarian organisations to rethink the integrity of existing modes of response. The evolution of a body of ethics in the built environment is reinforcing an autonomous actor model that has the potential to counter the negative implications of corporatising organisational behaviour. The humanitarian designer is in a unique position to expand his or her skill sets in real estate development and regulation, and so create a hybridised professional who has the professional and ethical responsibilities to do no harm. As educators, humanitarian designers have the opportunity to empower communities for the design and management of the built environment. As advocates, humanitarian designers have the opportunity to protect ill-defined property rights that don't fit squarely within a liberalising world economy. The humanitarian designer working in this capacity has the ability to effectuate positive change in the delivery of architecture, which has implications well beyond the historical conventions of the architectural profession.

Notes

1   Bernard Tschumi, 'Violence of Architecture', *Architecture and Disjunction*, MIT Press (Cambridge, MA), 1996, pp 121–37. See generally Teresa Stoppani, 'The Architecture of the Disaster', *Space and Culture*, vol 15, no 2, 2012, pp 135–50.
2   Bruce Nussbaum, 'Is Humanitarian Design the New Imperialism?', *Fast Company*, July 2010, www.fastcodesign.com/1661859/is-humanitarian-design-the-new-imperialism (accessed 10 January 2015).
3   Bhiku Parekh, 'Rethinking Humanitarian Intervention', *International Political Science Review*, vol 18, no 1, 1997, pp 49–69. See also HLA Hart, 'Positivism and the Separation of Law and Morals', *Harvard Law Review*, vol 71, no 4, 1957, p 593.
4   Boaventura de Sousa Santos, *Toward a New Legal Common Sense*, 11, Butterworths Lexis Nexis (London), 2nd edition, 2002, p 3.
5   Claudio Caratsch, 'Humanitarian Design and Political Inference: Red Cross Work in the Post Cold War Period', *International Relations*, vol 11, no 4, 1993, pp 301–13.
6   Cedric G Johnson, 'The Urban Precariat, Neoliberalization, and the Soft Power of Humanitarian Design', *Journal of Developing Societies*, vol 27, no 3, 2011, pp 445–75.
7   Clara Irazabal, 'One Size Does Not Fit All: Land Markets and Property Rights for the Construction of the Just City', *International Journal of Urban and Regional Research*, vol 33, no 2, 2009, pp 558–63. See generally, Henri Lefebvre, *Le Droit al Ville*, Anthropos (Paris), 1968.
8   Johnson, 'The Urban Precariat', p 448.
9   International Federation of Red Cross and Red Crescent Societies (IFRC), *Review of International Federation of Red Cross and Red Crescent Societies Recovery Operations: Summary Report* (2006). See generally, Tom Pope, 'Converting Donors: How to Retain Donors from Disaster Solicitations', *Non-Profit Times*, 15 February 2006.
10   Active Learning Network for Accountability and Performance in Humanitarian Action, *Tsunami Evaluation Coalition Report*, 2005.
11   See generally, Michael N Barnett, 'International Paternalism and Humanitarian Design', *Global Constitutionalism*, vol 1, no 3, September 2012, pp 485–521.

12 J Benton Heath, *Accountability in the United Nations Humanitarian System: the Consequences of Institutional Choice in Disaster Response*, paper presented at the American Society of International Law (ASIL) Research Forum, October 2012, p 21.

13 Madeline Kristoff and Liz Panarelli, Haiti: *A Republic of NGOs?* United States Institute of Peace Brief, April 2010.

14 Shaun Williams, 'Getting Back Home: Impact on Property Rights of the Indian Ocean Earthquake-Tsunami 2004', Oxfam International (Oxford), 2005, p 10.

15 Christian Aid, *Don't Be Scared, Be Prepared: How Disaster Preparedness Can Save Lives and Money* (London), 2005; United Nations Population Division, Department of Economic and Social Affairs, *World Urbanization Prospects: The 2009 Revision*, 2009.

16 Ibid.

17 Andrew Solomon, *Forced Displacement and Housing, Land, and Property Ownership Challenges in Post-Conflict and Reconstruction*, International Network to Promote the Rule of Law (INPROL) Consolidated Response (09-003), 5 March 2009.

18 Aka the 'Pinheiro Principles', are in support of the right to housing and property restitution as a core remedy to displacement.

19 United National Human Settlements Programme, *Land and Natural Disasters: Guidance for Practitioners*, 2010, p 84. See Protection and Early Recovery Clusters, *Humanitarian Coordinator and Resident Coordinator Checklist of Housing Land and Property Rights and Broader Land Issue*, 2009.

20 Tony Lloyd-Jones, *Mind the Gap! Post-Disaster Reconstruction and the Transition from Humanitarian Relief*, Report of the Royal Institute of Chartered Surveyors (RICS), June 2006, pp 13–15.

21 Ibid, p 16.

22 The Sphere Project, *Humanitarian Charter and Minimum Standards in Humanitarian Response*, The Sphere Project (Geneva, Switzerland), 2011.

23 The Max Lock Center, School of Architecture and the Built Environment, University of Westminster, *The Rough Guide to Community Asset Management*, 2005.

24 See generally, John FC Turner, *Housing By People: Towards Autonomy in Building Environments*, Pantheon Books, (New York, NY), 1977.

25 Best practices in ADR include a lowering of the evidentiary standards, accelerated procedural timelines and alternative definitions for class standing; see note 17.

Remediating Ecocide

Alice Min Soo Chun

Particularly in the context of humanitarian architecture, we are in
pursuit of radically ecological and natural methods of engaging with the
environment. Owing to current and historical trauma caused by industry and
petrol pollution, the land across continents has degraded to exponential
levels. Landscape has often been conceptualised as a natural environment
existing prior to human intervention. In this essay, the utilisation of
natural systems for the reform of brownfield and contaminated land
is demonstrated by Latz + Partner's land reform project. Latz designs
a project undertaken in a landscape that is in every way a man-made
environment. Design takes advantage of existing topographies, including
structures, and acts to remediate environmental damage to create an
oasis of public activated domains. Land reform itself requires its own set
of Ground Rules.

The environment has long been a metric for the ecological trauma that has pervaded
regions taken over by large corporations mining for oil. Industrial waste is a common
offender creating environmental distress. Nathanail and Bardos's 2004 book on land
contamination highlights numerous incidents that have captured the media's attention
internationally. This is best epitomised by the Minamata Disaster in Japan. Over 3,000
inhabitants in the village of Minamata suffered mercury poisoning due to the disposal of
petrochemical waste from plastics production off the coast of western Japan between
1932 and 1968.[1] Nathanial and Bardos also highlight how the perception of industrial
contamination has evolved from that of a few isolated catastrophes to far-reaching
infrastructural difficulties caused by the presence of long-term industrial waste processes.
These sites are now in an apparent state of degradation and disaster, perpetuating a
decline of entire districts and communities. Research shows that there are approximately
400,000–600,000 brownfield sites in the United States alone.[2]

Latz + Partner, Landscape Park,
Duisburg Nord, Ruhr Valley,
Germany, 1990–2002, Cowper
Square with Blast Furnaces
and Cowper Stoves. Industrial
ruins, scrap or debris are not at
all ugly and useless. The basic
structures, when possible, can
become elements in a landscape.
© Christina Panick.

On the southernmost edge of Nigeria, there exists one of the most amazingly rich and diverse ecosystems, which has also been the site of oil production for over 40 years. At the core of this delta region is Bayelsa State. Henry Seriake Dickson, the governor of the state and founding secretary of the Green Movement in Nigeria describes how it is, 'one of the "richest" and amongst the three largest wetlands in the world. Its treasures include the rain and mangrove (*Angala*) forests that it is home to, over 450 kilometres of coastline, and the rare and exotic species that are part of its unique biodiversity, including the Niger Delta red colobus and the pygmy hippopotamus.'[3] Bayelsa State encompasses a system of rivers and waterways flowing through forest reserves. This fragile ecosystem has been continuously exposed to haemorrhaging oil from petroleum and gas companies. Dickson cites how Nigeria's National Oil Spill Detection and Response Agency (NOSDRA) has recorded in Bayelsa State alone over 804 oil spills in a two-year period, making an average of over two spills every day. In May 2010 a report in the British newspaper, the *Guardian*, referred to a 2006 survey that calculated up to 1.5 million tons of oil – 50 times the earlier record pollution unleashed in the Exxon Valdez tanker disaster in Alaska – was spilled in the Niger Delta over the past half century. The same report observed that, 'more oil is spilled from the delta … every year than has been lost in the Gulf of Mexico [from] the explosion that wrecked BP's Deepwater Horizon rig.'[4]

This ecocide – or widespread destruction of the natural environment through man-made pollution – is demanding increasingly global land and water remediation strategies. More and more ecologically sensitive and responsive methods are exemplifying success in brownfield and contaminated land reformation.

Land reform and redevelopment works on multiple levels. If existing infrastructure can be used to cleanse contamination through the application of natural systems, green fields can be left in their natural state. In this way, repurposed brownfield sites may lead the way in sustainable planning. This strategy will thwart sprawl, reduce carbon emissions and encourage reinvestment in adversely affected communities. Designing with land and water, allowing the rich harmony of disparate natural elements, must be the new paradigm for land remediation. Landscape architects Anneliese and Peter Latz of Latz + Partner in Germany have made the issue of design a critical element of land reformation. The practice counters ecocide by using natural local materials and systems in their designs. In her essay 'Regenerative Landscapes: Remediating Places', Anneliese Latz describes the aesthetic demands on ecological design:

> The project, Landscape Park, Duisburg Nord: a Metamorphosis
> [O]ne of Latz + Partner's biggest tasks of the last fifteen years has been the redevelopment of the former Thyssen steelworks in Duisburg. This transformation of 568 acres (230 hectares) of industrial contaminated wasteland into a new urban landscape has had a strong economic and social impact on the local neighbourhoods in the immediate vicinity.[5]

Duisburg is located in the Ruhr region of Germany, one of the largest coal-mining and steel-manufacturing centres in 19th-century Europe. The design strategy for land reclamation in the city could ultimately transcend cultures, continents and scale, and be applied to brownfield sites in Africa or the remediation of poisoned ecosystems in Japan. Land and water design strategies provide rich opportunities to integrate less wasteful models of basic infrastructure and so create new public spaces with a social function and purpose. Such opportunities enable reciprocity between human wellbeing and a strategy for ecosystem services.

The Landscape Park retains structures that symbolise the site's industrial heritage as a former steel plant. These include a blast furnace and storage bunker. Latz + Partner took advantage of these emblems in their design by transforming them into iconic landmarks, engaging visitors in a collective history of the area. These elements provide the current structural overlay for the park, visually linking the park's spaces. The visibility of the elevated 'railway park', for instance, which is formed out of old raised railway beds, footbridges and promenades, helps to orientate visitors. Transforming the open wastewater channel of the 'Old Emscher', a tributary of the Rhine, into a clear water canal with bridges and footpaths created a lower lying 'water park'. These 'parks within a park' give coherence to the Landscape Park as a whole. The railway lines make up a system of vital arteries that extend outwards into the infrastructure of the surrounding city. The railway bridges articulate a unique and logical relationship of pathways across the site. These pathways eventually meet at the massive form of the 'rail harp', a series of railway tracks set like the strings of a harp, originally used for the distribution of goods. The harp's enormity can be experienced from the pathways and from the vantage point of the blast furnace observation platform.[6]

Water management is a common challenge in brownfield remediation. Since there was no natural water remaining on the Duisburg site, the higher areas of land had high levels of pollution that required addressing. The 'Old Emscher' tributary had carried untreated sewage across the entire park from east to west. As a first step towards cleansing the site, all sewage was transferred underground in a sealed clay channel. The former open sewer system of collecting wastewater became part of a new clean water system, to avoid contact with the polluted land. Collected rainwater travels in overhead pipes and new rivulets, which allows the water to oxygenate before finally falling into the former cooling basins. Aquatic life thrives in the clean water and water lilies and irises help to maintain and support the new water biotopes. The existing settling tanks once held tons of arsenic mud but this was cleared and now the tanks serve as a clean water reservoir. The 'old gasometer', a former gas tank, was filled with water and transformed into the world's largest indoor diving centre.

This strategy for 'water paths' allows visitors to be entertained by the sound and movement of the water as it oxygenates through the watercourses. Water is moved around the site by a water pump at the mill tower in the former sintering plant. The water pump's incredible 52-foot (16-metre) blades use wind power to drive the pump, moving the water to a series of waterfalls that douse various locations at the site. Water strategies are designed to be an open architectural element in the process of cleansing and maintaining the natural ecology of the park. The park is founded on an inherent respect for our natural environment, and the aim is to create a design solution that fully tackles the devastation caused by industrial pollution in a demonstration of positive and far-reaching problem solving.[7]

A recurring difficulty for land remediation schemes is the provision of a connected network of rainwater management, which is separate from wastewater. The biggest challenge is the implementation of rainwater harvesting because usually it is not incorporated in government water policies. Rainwater harvesting is an umbrella term that covers a plethora of strategies for collecting and storing rainwater either in soil, in containers or natural or synthetic dams, allowing for a more sustainable environment in times of drought. In many cases water management is based on renewable water, which is surface and ground water, with little consideration for rainwater. Rainwater is taken as a 'free for all' commodity with little or no design integration. The increased pressure for available water in many regions of the world has drained water resources drastically, reducing the availability of water for downstream users and the ecosystems they inhabit. In some places it has been sufficient to trigger water conflicts. For a sustainable use of water resources, it remains critical that rainwater harvesting is considered as vital a water source as ground and surface water.[8]

This brings critical questions into focus: Does rainwater harvesting offer increased health and welfare benefits to users and their ecosystems? Could an increase in rainfall harvesting be used innovatively and integrated into infrastructures at both small and large scales? What if harvesting rain could create synergies to nurture and sustain the growth of natural ecosystems?

As demonstrated by the design strategies implemented at Duisburg Nord, the task of dealing with environmental pollution has become an opportunity to create a multilayered section of past debris and new levels of urban metabolism. Technology, chemistry and ingenuity fill the gap left by industrial pollution, creating an ecologically literate, resourceful and spatially enchanting urban space.

Latz + Partner solved problems by developing strategies for remediating pollution in the park with water, movement and air. First, by disposing of contaminated demolition waste and building new strata. For example, the roof gardens on the bunker site not only cover but also filter any toxic material that is buried deep below the surface. A simple, natural mixture of lime and slag is used to encourage the immobilisation of heavy metals. In the former blast furnace, gas is allowed to slowly emit over many generations, reducing contamination over time. The contamination levels are low and still allow for activities such as walking and cycling in the immediate vicinity. Less contaminated demolition waste was reused as filler for plant underlays. The planting was specifically chosen for its resilience and ability to flourish in any soil substrate. Bricks and concrete were recycled for new construction work and steel was upcycled for walkways and stairs.

above: Latz + Partner, Landscape Park, Duisburg Nord, Ruhr Valley, Germany, 1990–2002, Footbridge, Overhead Railway and Gardens in the Former Storage Bunkers. A new elevated walk follows the former overhead railway and crosses large areas of the park. It allows views into the former storage bunkers, which were gradually developed into gardens. © Michael Latz.

overleaf: Latz + Partner, Landscape Park, Duisburg Nord, Ruhr Valley, Germany, 1990–2002, the new 'Old Emscher'. An open wastewater canal, the Old Emscher, used to carry untreated sewage to the Rhine. For the new clean-water system, the profile of the old construction was used to avoid contact with the polluted ground all around. The wastewater is now carried within an underground main. © Michael Latz.

above: Latz + Partner, Landscape Park, Duisburg
Nord, Ruhr Valley, Germany, 1990–2002, Former
Cooling Basins. Rainwater gets collected and led
through partly open rivulets and the existing
overhead pipe system to the new canal. On its way
it passes the former cooling basins, which became
new biotopes. © Michael Latz.

opposite: Latz + Partner, Landscape Park, Duisburg
Nord, Ruhr Valley, Germany, 1990–2002, Wind
Wheel on top of the Former Mill Tower. For an
oxygenation system, water is pumped from the
canal through an Archimedean screw, operated by
wind power. The water falls from several points
after having made its way through the gardens;
here, buried beneath the 'roof gardens' is polluted
demolition waste. © Michael Latz.

Located at the core of the blast furnace is the Piazza Metallica, which symbolises the transformation of the steel plant into a public space. Forty-nine cast-iron plates have been rejuvenated from a life of lining casting moulds and are positioned in the centre of this majestic piazza. As the weather reacts with the iron ore, new layers of erosion and depth occur on the surface of the plates, marking the passing of time. The surface displays a new landscape of erosion that reveals the promise of its new 'post-industrial' surroundings. Compared to building new constructions, this resourcefulness with leftover materials saved time and money. The decision to reuse existing weathered materials was a conscious design choice, which poetically evokes history and memory. Reimagining these materials created a harmony between the landscape design and the endeavour of ecological resilience.[9]

This socially sensitive municipal programme is proving to be an effective model for transforming formerly polluted landscapes into thriving public communal spaces. Design education is in a unique position to create a socially driven, culturally sensitive and ecologically resilient metabolism. The future of remediation for ecocide requires a number of relationships between academia, communities and governments, to ultimately heal the disrupted bodies of land, water and air. Here a series of terms have been outlined, inspired by the 10 principles for informal cities drawn up by the landscape architect and educator Christian Werthmann.[10] These are vital for a sustainable future, but not limited to these systems. The terms should be used to 'cross-pollinate', to fully transform the environment from states of ecocide to states of thriving eco-literacies.

above: Latz + Partner, Landscape Park, Duisburg Nord, Ruhr Valley, Germany, 1990–2002, Piazza Metallica. The symbol of the transformation is the 'Piazza Metallica'. The plates had lined casting moulds. Cleaned of ashes and of casting sediments, these cast-iron plates revealed their subtle patterns. In the future, they will show an image of rust and erosion. © Michael Latz.

overleaf: Latz + Partner, Landscape Park, Duisburg Nord, Ruhr Valley, Germany, 1990–2002, Sintering Park. Recycling is another form of transformation: the soil under this flowering meadow, which lies like a carpet in front of the ruin of the sintering plant, is a product of demolition. © Michael Latz.

1 Beauty: Every area of land, water and air has its own aesthetic, linked to history, culture and individual sensibilities. Designers especially must understand this and situate, project and appropriate in this context. The aesthetic posture of an intervention is an indispensable tool for empowering communities on a multitude of scales, from an individual to the face of a nation.

2 Holistic Systems: Transdiciplinary in nature, this approach demands the integration of many disciplines and government where no single discipline is dominant. Education, government, health, land, housing and economics are critically linked to the long-term success of thriving communities. This term requires democratic dialogue between communities, politicians, planners and designers. The development of new infrastructures in formal and nonformal cities necessitates simultaneity of processes at all levels whether local, regional or global.

3 Multifunctionality: Hybridised systems and design opportunities have to combine programmes not typically placed together, but ultimately make the most sense due to scale, materials and usage. For instance, sports fields or roofing systems that also serve for rainwater catchment, or walls that are also sewage treatment plants.

4 Water is the Key Infrastructure: Rainwater harvesting and management is pivotal to the future of health and safety in urban and rural areas. This will have a profound impact on the composition of all urban and rural ecologies and will be especially critical to areas suffering the ravages of industrial mining, waste management and extreme poverty.

5 Parallel Metrics: Ecology becomes economy and vice versa. The economy of formal and nonformal cities is inextricably linked to agricultural health. There are opportunities to reinvent ecologically beneficial infrastructures, to generate new jobs and provide services for everyone. People, water, material, energy and waste, should be considered at many scales; the parallel metrics, between health and economy, and the good health of children is the metric for a good healthy economy. The strength of education means strength in culture and history and so on.

The environment in which we live and thrive has a rich and vital heritage that deserves the attention of our watchful stewardship through innovative and ecologically sensitive interventions. Human interdependence on natural ecosystems requires a smart integration of biological systems, accommodating a catalogue of biodiversity. This understanding of the mutual reliance of human and natural systems is on the increase and we are seeing more local actions responding to local challenges, taking advantage of readily available materials and combining to have a positive global effect. What this demonstrates is the ability of communities to restore our environment at a grass-roots level to its fertile origins, having a restorative impact on the constellation of biodiversity that is our inheritance.

Notes

1   C Paul Nathanail and R Paul Bardos, *Reclamation of Contaminated Land*, Wiley (Chichester), 2004. See also 'Analysing Remediation Of Contaminated Land In Nigeria Environmental Sciences', (November 2013), www.ukessays.com/essays/environmental-sciences/analysing-remediation-of-contaminated-land-in-nigeria-environmental-sciences-essay.php?cref=1 (accessed 10 January 2015).

2   John Joseph Parker, *Global Initiatives, Brownfield Redevelopment, LSRPs, Green Buildings, Solar Power and Emissions Controls*, 8 November 2013, http://commercemagnj.com/global-initiatives-brownfield-redevelopment-lsrps-green-buildings-solar-power-and-emissions-controls/#sthash.xAUJQwM3.dpuf (accessed 10 January 2015).

3   Henry Seriake Dickson,'Voicing out from Bayelsa's Brown Fields, Mangroves and Seas', 5 June 2014, www.thisdaylive.com/articles/voicing-out-from-bayelsas-brown-fields-mangroves-and-seas/180227 (accessed 10 January 2015).

4   John Vidal, 'Shell faces payouts in Nigerian oil spill case', 20 June 2014, www.theguardian.com/environment/2014/jun/20/shell-faces-payouts-nigerian-oil-spill-case (accessed 10 January 2015).

5   Anneliese Latz of Latz + Partner, 'Regenerative Landscapes–Remediating Places', L Tilder and B Blostein, *Design Ecologies: Essays on the Nature of Design*, Princeton Architectural Press (New York), p 190.

6   Ibid, pp 192–4.

7   Ibid, p 195.

8   *Rainwater Harvesting: A Lifeline For Human Well-Being*, United Nations Environment Programme and Stockholm Environment Institute, 2009.

9   Anneliese Latz of Latz + Partner, Regenerative Landscapes–Remediating Places, p 195.

10   Christian Werthmann, 'Dirty Work: Landscape and Infrastructure in Nonformal Cities', Cynthia E Smith, *Design with the Other 90%: Cities*, Smithsonian, Cooper-Hewitt National Design Museum, (New York), 2011, pp 89–93. These five terms that I have redefined were inspired by Werthmann's 10 principles for informal cities; in redefining the principles into systems, my hope is to clarify the most critical areas of what is vital for remediating land, water and air.

Crisis in Health and Culture 3

As with most topics we are examining in relationship in this text, there are a number of varying issues that arise with regards to this broad field, many of which are temporal. Much humanitarian design work is undertaken in immediate response to natural disasters or human conflict, which have caused severe and urgent injuries in the affected population. Building responses to health crises must be streamlined and efficient to facilitate emergency response teams attempting to provide medical care in the fastest manner possible. The design criteria in such situations have certain commonalities with long-term medical provisions, for example, structures must be safe and sanitary ready, allowing for segregation of infectious diseases and so forth. However, long-term health care facilities must expand their functionality in order to provide efficient/cost-effective maintenance, be culturally appropriate for the community they serve and the subcommunity that staffs it. Public health, which one would think is all health, but in fact specifies health concerns of whole populations versus acute medical care, tends towards the long-term and broad issues of culture and economics. Crisis and health are inextricably bound up with culture and, we would argue, impact and shape cultures in such a way that a culture post-crisis is a new place.

Detroit, Michigan USA. Community members examine the rubble on the site of the former First Unitarian Church, which was destroyed in a suspicious fire in the summer of 2014. Preservationists, the Unitarian Universalist congregation and community members gathered for a memorial of yet another historic structure lost in the face of external development. © Irene E Brisson.

Crisis Architecture
Conflict, Cultures of Displacement and Crisis-Forms

J Yolande Daniels

This essay examines and classifies the ways architecture responds to a crisis. As a result, it operates within territories that are at the limits of architecture. The scale, sites explored and determining factors of the crises vary. Examining sites of building production and destruction requires an analysis that goes beyond form to uncover determinants, such as value and location. Characteristics of underlying forces that shape the crisis under study differ, but include natural resources, geography, land rights, zoning, shifting national borders and alliances, international law, citizenship rights, economic determinants, sociocultural differences, and struggles for economic power. The work provides a framework for understanding the forces that produce and maintain four critical structures: marginal, temporary, illegal/informal and post-conflict.

Conflict and Crisis Culture

The early 21st century has witnessed system-wide transformations and volatility across multiple levels: environmental, economic, technological and sociopolitical. This volatility surfaces serially in crises. As warnings or outcomes of conflict that foreshadow catastrophe, crises are typically viewed as departures from normal conditions. However, as the distance between cataclysmic global events has appeared to compress, cultural perspectives have reluctantly shifted to view continual occurrences of ecological, political and economic crises as adverse norms. While a state of continual crisis arguably existed on the global event scale prior to 24-hour media access, recognition of the criticality of multi-scalar interconnections between ecologies, nations and individuals indicates a paradigm shift.

The current public perception of crisis itself as a paradigm has been shaped by catastrophic events related to global climate change, and global political events, such as the decolonisation of Africa, the Israeli Palestinian conflict, the fall of communism in the Soviet Union and China, the Arab spring uprising and the attack on the World Trade Center towers in New York.

Despite their international style, the towers were implicated as specific cultural and political products of the West. The literal and symbolic destruction of the towers as specific cultural and political products of the West exposed a depth of crises ranging from building safety and security to national identity. At the time of the attack in 2001, the two towers, at 110 storeys each, ranked second and third as the tallest buildings in the United States behind the Willis/Sears tower. Although the contest to build the world's tallest buildings had already shifted to Asia in the late 1990s, the fall of the towers coincided with a shift towards Middle Eastern dominance in the market to build the tallest building as a symbol of global pre-eminence in the 21st century.[1]

Constructed environments are comprised of interconnected and layered political, spatial and social organisational systems that exhibit system properties, at multiple scales, and also tend towards diversity and self-organisation. Depending on the scale of the organisational systems of nations, cities and citizens, or, of global, national and urban regions, the dynamics of natural and man-made economies affect the construction and distribution of space and physical forms.[2]

The understanding of systems discretely through analyses that isolate and segregate has shaped attitudes towards the control of natural and man-made environments. Nation-states, derived from concepts of stable and geographically rooted homelands, foster control-oriented closed system approaches to nation making, urbanism and architecture. As a result, a contradictory conflict between the borderless (capital, travel, communication) and the bordered (labour, migration, economic disparity) is an accepted aspect of globalisation.[3]

The necessary fixity of nations and cities is drawn into crisis when borders are jeopardised. Owing to ice melting in Greenland and the Antarctic, rising seawater levels in the Pacific islands and the Arctic have resulted in shrinking landmasses, thereby drawing to extinction the way of life, homeland and identity of the Pacific Island and Inuit communities facing displacement.[4]

Conflict and Crisis-Forms

Crisis architecture maps the forms and spatial relationships produced by crisis-driven displacement through the relationships between physical territories and social value. Territorialisation occurs across levels and scales of economic, social, cultural and political conflicts; geographic location and natural resources; regional and national borders; international and local law and citizenship rights; property and land rights; zoning laws and development plans; population density and access to housing, infrastructure and services and so on.

Crisis-forms often exhibit overlapping features, such as marginal positioning, temporary status, economic instability and reliance on informal economies, impending illegality and the threat of conflict to erupt in violence. Whether economic, sociocultural or political, the origins, scale and determining factors of crises vary between internal or external territories at the local or global scale and produce differential effects.

Crisis-forms contain relations of time and space. Defined by distance, marginality is a crisis of hierarchically differentiated and territorialised space; temporality is a crisis of indeterminacy that is enacted over time; the informal is defined by territorial crises of economics, law and policy. Suspended in time, post-traumatic sites (such as the World Trade Center) are fixed within the relationship between a destructive event and consolatory constructions.

Crisis-forms are defined by crises in occupancy status that often result in displacement and dispossession, including appropriated settlements created by those economically shut out of the real estate market: institutional shelters for the homeless, immigrants, refugees and war internment. Displacement occurs in relation to identity, power, value and physical space.

Defined by cycles of deconstruction and reconstruction, crisis-forms that result from conflict-related violence are either complete if recycled into the general economy, or incomplete if displaced outside the general economy. In addition to being spatially displaced, incomplete crisis-forms prohibit occupancy and exist as uninhabitable territories.

Marginal Spaces of Displacement

Spatial displacement puts into question the subject and object in space, the privilege of critical distance, narratives of control and safety and the role of space and architecture as agents. At spatial margins, status is fixed within structural relationships and measured as 'other' relative to a dominant group or centre. States of marginality interrupt the privileged economy of the formal, physical and fixed. Marginalised people often occupy spaces of little to no value.

On the outskirts of Dublin, marginalised Irish 'travellers' occupied the Dunsink landfill where they lived in caravans without access to electricity, water or plumbing and fostered a recycling economy from illegal dumping. The 200-acre (81-hectare) Dunsink landfill had been the site of the Irish Power Plant since the 1990s. As plans arose to cap and develop the landfill in the early 2000s, the criminalisation of the travellers' occupancy on the site was a step towards the remediation of Dunsink, which furthered their marginalisation and displacement. In this example, transitory marginal spaces and the degradation of land values can be 'flipped' to yield profits without affecting the underlying structures of disparity.[5]

Class and ethnic conflicts are exhibited in occupancy and land rights struggles occurring at both local and global levels. While political borders are generally reinforced by physical margins, marginal and temporary territories transcend visible spaces of conflict to involve the mapping of displacement and exchange onto perceived-to-be stable relations of nations and cultures.

Social and political crises have spatial effects. The work of Eyal Weizman in Jerusalem and Palestinian settlements in Israel, reveals how social marginalisation in the spaces of the displaced is reinforced by physical isolation employing geography and infrastructure (especially walls).[6] Marginal occupancies occur outside the normative market; the politics of locality and the intertwined nature of identity and place are revealed through them. Although apart, marginal spaces are integral to formal economies.

States of 'temporariness' induced by occupancy crises measure time distinctly from temporality, in that identity and place and time are implicated. Although addressed as temporary conditions, displacement, migration and marginality call for a revised politics of locality based upon flexible localised approaches indexed to the built environment.

Social crises and divisions have the tendency to become 'naturalised' in a roster of marginalised identities represented in the 'homeless' or the 'refugee,' or marginalised places, such as the ghetto or slum that, while calling attention to class, identity and territorial conflicts, simultaneously mask underlying conditions. Naturalised states of being obscure the crises of place and localisation.

Mexico City, Mexico.
Stefan Ruiz ©2003.

Appropriated Crisis-Forms and Economic Displacement

Appropriated crisis-forms are a general response to the shortfalls of government actions to address economic displacement. While the United Nations Human Rights Council (UNHRC) monitors and services populations displaced by violent conflict globally, those displaced by economic crises and rendered homeless are not monitored by a central international agency. Instead their numbers are documented by various national, governmental and independent organisations that track commerce and trade. In the United States, although 'homelessness' increased with the economic downturn and shrinking of social services in the 1980s, the Department of Housing and Urban Development only began to monitor and address 'homelessness' on a national scale in 2007.[7]

Although 'street people' are prevalent in images of the homeless, most of the economically displaced are invisible. Underlying the spatial crises of homelessness are the economic and social crises of poverty and disempowerment. All human beings require sheltering from the environment to survive. In this context, homelessness, is not only a crisis of occupancy status; it is a crisis of human rights. In the United States, only New York City has enacted legislation to secure the homeless have a right to (emergency) shelter and a right to register to vote.[8]

Institutionalised spaces of displacement, whether conflict-related or economic-based, operate under similar constructs to temporarily shelter and centrally organise basic and limited services and supplies. Within existing urban environments, the homeless occupy and appropriate public spaces and land owned by the public trust and rely on the potential of peripheral existing infrastructure for shelter or services.

In Japan, the economic downturn that began in the 1990s and spiked again after the tsunami and Fukushima reactor incidents in 2011, resulted in an increase in the aged homeless population. The increase from 58.8 per cent in 2003 to 73.5 per cent in 2012 reflects not only larger numbers of elderly in the general population, but also the physical and economic vulnerability of the elderly poor and working class during periods of economic downturn.[9]

Self-Organised, Mass-Appropriated Crisis-Forms

Mass-appropriated urban settlements produced in response to crises rival governmentally authorised developments in scale and scope and can be as large as townships or cities. Although occupants risk the raising of settlements without compensation because they are illegal, for the economically displaced in countries such as Africa, Brazil, East Asia, Southeast Asia, Latin America, Turkey and others, the appropriation and settlement of unoccupied space in squats, shantytowns, slums, *barriadas*, *basti*, *favelas*, *gecekondu* and so on, is an alternative to the lack of opportunities within market-driven economies and, to limited or undesirable, institutionally organised alternatives.[10]

In the discourse surrounding mass-appropriated urban settlements, the logic of formal and informal economies remedies the derogatory associations of 'squatters' with criminality and the deflection of minority/majority discourse to address underlying conflicts

Food Distribution Centre, Lukole A,
Ngara, Tanzania, 2000. One of the food
distribution centres at the Lukole Refugee
camp. The refugees were from Burundi and
Rwanda. Stefan Ruiz ©2000.

of power that are a result of disjunctions between dominant and subordinate interests that impact economic, social, and by extension, spatial interactions and systems.[11]

The organisational and spatial specifics of economic displacement distinguish the squatter from the homeless. While squatter settlements are the dominant image of the poverty in Brazil, cities like Rio de Janeiro also have large numbers of homeless individuals and families on the streets. Economic displacement results in both small- and large-scale property appropriations. In contrast to the homeless on the street or in shelters in urban areas, squatters consist of individuals and families who organise as groups to acquire land and construct dwelling spaces quickly, without the proper permissions.

Mass-appropriated urban settlements are isolated spaces of displacement that are integral to the formal economy. Occupants of mass-appropriated urban settlements rely on informal and formal networks to fill gaps in services, alleviate economic and civil deprivations, and provide protection from crime.[12] Regionally specific, cultures of economic displacement produce settlements that are commonly characterised in dense living conditions of tiny intertwining lots, poorly constructed labyrinthine buildings, narrow streets with poor access, and makeshift infrastructure that is often illegally accessed from city utilities.

The geography of 'informal' settlements often heightens the need for structuring balance between human settlement, urbanisation and the environment. While residents are without a legal right to the land or property on which they build, the land is available because it is vacant, abandoned, undervalued, undeveloped or considered wasteland. In Rio de Janeiro, many of the approximately 500 *favelas* have been constructed on steep mountainsides once considered undevelopable. Tenuous geography coupled with the use of inadequate materials and substandard construction make the structures within many settlements hazardous and prone to collapse, as in the earthquakes in India in 2001, and in Turkey in 1999. Flood-plains in the United States and the earthquake-prone mountain regions of Turkey that are populated by the poor, are indicators of the social and geospatial politics of unbuildable sites globally and exemplify the relationship between poverty, geographic location and environmental risk.[13]

In mass-appropriated urban settlements in Brazil and India, governments have begun to reconsider the urban poor as de facto city builders. Favela-Bairro, was an urban upgrading project structured to transition 'slums to neighbourhoods' by integrating existing *favelas* into the urban fabric through de-densification, upgrading existing structures, and the provision of alternative low-cost housing along with investments in infrastructure, social services, land legalisation and limits on future land invasion.[14]

Rocinha, the largest and most developed *favela* in Brazil, is located on a mountainside to the south of Rio de Janeiro that affords ocean views. A tourist industry evolved there in the late 1990s supplying tours, bed-and-breakfast or homestay apartment rentals for travellers seeking inexpensive accommodation or exotic cultural exchanges. During the 2014 World Cup, *favelas* offered accommodation to tourists priced out of the standard hotel economy.[15]

Evident in both the concept of *favelisation* as a (positive or negative) contagion and in remediation projects that aim to bring the settlements into the formal economy, the appropriations of the traditionally disempowered have significance as models containing formal and procedural alternatives that emphasise the value of integration with the environment. The challenge in acknowledging such models, however, is to not overlook the severe economic disparities that give rise to them.

Temporary Crisis-Forms and Conflict Displacement

Temporary crisis-forms are the dominant response to conflict displacement. When boundary eruptions and transgressions result in the loss of a homeland, temporary occupancies become, for many, an unfortunate way of life. For 'refugees', the 'stateless' and some 'migrants', spaces of displacement are defined by conflict, transit and resettlement. Refugee resettlement typically occurs in camps centralised with the intention to provide basic services and basic infrastructure (food, clean water, shelter, sanitation and health care). Although refugees and the stateless may occupy urban areas, they often find refuge in peripheral border regions. Temporary approaches to shelter have left camps susceptible to a lack of services, faulty infrastructure and the increased incidence of disease. Spaces of displacement for those not yet granted asylum or refugee status, in addition to being spatially isolated, have even less permanence.[16]

Since the Second World War, the scale of displacement due to conflict has escalated globally in number and complexity, yielding an increase of war and refugee camps.[17] These 'temporary' sites of conflict displacement often become permanent. Despite improvised infrastructure, refugee settlements serviced by informal economies to provide increased access to goods and services have grown over time to resemble towns and cities. The scale and durability of many refugee camps has led to campaigns against 'refugee warehousing'.[18] Originally designed for 90,000, the refugee camp outside Dadaab, Kenya, one of the world's oldest and largest, houses over 332,000 primarily Somalian occupants.[19]

Cultures of displacement are at odds with the fixity of homelands. In eras defined by dissolving boundaries, dislocation and migration, the idea of the homeland that embodies the stability of a fixed identity of a people rooted to a specific geography and narrative of origin is very potent. While the 'right to return' is a concept specific to the Palestinian refugee crisis, the idea of a return that is dependent upon conceptions of a homeland is central for refugees and migrants.[20]

In some camps, generations of residents have existed without a formal economy awaiting the right to return to their homeland. The oldest refugee camps have housed Palestinians since the formation of the state of Israel in 1947 and the War of 1948. Founded in Bethlehem in 1949, Deheishe refugee camp has 13,000 residents. In Deheishe and camps of long duration, the United Nations Human Rights Council (UNHRC) has had to consider how to renovate the camps.[21]

Complete and Incomplete Crisis-Forms

Spatial displacement due to violence results in post-traumatic sites. Post-traumatic sites reveal the drama of conflict-related violence at the national scale through narratives of violence and loss. These narratives assist the amelioration of traumatised sites in the recuperative production of complete or incomplete crisis-forms. As consolatory constructions, crisis-forms may be complete and transcend catastrophes or remain incomplete, suspended between tragic events and competing narratives. In contrast to the states of occupancy discussed previously, conflict displacement that occurs in response to a catastrophic event yet prohibits the conditions for occupancy, results in unoccupied territories and incomplete crisis-forms. Complete and incomplete crisis-forms present a constructive and a deconstructive alternative.

Complete crisis-forms repair through replacement and override violent narratives of loss in new narratives and structures. The rebuilding and modernisation after the catastrophic fires of Chicago in 1871 confirmed the city's position as the premiere American city and the precursor of American industrial architecture at the beginning of the 20th century. Likewise, the reconstruction and rebuilding after fires in 1904 in Alesund, Norway, resulted in a reservoir of Art Nouveau architecture that has distinguished the city. As a replacement structure for the twin towers, One World Trade Center, as artefact, both erases and commemorates the tragedy and existence of the previous twin towers. As a complete structure, the artefact eclipses the event as it becomes more distant.

Incomplete crisis-forms are reflected in the built environment in strategies of memorialisation and abandonment that reconcile or heighten traumatic, national or global events, through a refusal to realise the potential profit of a developable site. Trauma has rendered the site nondevelopable. Sites of destruction, sites that remain under-siege and sites of reconstruction, as examples of incomplete crisis-forms, remain marginal, indeterminate and temporarily dislocated. Incomplete crisis-forms harbour non-occupiable territories. As a replacement structure, One World Trade Center is the symbol of American power amidst the escalation and shift in economies in the Eastern Hemisphere as evidenced by 'mega-tall' buildings.

Conflict borders that operate on a national scale: the green line in Jerusalem, the Korean Demilitarised Zone (DMZ), the former Berlin wall, the former green line in Beirut and others, memorialise crises and division in spatial demarcations of prohibition that are controlled and enforced through voided non-occupiable space.

Monuments and memorials are incomplete crisis-forms that embody and reproduce national narratives in the public imagination through the strategic production or restoration of artefacts and occupancy of territory. As commemoratory representations of state power, memorialised reconciliations of loss simultaneously idealise, reproduce and erase traumatising events and concretise narratives of blood and land. Memorialised conflict sites, such as the bomb sites reformed as parks and memorial museums in Japan at Hiroshima (the Peace Memorial Museum) and Nagasaki (the Atomic Bomb Museum), or, in the United States, at the New York City World Trade Center site (the 9/11 Memorial Museum), represent the collision of narratives of displacement and crisis brought to violent ends and narratives of 'homeland'.

Conclusion

The systemic inability of nation-states to address political, economic and environmental conflicts prior to crisis has produced cultures of displacement, resulted in ecologies of migration and elicited multiple states of homelessness. Contests for territory and resources that gave rise to 20th century world wars continue to shape the 21st century in ecologies of migration. They are factors contributing to the economic and political volatility that affects local and global regions. Whether voluntary or forced, they contribute to displacement and migration. Frequent and prolonged volatility due to economic and violent conflicts has produced cultures of displacement that counter stable narratives of a homeland as a locus of a people.

The examples presented as appropriated, mass-appropriated and temporary crisis-forms correspond to states of occupancy and displacement. These forms are, as outlined, crisis determined. Crisis-forms are 'temporary' when permanent, 'marginal' though integral, 'informal' or illegal, yet necessary. The required spatial forms and structures must address alternate forms of occupancy by transcending the conditions of economic and conflict displacement.

Notes

1 By 2020, the 20 tallest buildings in the world will include only one building in the United States, One World Trade Center. See 'The Tallest 20 in 2020: Entering the Era of the Megatall', Council on Tall Buildings and Urban Habitat (CTBUH), www.ctbuh.org (accessed 10 January 2015).

2 Hans Liljenstrom and Uno Svedin (eds), *Micro Meso Macro: Addressing Complex Systems Coupling*, World Scientific Publishing (Singapore), 2005, p 2.

3 Jan Nederveen Pieterse, *Globalisation or Empire?* Routledge (New York), 2004, p 86.

4 The World Bank, *Convenient Solutions to an Inconvenient Truth: Ecosystem-Based Approaches to Climate Change, Environment and Development*, The International Bank for Reconstruction and Development/The World Bank (Washington, DC), 2010, p 19.

5 Maurya Wickstrom, *Performance in the Blockades of Neoliberalism: Thinking the Political Anew*, Palgrave MacMillan (Houndmills, Basingstoke, Hampshire), 2012, pp 140–5.

6 Eyal Weizman, *Hollow Land: Israel's Architecture of Occupation*, Verso (London), 2007.

7 US Department of Housing and Urban Development (HUD), Office of Community Planning and Development, 2010 Annual Homeless Assessment Report to Congress, US Department of Housing and Urban Development (HUD), (Washington, DC), 2011.

8 In *Callahan v Carey*, it was ruled that the homeless have a right to emergency shelter in New York, and, in *Pitts v Black*, 1984, it was ruled that the homeless (even if residing in shelters or on the streets) be permitted to register to vote in New York. See *Callahan v Carey*, No 79-42582, Supreme Court New York County, 5 December 1979, International Network for Economic, Social and Cultural Rights, ESCR-net, and *Pitts v Black*, 608 F Supp 696, US District Court for the Southern District of New York, 9 October 1984, JUSTIA US Law, www.lawjustia.com (accessed 10 January 2015).

9 Ida Torres, 'Japan's New Problem: An Ageing Homeless Population', the *Japan Daily Press*, 1 March 2013, www.japandailypress.com (accessed 10 January 2015).

10 This is a sampling of the regional terms applied to appropriated settlements or shantytowns. See 'Shanty Town', Wikipedia, Wikimedia Foundation, en.wikipedia.org (accessed 10 January 2015).

11 Michel S Laguerre, 'The Informal Arena of Inter-Ethnic Relations', *The Informal City*, St Martin's Press (New York), 1994, pp 139–61.

12 Ibid.

13 Saleh Saeed, DEC 50TH Anniversary: Earthquake In Turkey 1966, Disasters Emergency Committee (DEC), 19 August 2013, www.dec.org.uk (accessed 10 January 2015).

14 'Case Examples: Favela-Bairro Project, Brazil', in *Upgrading Urban Communities: A Resource Framework*, The World Bank Group, 1999, www.worldbank.org (accessed 10 January 2015).

15 Eric Weiner, 'Slum Visits: Tourism or Voyeurism?' the *New York Times*, 8 March 2008. See also, Simon Romero, 'Now Taking World Cup Bookings, Rio's Slums', the *New York Times*, 21 December 2013, www.nytimes.com (accessed 10 January 2015).

16 For refugee and stateless population estimates, see Global Appeal, Office of United Nations High Commissioner for Refugees (UNHCR), 2015. For internally displaced population estimates, see Jeremy Lennard (ed) *Global Overview: People Internally Displaced by Conflict and Violence, Internal Displacement Monitoring Centre (IDMC)*, Norwegian Refugee Council (Geneva), May 2014, www.internal-displacement.org (accessed 10 January 2015).

17 History of the UNHCR, UNHCR News, Office of United Nations High Commissioner for Refugees (UNHCR), www.unhcr.org (accessed 10 January 2015).

18 Refugee Warehousing, USCRI Reports, US Committee for Refugees and Immigrants (USCRI), www.refugees.org (accessed 10 January 2015).

19 Global Report, Office of United Nations High Commissioner for Refugees (UNHCR), 2013, www.unhcr.org (accessed 10 January 2015).

20 David Morley and Kevin Robbins, 'No Place Like Heimat: Images of Home(land) in European Culture,' in *Becoming National: A Reader*, (ed) Geoff Eley and Ronald G Suny, UP (New York; Oxford), 1996, p 474.

21 Global Report, UNHCR, 2013.

Emergency Medical Structures

Sabrina Plum

In both emergency and long-term development situations, the provision of health care in adequate facilities is critical to sustainable communities. Drawing on her experience with Médecins Sans Frontières and architectural studies, Sabrina Plum provides a broad overview of how one medical humanitarian organisation operates in an emergency, and which emergency medical structures have been the most successful. Despite recent interest in design for humanitarian contexts, there has been a dearth of literature specifically focusing on emergency medical structures. Dialogue around emergency structures generally addresses shelter, and dialogue around medical structures typically addresses permanent construction. As medical structures require a high level of functionality and adherence to the required programme, and an emergency response dictates the need for rapid installation and operationality, we are presented with a highly specific design problem, and it is essential to understand the successes and challenges that have been experienced in the field.

Generally speaking, large-scale humanitarian emergencies are often the result of one or more of the following: armed conflict or widespread violence, epidemics and natural disasters. There are exceptions to this statement, but we will use this definition for the purposes of this essay. These crises are often followed by large-scale population displacement, which can potentially have devastating consequences on the health of those affected. Urgent solutions are needed, but as every context has its own challenges there is no one-size-fits-all solution. Therefore, this essay is not meant to be prescriptive, rather it provides the reader with a background framework from which to begin thinking about this design problem.

In the scope of this essay, the extensive experience of Médecins Sans Frontières/ Doctors Without Borders (MSF) in establishing and operating from emergency medical structures will be looked at as a case study. A number of other international aid organisations, such as the International Committee of the Red Cross and Merlin require medical interventions in similar crisis zones and utilise similar techniques and criteria. The structures discussed here are not unique to MSF but are reliable, available options that are used by many humanitarian actors, including NGOs, governments and United Nations agencies.

With an operating budget of nearly €900 million and 34,000 staff working globally,[1] MSF is one of the largest medical humanitarian organisations in the world. Founded in 1971, the organisation has over 40 years experience working in the world's crisis zones. At present, its activities range from the 'traditional' emergency medical interventions that it is well known for, to longer-term projects, including the treatment of HIV/AIDS and tuberculosis. Much of MSF's expertise has been developed through the organisation's work in camps for the displaced,[2] but these lessons learned have been applied to other contexts as its work has evolved.

When responding to a humanitarian emergency, the primary goal of a medical intervention is to reduce excess mortality and morbidity.[3] Interventions are defined following a rapid assessment of the medical needs of the target population and activities are adjusted as the needs evolve. An appropriate health structure is essential to a successful operation, as it aims to provide a minimum level of functionality, hygiene, security and visibility.

When intervening in an emergency, one generally has two options for establishing medical care structures. The first is to start activities in an existing structure if a sound structure is identified and can be used for medical activities, and the second is to establish activities in an independent structure.

Establishing Activities in an Existing Structure

The benefits of this option are typically: immediately operational as there is nothing to be assembled or built, and structural integrity as a permanent building is resistant to the elements and can provide some level of physical security. There is also the potential benefit that the building will already have water, electricity and waste management systems in place. If the existing structure were a health facility, ideally it would be designed for medical activities, and though this can be helpful, in some cases the structure could be maladapted to the specific activities planned for the intervention. Another challenge related to the permanent nature of a structure is that it is inflexible and might not be easily adapted to evolving needs. For example, additional space might be needed if there is a large influx of patients, or specific structural adjustments might be necessary if medical activities are added.

In addition to the structural considerations of setting up in an existing facility, there are also potential benefits and challenges related to ownership and management of the structure. This is especially relevant when intervening in an armed conflict where perception by the civilian population and parties to the conflict is directly related to security. This was exemplified in 2007 when the MSF operational centre in Paris[4] returned to Somalia after withdrawing a decade earlier following the assassination of one of its staff.[5]

Somalia had been plagued by insecurity and armed conflict since the collapse of its central government in 1991,[6] and was characterised by a complex security context with diverse and numerous warring parties. Médecins Sans Frontières returned during an escalation in the conflict between Al Shabaab — the radical military splinter group of the Islamic Courts Union — and the internationally backed Transitional Federal Government (TFG).[7] The objective was to establish a project in Mogadishu, as there were immense needs in the capital as a result of the conflict. The decision was made to identify an existing structure to help facilitate the negotiations to launch the project.[8]

A hospital in the northwest suburb of Dayniile was identified; it was in good condition and far enough from the front line for people to feel secure accessing it. It was managed, however, by a local sub-clan chief, who had links to more than one of the warring parties.[9] After a series of negotiations and the explanation that MSF's mandate was to provide accessible medical care for everyone, the local chief agreed to withdraw from the hospital. It was in his interest, and that of the opposing party, to allow MSF to work there.[10] This first obstacle theoretically overcome, the team found that as the context evolved, the location of the structure resulted in other challenges of perception and security. By 2010, the Islamist opposition had gained control of the area, and there were some political actors who viewed MSF as the 'opposition's war surgeons'.[11] The health structure and its site were inextricably linked to the political and security context, and consequently, played a significant role in the operations. There is no easy solution to a situation like this, and the risks and benefits are evaluated on an ongoing basis.

Establishing Activities in an Independent Structure

In cases where an appropriate existing structure cannot be found or is not desirable, for example, in contexts where the majority of infrastructure has been destroyed or is insecure, an independent solution can be the best option. This is particularly relevant in post-earthquake settings, where damaged buildings that are still standing could be at risk of collapse in the aftershocks. Depending on the urgency of the affected population's medical needs and the estimated duration of the intervention, MSF will use temporary installations, semipermanent structures or a combination of both.[12] These interventions can be complementary to one another, and MSF often employs a temporary, urgent fix before a semipermanent structure is built.

Temporary Structures

Despite innovations and progress in the development of temporary structures, comparatively speaking, the tent remains the most well-adapted short-term emergency option. As each context has its own set of critical considerations, a highly flexible structure is needed, but rapid installation and set-up are essential. The tent continues to be the most reliable option because: it is lightweight and transportable, easy to assemble, modifiable, and provides a minimum standard for most medical activities. Médecins Sans Frontières has a variety of tents it uses in emergency situations, but only the multipurpose tent and the Modular Field Hospital (MFH)[13] will be discussed here. The 484-square-feet (45-square-metre) multipurpose tent is the most widely used temporary structure that MSF deploys,[14] and the MFH has proven a great added value in interventions that have specific hygiene needs, such as surgery.[15] Both have been developed in collaboration with the manufacturer, according to the specific needs of MSF, and are re-evaluated and improved on a regular basis.

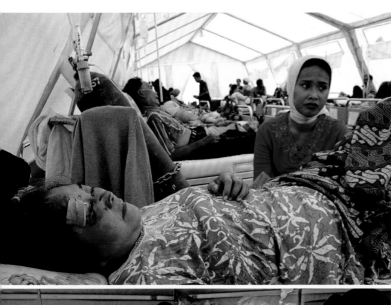

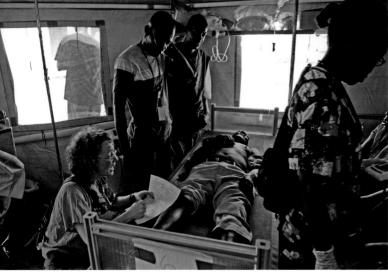

top: Simeulue Island, Indonesia, March 2005. Interior of
a multipurpose tent serving as a temporary hospital for
injured Indonesians following an earthquake in the town of
Sinabang. © Tarmizy Harva (Rights Managed – Corbis).

above: Port-au-Prince, Haiti, February 2010. Interior of
a multipurpose tent with additional features of screen
openings and framed walls. This was a temporary medical
tent operated by the International Medical Corps outside
the Port-au-Prince General Hospital. © Peter Turnley
(Rights Managed – Corbis).

right: Bir Ayyad, Libya, 2011. A medical worker prepares an emergency medical reception point in an abandoned cafe near a checkpoint. © Anis Mili (Rights Managed – Corbis).

below: Buranga, Rwanda, October 1994. Dome-shaped temporary structures mark the location of the AmeriCares clinic. © Rick D'Elia (Rights Managed – Corbis).

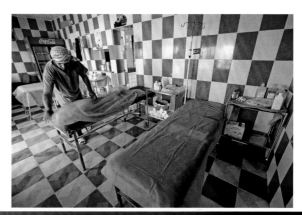

Multipurpose Tent

At only 430 pounds (195 kilograms), the multipurpose tent is easy to transport and can be assembled in 30 minutes with a team of six people.[16] It is wind resistant, waterproof, rot proof and is designed for frequent set-up with a minimum life span of one year of continuous use in a tropical climate. It is modular in nature and can be connected to create larger interior spaces as needed. There are additional options available to improve ease of use and flexibility – most notably, shade netting, interior partitions and a fitted ground sheet (which has replaced the use of plastic sheeting).

As the name indicates, it is not strictly employed for medical activities, but modifications have been made to make it more amenable for this purpose. The interior space can accommodate up to 10 field hospital beds and the PVC-coated groundsheet facilitates hygiene maintenance.

Though the multipurpose tent is well suited to certain medical interventions, such as cholera treatment, vaccination and outpatient consultation, it does not provide the level of functionality and hygiene needed for more complex interventions, such as surgery and hospitalisation of burns victims. For these types of interventions MSF has developed and used the Modular Field Hospital (MFH).

Port-au-Prince, Haiti, 2010. Treatment for cholera requires particular attention to easily cleaned set-ups to maintain hygienic environments. Here a man is being treated for cholera in Port-au-Prince at a Samaritan's Purse clinic. © Julie Dermansky (Rights Managed – Corbis).

Modular Field Hospital[17]

Following the tsunami response of late 2004 in Banda Aceh, Indonesia, MSF conducted an analysis of the different medical structures being used by the various international nongovernmental organisations (NGOs) and military actors. The objective was to find a mobile unit that could be adapted to MSF's more complex medical activities — specifically surgery — and an inflatable tent in use by the Singaporean military was identified. MSF contacted the manufacturer and a similar unit adapted to MSF's specifications was developed into what is known today as the Modular Field Hospital (MFH).

The MFH is particularly well adapted to medical needs that require a sterile environment, specifically: surgery, recovery, intensive care, hospitalisation for post-operative internal fixation patients and patients with burns that cover a large surface area. It is equipped with an interior shell that can be completely closed, and can be cleaned easily with disinfection products.[18] It has the capacity to be connected to autonomous sources of electricity and water, and is adapted to accommodate proper waste management. Médecins Sans Frontières has developed supporting kits that are deployed with the MFH not only to facilitate the installation of these systems, but also to ensure that the proper medical equipment necessary to start activities is available at installation.[19] The MFH is outfitted for climate control, although this has proven to be a challenge in practice.

The MFH was deployed in six emergency contexts from its development in 2005 until 2010, in addition to being used in three nonemergency projects. Half were in response to earthquakes (Pakistan 2005, Indonesia 2006, Haiti 2010) and half were in response to armed conflict (Yemen 2008, Occupied Palestinian Territories 2009, Sri Lanka 2009). Each emergency intervention had different objectives and constraints, so the MFH was adapted accordingly, with the number of tents ranging from one to nine (the complete hospital).

The full nine-tent set-up was used once in Pakistan following the earthquake of 2005, and again nearly five years later when an earthquake of magnitude 7.0 struck the city of Port-au-Prince, Haiti, in January 2010.[20] The existing MSF health structures were either partially or fully destroyed, along with over 50 hospitals and health centres, the presidential palace, the Parliament, the courts, and most of the ministry and public administration.[21] With literally no structurally sound options available for an adequate emergency response, a football field was identified as an adequate site to install the largest MFH configuration yet. Initially, there were nine inflatable tents that housed two operating theatres, sterilisation, recovery, emergency, observation, hospitalisation, an intensive care unit and a transit area that included storage and changing rooms. In early April, additional units were added to accommodate a burns department, the only specialised burn treatment centre in Haiti at the time.[22]

The benefits of the MFH are evident but there are still a number of challenges and limitations. In many of the contexts where the MFH was used, there were delays between the onset of the emergency (ie violence, earthquake and so on), and the time the MFH was operational. Reasons for these delays have ranged from problems with transport,

above: Port-au-Prince, Haiti, 2010. A team erects one of the inflatable tents during the MFH installation. The MFH was built on the football field of high school St Louis de Gonzague in Delmas 31, and was fully operational just 12 days after the 2010 earthquake struck. © Benoit Finck.

left: Port-au-Prince, Haiti, 2010. The interior of one of the inflatable tents that was used as a hospitalisation ward in the Médicins Sans Frontière St-Louis Hospital. © Yann Libessart/MSF.

customs and importation, to lack of expertise on site to facilitate a rapid set-up. Since then MSF has taken steps to improve the skills of their human resources to address the final factor. Issues with transport and importation cannot be as easily remedied as they are linked directly to the specific context and situation. Timing is critical because emergency surgery should begin as soon as possible after the onset of a crisis in an effort to save lives and alleviate trauma. Though there were ongoing surgical needs that the MFH served, ideally its deployment should have been more rapid.

Additionally, as with all tent structures, the MFH offers only the minimum of protection from theft, rodents or harsh weather, and continues to present problems with climate control. Though the inflatable tents are equipped for cooling and heating systems, these are costly to install and run, especially with regard to cooling. The disadvantages are tolerable in the short term, but if activities are projected to last in the medium term, a semipermanent option is often the best way forwards.

Semipermanent Structures

Médecins Sans Frontières has often constructed semipermanent structures to replace temporary tent structures. Material used for these structures has depended on what is available locally in a given project, but usually they are constructed with wood or metal framing. A set of standards has been issued by MSF that outline the internal guidelines for this type of basic construction; containers and prefabricated systems have also been used as needed. The example of Haiti can further elucidate this process and some lessons learned.

As previously mentioned, the earthquake of 2010 destroyed much of the infrastructure in the city of Port-au-Prince. Despite the fact that the three existing MSF facilities were severely damaged or destroyed, the organisation was able to respond immediately to urgent medical needs. Within the first 48 hours, MSF was performing emergency surgery in makeshift tents, shipping containers and the limited available space in existing local health structures.[23] Ten days after the earthquake, the MFH was installed and receiving its first patients.[24] With the mass devastation and overwhelming medical needs, it was clear that MSF's intervention in the country would go beyond the initial emergency response. Four of the MSF operational centres[25] present in the country began plans for replacing their temporary structures with a semipermanent solution. Several options were considered, but all four centres decided to install some version of a container hospital. The containers not only met the hygienic and programmatic requirements of medical activities – climate control, hygiene and waste management – they could also be erected relatively rapidly and were more resistant to hurricanes and inclement weather.[26]

The modular containers are flexible and can be tailored to suit medical needs. The objective was to optimise this flexibility and quickly build an effective health structure.[27] As with all medical structures, incorporating the medical programme into the building design was a critical component of the process. This challenge was complicated by the urgency of building semipermanent structures to replace temporary ones, and lessons learned will undoubtedly be applied in future projects.

Port-au-Prince, Haiti, 2010. The exterior of the container hospital, Nap Kenbe. This emergency surgery facility provides trauma, orthopaedic and visceral surgery. © Yann Libessart/MSF.

The Expanding Role of Architects

Emergency response NGOs engage architecture and design professionals as necessitated by their activities. For example, organisations such as Emergency and Merlin have engaged external architectural service providers,[28] whereas the International Committee of the Red Cross (ICRC) and MSF have on-staff architects to provide technical expertise on a full-time basis.[29] The operational needs dictate what model works best for each individual NGO.

At the time of writing, all five MSF operational centres had technical advisors based in their respective headquarters to assist the field teams on structural matters. These on-staff experts – architects, designers and construction managers – help to develop, guide and implement MSF's construction policies. At the field level, once the medical needs of a project are established and construction options need to be explored, a technical expert is sent to the field to do a feasibility study. This evaluation includes investigations into site, budget, locally available resources and standards of quality, as well as human resources necessary to execute the construction programme. It is at this point that the need for a project architect will be determined, and whether there is local talent to fill that role. This person has many responsibilities, not just overseeing design and construction, but also managing the financial and legal aspects that are associated with the project.

Additionally, logistics staff based in the headquarters are dedicated to finding improved alternatives and new innovations for both temporary and semipermanent structures. As advancements are made and modifications are adopted, one key concern remains indisputable – that the design is always driven by the medical need.

Many thanks to Laurent Dedieu, Francisca Bastos, Eric Boivin, Vincent Brown and Michael Goldfarb for their input and support.

Notes

1   Médecins Sans Frontières, *Médecins Sans Frontières Activity Report 2011*, 2011, p 114.
2   Claudine Vidal and Jacques Pinel, 'MSF "Satellites": A Strategy Underlying Different Medical Practices', *Medical Innovations in Humanitarian Situations: The Work of Médecins Sans Frontières*, (eds) Jean-Hervé Bradol and Claudine Vidal, Médecins Sans Frontières (Charleston), 2011, p 25.
3   The Sphere Project, *Humanitarian Charter and Minimum Standards in Humanitarian Response*, 2011, p 292.
4   An 'Operational Centre' (OC) is an MSF office that manages operations in the field. At the time of writing, there are five operational centres: Amsterdam, Barcelona, Brussels, Geneva and Paris.
5   Michael Neuman and Benoit Leduc, 'Somalia: Everything is Open to Negotiation', *Humanitarian Negotiations Revealed: The MSF Experience*, (eds) Claire Magone, Michael Neuman and Fabrice Weissman, Columbia University Press (New York), 2011, p 79.
6   Note that in August 2012, a new central government was established. See Mohammed Ibrahim, 'New Parliament is Convened in Somalia', *The New York Times*, 20 August 2012, www.nytimes.com (accessed 10 January 2015).
7   Neuman and Leduc, 'Somalia: Everything is Open to Negotiation', p 79.
8   Ibid, pp 83–4.
9   Ibid, p 84.
10 Ibid, pp 84–5.
11 Ibid, p 87.
12 The definition of 'temporary' and 'semipermanent' varies, but for the purposes of this essay, they will be defined as structures with the following life-span: less than one year (temporary), one to five years (semipermanent).

13 Though the term Modular Field Hospital (MFH) can include the use of multipurpose tents, in this essay it refers only to inflatable tents.

14 For example, in 2012, MSF Logistique (the supply unit which serves MSF operational centres Barcelona, Geneva and Paris) sent 140 multipurpose tents to the field.

15 Matthew Cleary and Vincent Brown, *Evaluation of the use of a Modular Field Hospital with Inflatable Tents in MSF-OCP*, Médecins Sans Frontières, April 2010, unpublished.

16 All specifications provided were sourced from Médecins Sans Frontières, *2012 MSF International Technical Coordination Logistic Catalogue*, Médecins Sans Frontières (Belgium), 2012.

17 Cleary and Brown, *Evaluation of the use of Modular Field Hospital*, April 2010. Note that all information related to the MFH was sourced from this document unless otherwise noted.

18 Xeni Jardin, 'How to Set Up a Plug and Play Hospital – Doctors Without Borders', *Boing Boing*, 21 January 2012, boingboing.net/2010/01/21/haiti-howto-set-up-a.html (accessed 10 January 2015).

19 Ibid.

20 *US Geological Survey*, 12 January 2010, www.usgs.gov (accessed 10 January 2015).

21 Ibid.

22 'Haiti: A Boy Recovers From His Burns', *Médecins Sans Frontières/Doctors Without Borders*, 12 May 2010, www.doctorswithoutborders.org (accessed 10 January 2015).

23 Médecins Sans Frontières, *Haiti: One Year After*, 10 January 2011.

24 Ibid, p 12.

25 Amsterdam, Brussels, Geneva and Paris.

26 Médecins Sans Frontières, *Haiti: One Year After*, 10 January 2011; and 'Haiti: A Hospital in Containers Built to Last', *Médecins Sans Frontières/Doctors Without Borders*, 16 October 2010, www.msf-me.org (accessed 10 January 2015).

27 'Haiti: A Hospital in Containers Built to Last', *Médecins Sans Frontières/Doctors Without Borders*, 16 October 2010, www.msf-me.org (accessed 10 January 2015).

28 See Raul Pantaleo, 'On Beauty, Architecture, and Crisis: The Salam Centre for Cardiac Surgery in Sudan', *Beyond Shelter*, (ed) Marie J Aquilino, Metropolis Books (New York), 2011; and Architecture for Humanity, 'Caravelle Clinic for Medical Relief International (MERLIN)', *World Changing*, 2012, http://openarchitecturenetwork.org/projects/merlin-caravelle (accessed 10 January 2015).

29 ICRC Recruitment Unit, *Working for the ICRC*, International Committee of the Red Cross (Geneva), 2012.

MASS Design Group, Butaro Hospital, Burera District, Rwanda, 2011. In a permanent structure, design is also driven by medical needs. But greater emphasis can be made on circulation, lighting and peripheral spaces, in addition to the main treatment areas. © Iwan Baan.

top left: Streets in Makoko, Lagos, Nigeria, 2011. The flooding narrow streets are filled with sewage water for most of the year as the incoming tides run into the walkways. There is no sanitary sewage system. © Alice Min Soo Chun.

top right: Sluice Gate, Ducis, Haiti, 2011. Community-managed irrigation channels bring fresh water to rural croplands in southern Haiti. © Irene E Brisson.

above: Stilt House in Makoko, Lagos, Nigeria, 2011. Houses in the slum of Makoko are built elevated on stilts to make use of the water in a neighbourhood without land. While water is everywhere, clean water is scarce and sanitation concerns are numerous. © Kimberly Tate.

Water and Sanitation 4

No discussion of humanitarian design could be complete without addressing the needs and issues surrounding water – a critical resource and powerful threat. As a resource, water is necessary for basic health and sanitation. While two thirds of Earth's surface is covered in water, only 0.01 per cent of the moisture in Earth's ecosystem is available for use, much of which is polluted or otherwise made unfit for human consumption. The United States government agency, USAID, reports that 450 million people in 31 countries face shortages of fresh water and project that by 2025, 2.8 billion people will face severe and ongoing water shortages. Water also presents a great danger – not just water insecurity and droughts – in excess it arrives in the form of flooding, tsunamis and hurricanes, which have caused some of the greatest humanitarian disasters in recent history. Because of the chronic lack of sanitation infrastructure – exacerbated in disaster situations – more than 1.2 billion people are at risk of disease and infection due to a lack of access to clean water. There are approximately 2.5 million deaths each year due to water-related diarrhoea illness.

Throughout history access to, protection from, transportation on and of water, all have played a key role in human settlements and migrations, patterns of urban and regional development, rituals and traditions, trade and recreation, around the globe. All architects are tasked with managing how water will be accessed in the built environment and controlling the impact of buildings on water resources. It is our responsibility to be thoughtful in all contexts where designs will impact water consumption and management. In crisis situations, where people are displaced from permanent structures and infrastructure, dependency upon clean water clearly becomes an immediate concern. Temporary and sustainable design responses have addressed this problem in a multitude of manners, but there is still significant room for improvement in the management of our water resources. Such improvements will determine the success of humanitarian design interventions.

Varanasi,Uttar Pradesh,
India, 2011. The roof
of a flooded building is
just visible above the
overflowing Ganges.
© Elizabeth Parker.

Fluid Matters
On Water and Design

Elizabeth Parker

The excess or scarcity of water has precipitated a great number of natural and humanitarian disasters in history. In many ways the architectural moves made by humans historically, and currently, can have drastic effects on the outcome of these situations. In this essay, Elizabeth Parker, drawing on her research travels through the subcontinent of India, traces the complex relationships between humans, architecture and water. She identifies a number of design projects that exemplify the need to engage with water resources at many spatial and temporal scales. She also considers critically the need for foundational community engagement by designers, to engage effectively with water management. Parker describes water resources and management fluidly across scales because more than any other environmental factor, water resources function, and must be met as a holistic system that cannot be truly separated into components, such as access, sanitation, run-off, storm protection and so forth. While describing the complexity of these systems she calls on architects to rise to the challenge, to try positively rather than negatively to impact our relationship with water.

In December 2004, a tsunami ripped across the Indian Ocean, killing over 225,000 people,[1] and in 2013, globally, it is estimated that one child under five dies every 56 seconds from diarrhoeal diseases, which can be linked to unclean water. Twenty-five years ago, the situation was far worse; children under five died from diarrhoea roughly every six seconds,[2] and while flooding has impacted an increasing number of people over the last 30 years, the number dying from floods has decreased, largely because of disaster response work.[3] We are both sustained and destroyed by water. But while we are vulnerable amidst its floods, we can be powerful in its management. Particularly at this time of unprecedented climate extremes, it becomes increasingly reckless to ignore the degree to which, more than any other resource, our relationship with water will determine our survival as a species.

How Water Guides Us

When access to water dries up altogether, it can dislocate entire cultures and begin wars. Recently, the Syrian government's water table mismanagement and a subsequent five-year drought destroyed the livelihoods of over 800,000 Syrian farmers and herders. Without work or fertile land to farm, many 'drought refugees' became active participants in an uprising to overthrow the then president, with many citing their disillusionment over water issues as the catalyst.[4] This link between water shortages and social unrest is observed across the world, perhaps most famously in Sudan, where desertification of once-fertile farmland has been linked to territorial disputes and subsequent bloodshed in Darfur.[5] Lack of water also kills directly, but with remarkable regional variations; between 1980 and 2006, more than 99 per cent of reported human drought fatalities across the globe were in Africa.[6] In the face of direct or indirect water shortages, we suffer tremendous loss of life.

Too much water is also tremendously disruptive; water-related events are responsible for roughly 90 per cent of the damages suffered from all disasters.[7] Between 2000 and 2006, 2,163 water-related disasters were reported globally. These disasters impacted 1.5 billion people, killed more than 290,000, and cost more than US$422 billion in damages.[8] They destroyed homes and led to the spread of water-borne epidemics, which have risen at an alarming rate since the 1990s.[9] Asia flooded more than any other region between 1980 and 2006 and suffered the highest number of flood fatalities during that period, followed by the Americas, Africa, Europe and Oceania. But flooding is not a regional issue; across every world region, the frequency of floods increased between 1980 and 2006,[10] displacing tremendous numbers, killing indiscriminately and destroying millions of acres of property.

Water problems are rarely as simple as having too little or too much water; central to a successful relationship with water at any scale is effective drought and flood management. The cost of not managing this cycle of abundance and scarcity is high, because countries failing at this task are unlikely to develop.[11] In years to come the global waterscape will change significantly; places that have had generous access to water will go without, and places once dry will have too much.[12] Increasing greenhouse gas concentrations and a warming global climate will inevitably, and unavoidably, impact water resources, raising the likelihood of both floods and drought[13] and the costs of unsuccessful water cycle management.

With and without flood and drought, the issue of water cleanliness is essential to survival. Without clean water we get sick and our economies do not develop as quickly. Annually, 3.4 million people die from water-related diseases, 99 per cent of those deaths occurring in the developing world.[14] Approximately, only 10 per cent of wastewater is treated, with the rest flowing into natural bodies of water. Around the world, approximately 2.5 billion people lack access to improved sanitation facilities, defined as facilities that hygienically separate excreta from human contact.[15] It is estimated that half of the hospital beds globally are filled with people suffering from diseases that result from the consumption of unclean drinking water, inadequate sanitation and poor hygiene.[16] It is estimated that these factors are responsible for roughly 88 per cent of the diarrhoea cases in the world,[17] an illness easily cured in developed countries. The second most common cause of death among children under five is diarrhoea. Ninety per cent of deaths from this illness (1.5 million per year), are children younger than five.[18] But despite its power over our lives, we have tremendous influence over our relationship with water.

How We Guide Water

When local infrastructure cannot clean the water, it can be filtered for consumption. The *LifeStraw* is perhaps the most direct water remediation tool yet designed. Shaped like a small cigar, it removes the bacteria and parasites responsible for common diarrhoeal diseases in roughly the 6-inch (15-centimetre) distance between the surface of the water and your lips.[19] In Cambodia, the provision of ceramic water filters – the porosity of which also filtered bacteria and protozoa out of the water – halved the incidence of diarrhoeal illnesses in households using the filters.[20] Designs can also clean water as it is polluted. Winning entries to the Bill and Melinda Gates Foundation's *Reinvent the Toilet Challenge* transformed waste into hydrogen and electricity, and sanitised waste into clean water.[21] In Gansu Province, China, BaO Architects designed a bathhouse to be used by approximately 700 students during the week and the local community on the weekends. Self-sustaining with solar hot water, greywater filtration and dry toilets, the bathhouse remains disconnected from traditional sewer lines, relying on phytoremediation basins filled with bamboo to filter run-off wastewater from the showers before it flows back underground.[22] Whether cleaned immediately before consumption or immediately after pollution, a variety of examples of effective water remediation already exist for implementation by designers. Those examples must be adjusted only with consideration for local interests, customs and interpersonal relationships, as discussed later in this essay.

Beyond remediation, water retention during times of plenty is an established and important resource management technique. *WATERBANK School* in Laikipia, Kenya, was designed by PITCHAfrica and ATOPIA Research to harvest, filter and store rainwater for later use in the semi-arid region. On the typical budget available for a rural school, this design provides four classrooms, gardens for food cultivation and a variety of rooms for teachers and the community. Its 76,989 gallons (350,000 litres) per year harvesting capacity and 32,995-gallon (150,000-litre) reservoir collects water from 6,458 square feet (600 square metres), providing 300 children with seven pints (four litres) of water each day, year round. Partnering again at a far smaller, and more flexible scale, ATOPIA Research and PITCHAfrica have also designed *Rainchutes*, which harvest water using decommissioned parachutes. Given the rain levels on more than half of the African continent, a fairly average size parachute can be expected to harvest 5,499 gallons (25,000 litres) of water annually. Coupled with standard storage and ceramic water filtration systems, one parachute can provide 14 people a day with water throughout the year.[23] Without using these built or flexible methods for retaining water, locals might face greater water insecurity, spending significant time and labour transporting water from potentially unreliable and unclean sources.

---

overleaf. Fatehpur Sikri, Uttar Pradesh, India, 2011. Built by Emperor Akbar in the 16th century, Fatehpur Sikri's design demonstrates a consideration of water remediation, circulation and retention no longer celebrated in much of India's contemporary buildings. © Elizabeth Parker.

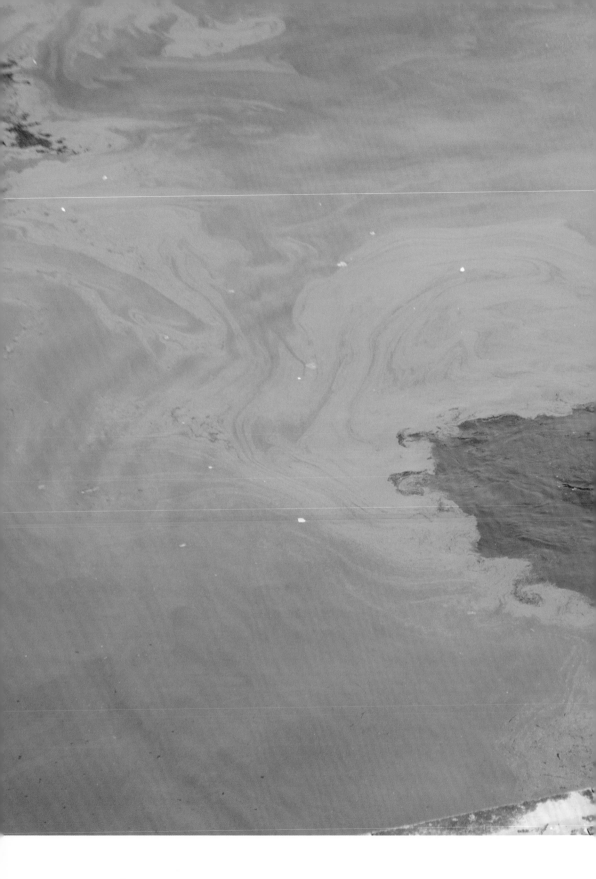

We can retain water, and we can also reroute it. In perhaps one of this century's most massive engineering feats, China is undertaking the *South–North Water Transfer Project*, which as its name suggests, will seek to transfer vast amounts of water northward into eastern, central and western China from the south. Tunnelling under the Yellow River and over part of the Himalayas, this massive rerouting may successfully move water from one place to another for a time. But warming in the Himalayas is expected to lower water tables across the nation and, eventually, simply transferring the water will not be enough to support a massive population's need for the resource. There are myriad examples, however, of fairly sustainable water rerouting. As a student at the University of Oregon, Nadia Kasko designed a tsunami-resistant project, which proposed to create six layered buffers between the edge of the ocean and the town of Ishinomaki on the north coast of Japan. Based on the understanding that if a wave encounters friction as it approaches the shore its energy will dissipate, Kasko proposed a variety of techniques ranging from a restored sand dune, to a terraced seaside park, to an urban plan oriented to avoid direct penetration of the wave, and designed to reroute the force of the tsunami. [24]

If it is not possible to move water, however, it is possible to float over it. The architecture, design and urbanism practice, NLÉ, focused on developing cities and designed the *Makoko Floating School*, a prototypical structure intended for the water community of Makoko in Lagos, Nigeria. The school, designed in the light of frequent flooding and anticipated climate change, is a triangular A-frame with a low centre of gravity for flotation. With three floors, two to four classrooms and enough space for up to 100 pupils, the structure addresses renewable energy, waste reduction and water and sewage treatment. The cost of construction was low at just over US$6,000.[25] Floating designs exist at a number of scales; Design Academy Eindhoven student Asnate Bockis created two pieces of furniture intended to float in times of floods. The first, an urban bench, is designed to float upwards in the instance of flooding, becoming a small refuge. *Cloud*, a stuffed boat-shaped sofa, is intended to reside in the domestic interior until, in times of flood, it flips over and is used as a boat, complete with rudder.[26]

New Delhi, Delhi, India, 2011. Residents stand in front of the community toilets they successfully lobbied to control with assistance from a local non-profit organisation. © Elizabeth Parker.

Many more dynamic designs exist that enable humans to float over, retain, reroute, and filter water. Designs that profoundly impact their intended beneficiaries, however, all share one quality: they engage the cultural, spatial and temporal contexts at the heart of any water successful remediation or management effort.

Issues to Consider When Designing for Water

At its core, successful water management and remediation is about human relationships. Engaging locals across genders and wealth levels during planning, implementation and management stages leads to water supply and sanitation projects with more effective and better sustained impact.[27] In New Delhi, India, access to community toilets built by the government and managed by a private party grew so expensive that they were seldom used, and without maintenance the public toilets fell into disrepair. Open defecation was common throughout the slums because household toilets were rare. After several years, mobilised with support from a local development organisation, the community's campaign to gain control of the toilets was successful and the government restored the facilities to working order. Managed by the community and an oversight committee, the cost of toilet use fell drastically, becoming readily affordable. Children under 12 and the handicapped no longer had to pay for access, and soap, running water and other sanitary measures were introduced. Children planted flowers around the bathrooms and open defecation became rare.[28] In this instance, the form of the designed environment did not drive its impact on the community; rather, interpersonal management issues and the desire of the local community determined almost entirely the design's success. This example is not unique; designs are only successful if they exist in a social environment that is conducive to their ongoing use and maintenance.

Designers aiming to successfully engage with water issues, then, need to design in the light of local interpersonal dynamics. Within the development sector, the term *capacity building* refers to efforts to nurture and strengthen the ability of developing countries and communities to plan for the long term in addition to their ability to respond to crisis. In the United Nations Development Programme's five-step approach to capacity building, engaging stakeholders is first, prior to assessing capacity assets and needs.[29] Transferred into a design context, this means getting to know many of the local actors prior to designing anything. This is essential, but not always common to architectural practices. It is a way of working that is often difficult for development agencies, despite their community-engagement goals, and especially during times of emergency and post-emergency when the skills and resources of local groups are often under utilised.[30] When not included in the rebuilding, local groups are left jockeying for access to the provided resources, a dynamic that can lead to tensions between various parties, undermining rather than strengthening the local community.

For projects that effectively engage water issues, knowing with whom to partner is essential, and the best local partners are not always the most obvious. Certainly, cultural traditions make different genders, religious communities, traditional leaders and other parties more or less suited to effective partnership. In many instances, however, because of their primary responsibility for collecting and transporting water, women are effective partners in water issues. Globally, they spend roughly 200 million work hours each day collecting the resource and, coupled with children, are estimated to be the most likely water collectors in approximately 76 per cent of households across 45 developing nations.[31] Perhaps for this reason, one study surveying water and sanitation projects across 88 communities across 15 countries found that projects conceived by, and implemented with the full participation of women, tended to have a larger impact for longer than projects that did not.[32] In some situations, of course, other groups may be more effective partners. Regardless, across the globe, designs that seek to engage water issues will not succeed if not built on informed relationships with local communities.

At the same time, designs driven by community consensus can fail to address potentially successful, but less popular opportunities. Some types of remediation receive a great deal of attention while other vital techniques remain unaddressed; in 2011, for example, water remediation experts interviewed by this author knew of only one project seeking to clean groundwater run-off in India. That project had been very successful, transforming Man Sagar Lake in Jaipur, Rajasthan from its methane-bubbling state in 2005 to a body of water sufficiently clean to support a variety of fish and wildlife just a few years later. Despite its success, no other similar projects were being developed in the rest of the country; the focus of the aid community attended primarily to drinking water access and sanitation issues.[33] With this anecdote in mind, designers should seek local partners but not rely solely on the existing water remediation and management infrastructure as a road map for a successful project.

In fact, successful designs in some cases seem counterintuitive, as in the case of a project by a team of University of Oxford researchers using mobile phones to manage the resource. Acknowledging that more people have access to GSM phone signals than filtered water, and that approximately one third of hand pumps do not work at any given time, with repairs often taking longer than a month, the team set out to test data transmitters, which automatically reported a broken rural pump to district and national managers. Initial project findings suggest that this technique might provide greater water security for millions accessing water through hand pumps.[34] Successful designs engaging water not only understand the existing human context, but also tackle those needs that may not have been addressed by local aid communities, exploring design opportunities informed by water remediation techniques of a different precedent.

Because water transcends scale no understanding of individual actors and their water remediation needs is enough to inform a holistic architectural response to local water issues. This is particularly important in instances where upstream demands on water influences downstream consumption. For example, a tremendous amount of India's water originates in Tibet. Given China's growing demands for the resource and anticipated climate warming in the Himalayas, we can expect that these upstream needs will eventually restrict access to water across India. Designers working on projects in India will benefit their clients by anticipating this issue and designing self-sustaining systems. Accordingly, designing successfully for the human, local scale of water use requires an understanding of the natural issues associated with water at a regional level.[35]

Varanasi, Uttar
Pradesh, India,
2011. Daily morning
rituals coexist on
the Ganges River.
© Elizabeth Parker.

Water also transcends temporal scales. Many designs will seek to address and anticipate water conditions for a given site over time, but because of ongoing natural variability and computational limitations, scientific models of future precipitation cannot precisely forecast how local water conditions will evolve.[36] Given this unpredictability, if intended for maximum utility, future designs engaging water will need to be adaptable and resilient, facilitating multiple management and remediation techniques over time.

Architectural techniques have elegantly navigated water's ebbs and flows before, with centuries-old designs attesting to the discipline's care for this resource. Currently, however, the remediation and management of water is considered to primarily be the disciplinary wheelhouse of non design-oriented developmental aid agencies and non-profit organisations or governments. At the heart of any successful response to water issues is the spatial, temporal and technical management of physical material informed by human relationships and practices. It is at this intersection where architecture resides, but only if designers engage with the complexity surrounding this vital resource. And although this essay cites several examples of effective engagements with water, there are no easy, absolute solutions to the immensely complicated, dynamic and widespread issues of local water remediation and management. Identifying a way to successfully remediate and manage this resource is essential to human survival. So as designers, we must try.

Notes

1   Yoganath Adikari and Junichi Yoshitani, *Global Trends in Water-Related Disasters: An Insight for Policymakers*, UNESCO (Paris), 3rd edition, 2009, p 8. United Nations World Water Assessment Programme Side Publication.
2   'Global Health Observatory Data Repository: WORLD Diarrhoeal diseases', World Health Organisation, no publisher, 2 October 2014, p 5, http://apps.who.int/gho/data/view.main. CM100WORLD-CH3?lang=en (accessed 10 January 2015).
3   Adikari and Yoshitani, *Global Trends in Water-Related Disasters*, 2009, p 2.
4   Thomas L Friedman, 'Without War, Revolution', *New York Times*, New York edition, 19 May 2013, Op-Ed section, p SR1.
5   *Sudan: Post-Conflict Environmental Assessment*, United Nations Environment Programme (Nairobi), 2007.
6   Adikari and Yoshitani, *Global Trends in Water-Related Disasters*, 2009, table 3.1, p 11.
7   'Jerry Delli Priscoli on Water and Development', interview by Scott Aughenbaugh, Center for Strategic and International Studies, 6 May 2009, www.csis.org (accessed 10 January 2015).
8   Adikari and Yoshitani, *Global Trends in Water-Related Disasters*, 2009, p 1.
9   Ibid, p 11.
10 Ibid, fig 3.6, p 10.
11 'Jerry Delli Priscoli on Water and Development', 2009.
12 Ibid.
13 Kathleen Miller, *Science, Politics and Crystal Balls – Building Effective Approaches to Water Adaptation Planning*, Water and Climate Spring 2010 Lecture Series, National Center for Atmospheric Research (Boulder), 14 April 2010, and Kathleen Miller, interview by the author, 10 February 2015.
14 Annette Prüss-Üstün, Robert Bos, Gore Fiona and Jamie Bartram, *Safer Water, Better Health: Costs, Benefits and Sustainability of Interventions to Protect and Promote Health*, World Health Organisation (Geneva), 2008.
15 *Progress on Sanitation and Drinking Water: 2013 Update*, World Health Organisation/UNICEF (Geneva/New York), 2013.
16 Kevin Watkins, Liliana Carvajal, Daniel Coppard, Papa Seck and Shahin Yaqub, *Beyond Scarcity: Power, Poverty and the Global Water Crisis*, Human Development Report, (trans) Chiara

Giamberardini, 2006 edition, United Nations Development Programme (New York), 2006.

17   Patrick Vaughan, Anthony Rodgers, Thomson Prentice, Tessa Tan-Torres Edejer, David Evans and Julia Lowe, *The World Health Report 2002: Reducing Risks, Promoting Healthy Life*, Rep. Comp. Christopher Murray and Alan Lopez, (ed) Barbara Campanini, World Health Organisation (Geneva), 2002.

18   *Tackling a Global Crisis: International Year of Sanitation 2008*. UN Water, 2008.

19   Vestergaard Frandsen, *LifeStraw*, Vestergaard Frandsen: Disease Control Textiles, www.vestergaard.com (accessed 10 January 2015).

20   Joe Brown, Mark Sobsey and Sorya Proum, *Improving Household Drinking Water Quality: Use of Ceramic Water Filters in Cambodia*, Tech. Water and Sanitation Program/UNICEF (Washington, DC), 2007.

21   Bill and Melinda Gates Foundation, *Bill Gates Names Winners of the Reinvent the Toilet Challenge, Gates Foundation Press Room*, 15 August 2012, www.gatesfoundation.org (accessed 10 January 2015).

22   'Shanmen Public Bathhouse', *BaO Architects*, www.bao-a.com/gansubathhouse.html (accessed 10 January 2015).

23   'The Rainchute Campaign', *PITCHAfrica*, http://rainchutes.org (accessed 10 January 2015).

24   Nadia Kasko, 'Fury and Fragility: Tsunami Resistant Regenerative Design', *Archiprix Moscow 2013*, Archiprix, http://archiprix.org (accessed 10 January 2015).

25   'Makoko Floating School, Lagos, Nigeria 2012', http://www.nleworks.com (accessed 10 January 2015).

26   'Product: Floating Among Clouds 1', Asnate Bockis, http://www.asnatebockis.nl (accessed 10 January 2015).

27   Bruce Gross, Christine Van Wijk and Nilanjana Mukherjee, *Linking Sustainability with Demand, Gender and Poverty: A Study in Community-Managed Water Supply Projects in 15 Countries*, IRC International Water and Sanitation Centre (Delft, The Netherlands), 2001, p 2.

28   Shri Om, director of Model Rural Youth Development Organisation, interview by the author, 2 August 2011.

29   *Fast Facts: Capacity Development*, Publication, United Nations Development Programme, 1 October 2011, www.undp.org (accessed 10 January 2015).

30   Ian Smillie, *Patronage or Partnership: Local Capacity Building in Humanitarian Crises*, Kumarian Press (Bloomfield, CT), 2001, p 7.

31   *Progress on Sanitation and Drinking Water: 2010 Update*, World Health Organisation/UNICEF (Geneva/New York), 2010.

32   Bruce Gross, Christine Van Wijk and Nilanjana Mukherjee, *Linking Sustainability with Demand, Gender and Poverty*, 2001, p 27.

33   Ishaprasad Bhagwat, interview by the author, 2 August 2011.

34   R Hope, T Foster, A Money, M Rouse, N Money and M Thomas, *Smart Water Systems*, Final Technical Report to UK Department for International Development, Oxford University (Oxford), 2011.

35   Scott Moore, 'China's Massive Water Problem', *The International Herald Tribune*, Global Opinion section (New York), 29 March 2013, www.iht.com (accessed 10 January 2015).

36   Kathleen Miller, interview by the author, 10 February 2015.

Water, Sanitation and Hygiene Interventions
Household Water Treatment and Safe Storage to Reduce the Burden of Diarrhoeal Disease in Developing Countries

Daniele Lantagne

A great number of high profile humanitarian design interventions integrate some form of water catchment, storage or delivery system, responding to the great need for localised water access in many developing contexts, both rural and urban. Collection at the point of use by architectural means, such as roof catchment, can be a step towards alleviating water access concerns but requires additional technologies to provide a potable water source. In this essay environmental engineer, Daniele Lantagne, gives a brief account of the costs and benefits of a number of household water treatment options. While not architectural in scale, these technologies are key components of any building-integrated storage system in order to provide safe and portable water as an output. These are inherently decentralised strategies that do provide the same economies of scale and monitoring as a centralised system. Based on years of field experience in training, monitoring and testing water treatment programmes across the globe, Lantagne presents the interconnected factors governing the more or less effective selection and implementation of household water treatment systems.

The burden of diarrhoeal diseases is largely borne by developing countries. An estimated nearly 1.7 billion cases of diarrhoea (Fischer Walker, 2012) and 1.87 million deaths in children under five occur each year (Boschi-Pinto, 2008), primarily caused by unsafe drinking water and inadequate sanitation and hygiene. The accumulated burden of repeated diarrhoeal diseases results in decreased food intake and nutrient absorption, malnutrition, reduced resistance to infection and impaired physical growth and cognitive development (Baqui, 1993; Guerrant, 1999). The World Health Organisation (WHO) estimates that improving water, sanitation and hygiene (WASH) could prevent approximately 9.1 per cent of the entire global burden of disease and 6.3 per cent of all causes of death worldwide (Pruss-Ustun, 2008).

The interventions commonly promoted to reduce the worldwide burden of diarrhoeal disease fall into four categories:

1   Water supply provision, particularly the installation of 'improved' water sources such as piped water supplies, protected wells or protected springs.
2   Promotion of household water treatment and safe storage (HWTS) options, such as boiling, chlorination or filters.
3   Improved sanitation options such as latrines to isolate faeces from the environment.

4   Hygiene promotion, such as handwashing, to improve personal and household hygiene.

All four of these interventions reduce diarrhoea, one metric used to measure intervention effectiveness, by approximately 20–60 per cent, depending on context and intervention type. Water and sewer infrastructure have other benefits that have not yet been exactly quantified, including but not limited to: economic savings, reduction in health impacts of hauling water, time savings for the family, increased work and school attendance and increased household and environmental hygiene.

Worldwide, an estimated 780 million people drink water from unimproved sources, such as rivers, ponds and open wells, and millions more drink contaminated water from improved sources (UNICEF/WHO, 2012). Providing safe, reliable, centrally treated piped water to every household is the ultimate goal and doing so yields optimal gains, as described above. While remaining strongly committed to this goal, the WHO also supports incremental improvements in water supplies, wherever possible, to accelerate the heath gains associated with safer drinking water for those whose water supplies are unsafe (WHO, 2011b).

One such interim improvement is the promotion of HWTS options to prevent or remediate contamination of water during collection, transport and use in the home. In 2009, WHO and UNICEF announced a seven-point strategy for the treatment and prevention of diarrhoea among children that includes HWTS, calling for the adoption of 'household water treatment and safe storage systems, such as chlorination and filtration, in both development and emergency situations to support reductions in the number of diarrhoea cases' (UNICEF/WHO, 2009) and in WHO's *Guidelines for Drinking-Water Quality* (GDWQ): 'HWT technology has the potential to have rapid and significant positive health impacts in situations where piped water systems are not possible and where people rely on source water that may be contaminated, or where stored water becomes contaminated because of unhygienic handling during transport or in the home' (WHO, 2008).

A growing body of evidence demonstrates that the use of HWTS technologies improves the microbiological quality of household water and reduces the burden of diarrhoeal disease in users (Fewtrell, 2005; Clasen, 2007; Waddington, 2009). The foci of research conducted to date on HWTS have been on the efficacy of HWTS technologies in controlled circumstances, with little research on effective use in actual real-world programmes. The research results to date provide insight into the potential of scaling-up HWTS interventions in vulnerable populations, and are described below.

Efficacy Research Conducted in Controlled Conditions

Several HWTS methods have been shown to significantly improve drinking water quality by removing some, or all of the organisms that cause diarrhoeal disease, including protozoa, bacteria and viruses (WHO, 2011a). These methods include free chlorine disinfection; membrane, porous ceramic or composite filtration; granular media filtration; solar disinfection; UV light technologies; boiling; sedimentation and flocculation/disinfection combined technologies. The log reductions associated with each method vary. For example, free chlorine disinfection is relatively less effective at removing the protozoa cryptosporidium; locally made filters are relatively less effective at removing viruses and boiling, solar disinfection, high-quality filters and combination approaches are the most effective at removing all three classes of organisms.

Furthermore, some of these options – including chlorination, filtration through sand or ceramic, flocculation/disinfection and solar disinfection – have also been shown to significantly reduce diarrhoeal disease in randomised, controlled intervention trials. In three meta-analyses conducted, the average diarrhoeal disease reduction associated with HWTS options in each case was 35 per cent, 47 per cent and 42 per cent, which was similar to the reductions associated with water supply, hygiene, and sanitation interventions (Fewtrell, 2005; Clasen, 2007; Waddington, 2009). Of note is that boiling, which achieves the greatest removal of pathogens, has not been evaluated for diarrhoeal disease reduction. Since boiling leaves water susceptible to recontamination, and studies of the microbiological effectiveness of boiling have shown mixed results (Gupta, 2007; Clasen, 2008; Sodha, 2011), a definitive conclusion on the health impacts of boiling cannot be made at this stage. Additionally, only one study has evaluated the health impact of safe storage alone, and results have indicated a nonstatistically significant reduction in disease (Roberts, 2001).

While this efficacy research has consistently shown a reduction in diarrhoeal disease associated with HWTS use, there are critiques of these results (Arnold, BF, 2007; Sobsey, 2008; Hunter, 2009; Schmidt, 2009). These include 1) that the few blinded studies that have been completed have shown no health impact; 2) that the outcome metric – self-reported diarrhoeal disease – is subject to reporting bias; 3) that the intervention trials to assess health impact are conducted during short study times with unrealistic implementation conditions, and that health impacts decrease over time in these studies; 4) that consumable HWTS options are less sustainable than durable products; 5) that the local water quality and routes of diarrhoeal disease transmission are not considered in implementing HWTS programmes and, 6) that the impacts of HWTS technology use on other waterborne diseases or chemical contaminants of concern have not been addressed.

In summary, it is not clear from the laboratory data on log reduction of organisms of concern and the randomised, controlled trials estimating the diarrhoeal disease reduction benefits associated with HWTS that there is sufficient evidence to support the widespread, indiscriminate scaling-up of HWTS technologies.

Effective Use in Field Implementations

In comparison to the extensive research detail above on efficacy of HWTS interventions in controlled circumstances, comparatively little work has been done to understand the extent to which HWTS interventions are being used correctly and consistently by vulnerable populations to make their water safe for drinking in real-world conditions. The *effective use* of HWTS technologies (the percentage of the population that actually uses the intervention distributed to make contaminated source water safe to drink) requires

Home Water Treatment and Sanitation Methods. Categories of filtration methods include physical filtration, chemical and heat treatments. Source: CAWST – The Centre for Affordable Water and Sanitation Technology (www.cawst.org).

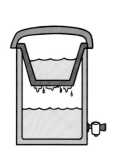 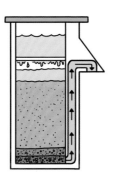 

Filtration: ceramic, porous, membrane filtration.

Chemical disinfection.

Heat: including boiling, pasteurisation and UV radiation.

Flocculant/ disinfectant.

considerably more effort to assess than more common monitoring and evaluation metrics, such as the number of product distributed, and in the little research available, there is increasing evidence that effective use may be a major challenge.

These challenges have been described in three fields of investigations. First, as referenced above, a series of field studies examining the microbiological effectiveness of boiling, by far the most common self-reported HWTS method used (Rosa, 2010), found it effective but sub-optimal in improving water quality. In general, shortcomings in performance were ascribed to inconsistent use and recontamination, factors that cannot be deduced from simple observation or surveys. Second, research on two long-term solar disinfection programmes found no impact on diarrhoeal disease in children (Arnold, B, 2009; Mausezahl, 2009). Third, research in the emergency context documented a large range of effective use (0-67.5 per cent of the targeted population using the distributed HWTS technology to improve the water quality in their home) across four acute emergency contexts (Lantagne, 2012a). The HWTS projects with the highest rates of effective use combined three factors: 1) they targeted households with contaminated water, such as those using unimproved sources; 2) they provided an HWTS method that effectively treated the water and, 3) they provided this method to a population who was familiar with that product, willing to use it, and trained in its use with the necessary supplies provided. Effective use was less than 15 per cent in all distribution-only projects, with products with more than two steps to operate, and when training was not provided. The two programmes with the highest effective use (Aquatabs distributed in Haiti (67.5 per cent effective use) and boiling in Indonesia (21.1 per cent effective use)) both existed in-country before the emergency occurred and had a safe water storage component.

All of the above results, which investigate the effectiveness of real-world, non-trial implementation programmes, provide a sobering view on whether or not HWTS interventions can be as effective in actual implementations as they are in trial circumstances.

However, there are two examples of more successful, real-world long-term HWTS implementations. The first is in a ceramic filter programme in Cambodia, which had reached over 2,000 households in four years before the evaluation. Households that had received a ceramic filter 0–44 months before the study were compared to matched controls (Brown, 2007). In a cross-sectional evaluation, 156 of 506 (30.8 per cent) households were still using the ceramic filter at the time of the visit, and the geometric mean *E coli* concentration in filtered water was 14 Colony Forming Units (CFUs) per 100 millilitres, as compared to 474 in unfiltered water. The main reason for filter disuse was breakage, as there was a 2 per cent breakage rate per month. A concurrent longitudinal diarrhoeal disease reduction study also documented a reduction in self-reported diarrhoeal disease of 46 per cent. The second programme is a liquid chlorine programme in rural Haiti, which began in 2002 and has subsequently reached over 4,000 families over 10 years (Harshfield, 2012). A total of 201 programme participants were randomly selected for a cross-sectional survey and compared to controls. Participants had been enrolled in the programme an average of 53 months at the time of the survey. Overall, 56 per cent of participants (versus 10 per cent of controls) had free chlorine residuals of 0.2–2.0

milligrams per litre, indicating correct water treatment. Additionally, significantly fewer children in participant households had an episode of diarrhoea in the previous 48 hours (31 per cent versus 52 per cent, p=0.001) with 59 per cent reduced odds (OR=0.41, 95 per cent CI 0.21–0.79). A commonality between both of these long-term, successful HWTS programmes is that they had extensive oversight and technical assistance by highly qualified programme managers over the long-term nature of the programme.

Overall, when reviewing the extensive research available on HWTS in developing countries, questions are raised about the actual impact of HWTS on improving health. It is clear from the data that: some HWTS technologies are highly effective in the laboratory context at removing the bacterial, viral and protozoal organisms that cause diarrhoeal disease; some HWTS options have been shown to reduce diarrhoeal disease in randomised, controlled intervention trials and, there are a few examples of long-term programmes with documented diarrhoeal disease reduction.

As such, there is an ongoing tension between the desire of some manufacturers and implementers to scale-up HWTS technologies widely, the research on health impacts, which questions the efficacy of HWTS, and the long-term goal of every household having access to a sustainable piped water supply that provides the maximum health gains. Clearly, HWTS technologies have a role in particular circumstances – as HWTS has advantages compared to other options in terms of being rapidly deployable, fast to distribute, and shown to improve the quality of stored household water. However, HWTS has drawbacks too, including placing the responsibility for water treatment at the individual household rather than the centralised level; necessitating training and follow-up; the availability of appropriate materials and, understanding and accepting that a (potentially large) portion of the target population will not use the method correctly to improve their water quality. There is little information on how to ensure that effective, appropriate HWTS options are correctly and consistently used by vulnerable target populations on a sustainable basis, and even less information on how to determine which populations are appropriate for targeting with HWTS technologies as opposed to other water, sanitation and hygiene interventions.

Example of Household Water Treatment and Safe Storage technologies.

A woman in Madagascar chlorinating water. © Daniele Lantagne.

Examples of Household
Water Treatment and
Safe Storage technologies.

from top:

A ceramic filter (Potters
for Peace). © Daniele
Lantagne.

A biosand filter (Hydraid).
© Daniele Lantagne.

A woman in Nepal using
the SODIS system.
© Eawag/Sandec.

SODIS user in India.
© Eawag/Sandec.

below: A boy in Vietnam
using the SODIS system.
© Eawag/Sandec.

Additionally, while there is a tendency to search for the 'silver bullet' HWTS technology that will be appropriate for all contexts, in actuality, the most appropriate HWTS method for a particular location is highly contextual and depends on a number of interconnected factors. These include:

1   existing diarrhoeal disease burden and pathogens of concern, as the HWTS technology selected to respond to a cholera outbreak (such as chlorine) may be very different than to respond to ongoing child diarrhoea attributed to rotavirus (such as vaccination) or cryptosporidium (such as filtration);
2   water and sanitation conditions and drinking water source quality, as in areas with insufficient water supply or poor water quality with high turbidity, HWTS technologies may be recommended only after source improvements have been made;
3   cultural acceptability and appropriateness, as some options (such as disinfectants) have chlorine-taste barriers in some cultures and other options (such as boiling) are more appropriate in areas with reliable fuel supplies and without deforestation concerns;
4   implementation feasibility, as concerns such as whether the appropriate amount of training is feasible to provide, or whether it is possible to transport the product to the vulnerable population, are critical;
5   financing, as some HWTS technologies are affordable by the vulnerable populations and some must be made available as either subsidised or free distribution. Responders must often weigh the question of whether to provide a higher-efficacy more expensive method or a less expensive method with higher effectiveness and,
6   availability, as simple product availability in the area at the time of need is crucial to ensuring that the product is used.

Given the variability in these factors there is clearly no silver bullet solution. This can be overwhelming to implementers, as the decision-making process for which HWTS option, if any, to implement can appear opaque. At this point in time, there is no standardised decision-making tool for HWTS option selection; individual implementers weigh the above and make option selection decisions. Implementers are increasingly providing a suite of HWTS options – similar to providing a suite of options for family planning to account for individual preference and needs – to allow for consumer choice and foster greater and sustained uptake.

Despite this variability in appropriate option based on individual context, however, there exists a strong desire from manufacturers to enter the HWTS space with new, untested, silver-bullet products. Before use, these new products need to be rigorously tested in both the laboratory and field contexts. It is highly recommended that all future research combine laboratory efficacy with field effectiveness analysis to understand both what technologies may be most effective, and also understand what technologies provide the greatest risk reduction in real-world circumstances.

In summary, the research all points to the need to carefully assess uptake and performance of interventions as part of implementing any HWTS programme or technology. The WHO and UNICEF have responded to this need by developing a document entitled *A Toolkit for Monitoring and Evaluating Household Water Treatment and Safe Storage Programmes*, which is an invaluable resource for implementers (Lantagne, 2012b). The lessons documented in the Toolkit, and herein, are not unique to household water treatment and safe storage programmes, but instead, consistent with experience in water supply, sanitation, hygiene and other household-level health interventions that require individual behaviour change to be successful.

Household interventions, such as household water treatment and safe storage, decentralise health management to the individual level, and inherently place an increased burden on those with fewer resources. They are not simple to implement and time, training and support are needed to design and build programmes that result in the behaviour change necessary to yield beneficial health outcomes. Successful intervention is possible, however, and these household interventions may be the preferred option in areas where centralised or community options are not available.

References

Arnold, B, Arana, B, Mausezahl, D, Hubbard, A and Colford, JM, Jr (2009). 'Evaluation of a pre-existing, 3-year household water treatment and handwashing intervention in rural Guatemala', *International Journal of Epidemiology, 38*(6), 1651–61

Arnold, BF and Colford, JM, Jr (2007). 'Treating water with chlorine at point-of-use to improve water quality and reduce child diarrhea in developing countries: a systematic review and meta-analysis', *The American Journal of Tropical Medicine and Hygiene, 76*(2), 354–64

Baqui, AH, Black, RE, Sack, RB, Chowdhury, HR, Yunus, M and Siddique, AK (1993). 'Malnutrition, cell-mediated immune deficiency, and diarrhea: a community-based longitudinal study in rural Bangladeshi children', *American Journal of Epidemiology, 137*(3), 355–65

Boschi-Pinto, C, Velebit, L and Shibuya, K (2008). 'Estimating child mortality due to diarrhoea in developing countries', *Bulletin of the World Health Organisation, 86*(9), 710–17

Brown, J, Sobsey, M and Proum, S, *Use of Ceramic Water Filters in Cambodia*. Water and Sanitation Program of the World Bank/UNICEF, Cambodia, 2007, www.wsp.org/UserFiles/file/926200724252_eap_cambodia_filter.pdf (accessed 10 January 2015)

Clasen, T, Schmidt, WP, Rabie, T, Roberts, I and Cairncross, S (2007). 'Interventions to improve water quality for preventing diarrhoea: systematic review and meta-analysis', *BMJ, 334*(7597), 782

Clasen, T, Thao do, H, Boisson, S and Shipin, O (2008). 'Microbiological effectiveness and cost of boiling to disinfect drinking water in rural Vietnam', *Environmental Science and Technology, 42*(12), 4255–60

Fewtrell, L and Colford, JM, Jr (2005). 'Water, sanitation and hygiene in developing countries: interventions and diarrhoea – a review', *Water Science and Technology, 52*(8), 133–42

Fischer Walker, CL, Perin, J, Aryee, MJ, Boschi-Pinto, C and Black, RE (2012). 'Diarrhea incidence in low- and middle-income countries in 1990 and 2010: a systematic review', *BioMed Central Public Health, 12*, 220

Guerrant, DI, Moore, SR, Lima, AA, Patrick, PD, Schorling, JB and Guerrant, RL (1999). 'Association of early childhood diarrhea and cryptosporidiosis with impaired physical fitness and cognitive function four–seven years later in a poor urban community in northeast Brazil', *The American Journal of Tropical Medicine and Hygiene, 61*(5), 707–13

Gupta, SK, Suantio, A, Gray, A, Widyastuti, E, Jain, N, Rolos, R, Hoekstra, RM and Quick, RE (2007). 'Factors associated with E coli contamination of household drinking water among tsunami and earthquake survivors, Indonesia', *The American Journal of Tropical Medicine and Hygiene, 76*(6), 1158–62

Harshfield, E, Lantagne, D, Turbes, A and Null, C (2012), 'Evaluating the Sustained Health Impact of

Household Chlorination of Drinking Water in Rural Haiti', *The American Journal of Tropical Medicine and Hygiene, 87*(5), 786–95

Hunter, PR (2009), 'Household water treatment in developing countries: comparing different intervention types using meta-regression', *Environmental Science and Technology, 43*(23), 8991–7

Lantagne, D and Clasen, T (2012a). 'Use of household water treatment and safe storage methods in acute emergency response: case study results from Nepal, Indonesia, Kenya, and Haiti'. *Environmental Science and Technology, 46*(20), 11352–60

Lantagne, D, Khush, R and Montgomery, M (2012b). *A Toolkit for Monitoring and Evaluating Household Water Treatment and Safe Storage Programmes*. World Health Organisation, Geneva, Switzerland

Mausezahl, D, Christen, A, Pacheco, GD, Tellez, FA, Iriarte, M, Zapata, ME, Cevallos, M, Hattendorf, J, Cattaneo, MD, Arnold, B, Smith, TA and Colford, JM, Jr (2009). 'Solar drinking water disinfection (SODIS) to reduce childhood diarrhoea in rural Bolivia: a cluster-randomised, controlled trial', *Public Library of Science Medicine, 6*(8), e1000125

Pruss-Ustun, A, Bos, R, Gore, F and Bartram, J (2008). *Safe water, better health: costs, benefits and sustainability of interventions to protect and promote health*. World Health Organisation, Geneva, Switzerland

Roberts, L, Chartier, Y, Chartier, O, Malenga, G, Toole, M and Rodka, H (2001). 'Keeping clean water clean in a Malawi refugee camp: a randomised intervention trial', *Bulletin of the World Health Organisation, 79*(4), 280–7

Rosa, G and Clasen, T (2010). 'Estimating the scope of household water treatment in low- and medium-income countries', *The American Journal of Tropical Medicine and Hygiene 82*(2), 289–300

Schmidt, WP and Cairncross, S (2009). 'Household water treatment in poor populations: is there enough evidence for scaling up now?' *Environmental Science and Technology, 43*(4), 986–92

Sobsey, M, Stauber, CE, Casanova, LM, Brown, J and Elliott, MA (2008). 'Point of use household drinking water filtration: A practical, effective solution for providing sustained access to safe drinking water in the developing world', *Environmental Science Technology, 42*(12), 4261–7

Sodha, SV, Menon, M, Trivedi, K, Ati, A, Figueroa, ME, Ainslie, R, Wannemuehler, K and Quick, R (2011). 'Microbiologic effectiveness of boiling and safe water storage in South Sulawesi, Indonesia', *Journal of Water Health 9*(3), 577–85

UNICEF/WHO (2009). *Diarrhoea: why children are still dying and what can be done.* World Health Organisation, United Nation's Children's Fund, Geneva, Switzerland, www.who.int/maternal_child_adolescent/documents/9789241598415/en (accessed 10 January 2015)

UNICEF/WHO (2012). *Progress on Drinking Water and Sanitation: 2012 Update*. United Nation's Childrens Fund; World Health Organisation, New York, NY, USA; Geneva, Switzerland, www.unicef.org/media/files/JMPreport2012.pdf (accessed 10 January 2015)

Waddington, H, Fewtrell, L, Snilstveit, B and White, H (2009). *Water, Sanitation and Hygiene Interventions to Combat Childhood Diarrhoea in Developing Countries*, 3ie Review, London, UK

WHO (2008). *Guidelines for drinking-water quality: Third edition incorporating the first and second addenda. Volume 1: Recommendations*. World Health Organisation, Geneva, Switzerland

WHO (2011a). *Evaluating household water treatment options: health-based targets and performance specifications*, World Health Organisation, Geneva, Switzerland

WHO (2011b). *Guidelines for Drinking-water Quality*, 4th edition. Geneva, Switzerland

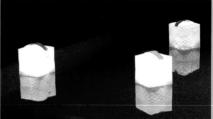

top left: An orphaned girl at the Reveil Matinal Orphanage Foundation (ROMF), in Port-au-Prince, Haiti, does her homework at night with the SolarPuff. © Damian Fitzsimmons.

top right: The SolarPuff, a patent pending solar inflatable lantern is designed to replace kerosene lanterns for the 1.6 billion people in the world without access to electricity. People in extreme poverty spend up to 30 per cent of their income on kerosene. This lantern is solar powered, adaptable, flat packable and low cost. The SolarPuff is designed to float so that fisherman in Makoko can use it at night instead of candles to attract fish. Fishing is a common trade in Makoko, some fisherman travel for days to the ocean to catch fish. © Alice Min Soo Chun.

above: In Makoko, Lagos, Nigeria, a cup is filled with kerosene and a string is lit to provide lighting at night. The smoke from this is toxic. The United Nations Development Programme (UNDP) reports two million children die each year because of poor indoor air quality. © Alice Min Soo Chun.

Ecology and Humanitarian Design

5

First defined in the mid-19th century, ecology was a vastly different matter compared to today. Ernst Haeckel, defined ecology as the comprehensive study of the relationship of organisms with their environment. In the intervening century and a half, other definitions of ecology have been proposed to reflect growth-pervasive definitions of ecology. Eventually the meaning of ecology evolved to be the study of the distribution and abundance of organisms and the study of ecosystems. The decline of our natural ecosystems calls for the combining of ecological design with integrated energy harnessing and human ecology in order to make a significant impact. This strategy could generate ethical methods of food production and sustainable systems for individualised infrastructure. Energy for lighting and communication is critical for livelihoods. Most regions in extreme poverty have decreased agricultural industry and live without a power grid. In Africa, there are 1,482,632,289 acres (600 million hectares) of uncultivated arable land, roughly 60 per cent of the global total. Farmers selling their goods must get up before sunrise to make it to market on time. There is no electricity so most use kerosene lanterns to light their way. Globally 1.6 billion people do not have access to electricity and rely on kerosene, a fossil fuel, for lighting. The smoke from these lanterns is toxic and causes burns, cataracts and two million childhood deaths per year due to bad indoor air quality.

New solutions, such as the SolarPuff — an inflatable solar lantern, allow localised infrastructure to redirect money from kerosene to food or education. Once a SolarPuff is purchased, lighting is free. In business, be it farming, education or health, the need for affordable and safe lighting is critical to daily life. By helping smallholders to move from subsistence to surplus, innovative solar energy used by millions at the local scale, could substantially offset carbon pollution at a global scale.

Höweler + Yoon Architecture, LLP,
Hover, New Orleans, Louisiana, USA,
2007, view from below. LED lighting
embedded in the canopy fabric is
powered by a solar-charged battery.
© Höweler + Yoon Architecture, LLP.

Architectures of Eco-Literacy

Eric Höweler and J Meejin Yoon

Access to, and production of, energy is widely uneven and unsustainable across the world. While in developing countries large portions of the population live without electricity and depend on expensive and toxic alternative fuels for lighting and cooking, in developed countries, the by-products of electricity generation are pushed to peripheries to cause major unseen environmental damage. Designing strategies for alternative energy must be a layered approach dealing not only with infrastructure and economies, but also cultural expectations and behaviours. Höweler + Yoon Architecture, a multidisciplinary practice that operates between architecture, art and landscape, presents here a series of installations that respond to the fragility of urban ecosystems. Their practice instigates discussion of energy and sustainable ecology by highlighting the ubiquitous resources of wind and sun, relating them to their social contexts. While new energy technologies proliferate, Höweler + Yoon Architecture uses beauty and play to encourage the changing of our energy behaviours. Here the vision of a thriving society reverberates with intelligent alternatives to energy consumption and production by utilising technology as a tool for education and resilience.

In the period following Hurricane Katrina, the reconstruction of New Orleans and its neighbourhoods proceeded at a painfully slow pace. There was a sense that the city might never recover completely to its pre-Katrina days. In October 2007, we were invited to participate in the Des Cours festival, which sought to animate hidden sites within the city with temporary installations designed by architects. Our proposal *Hover* was installed in the courtyard of a traditional house in the French Quarter. Recognising that the residents of New Orleans were still reeling from the experience of the hurricane, and wanting to activate the city, we proposed an illuminated canopy that would run on solar power. The fabric canopy would create a festive atmosphere during the day and early evening, but would also be entirely off-grid. The city's power grid and infrastructures in general proved to be highly vulnerable during the storm, and an off-grid solution demonstrated a kind of energy self-reliance that could inspire new attitudes towards resilience as vital city systems came back on line.

Hover, comprised of a series of yellow fabric canopies, shaped by a rigid aluminium frame to create a pentagonal tile. The tiling system allows the canopy to occupy any number of courtyard shapes and still pack into a complete surface. The cone-shaped surfaces of the canopy are specifically biased towards the solar orientation for New Orleans in October, thereby creating a solar collecting surface for a flexible photovoltaic panel (PV). The panel is connected to a custom microcontroller and a small rechargeable battery. When the PV is exposed to the sun the microcontroller switches to charging mode. When the PV is not charging the microcontroller acts as a switch to power an LED rope light that is sewn into the fabric. The effect was of a bright luminous cellular structure, under which outdoor events and impromptu jazz performances were held.

During the time that *Hover* was installed, the structure called attention to the sun as an abundant and reliable energy source, and that translated into a luminous structure representing greater implications. Explicit connection was made between smarter energy-conscious infrastructures and smarter building, rather than fetishise lone technologies grafted onto the status quo of architecture and urban living. It produced and consumed solar energy on the spot. It also made a point about energy independence and being able to function without reliance on a fragile infrastructure. But most importantly, the project was bright and festive, making a statement about the vibrancy of the city, and refusing to allow the storm to dampen the festive character for which the city is known.

Hurricane Katrina – and more recently Hurricane Sandy – served as a wake up call for environmental action, with many calls for more improved coastal management practices and energy infrastructures. At a greater scale the hurricanes have pointed to a larger cultural consciousness about extreme weather, global warming, the impact of human inhabitation on our eco-systems and the general instability of urban landscape contrary to existing faith in the impregnable modern city. For many, this has intensified an interest in sustainable and green design. Since 2005, there has been an explosion in interest in ecological architecture, environmentally friendly products and green design practices. Rightly or wrongly, the storm and its aftermath created visible evidence of the fragility of urban infrastructure and the necessity of environmental design.

It is impossible to speak of architectural discourse today without mentioning questions of energy, the environment, the larger ecology of discourses in which it is embedded. While contemporary architectural culture may find itself in the post-postmodern period, which is characterised by a proliferation of positions, without clear sides or stakes, it is clear that there is one dominant contemporary issue in architecture: ecological design. Ecological, sustainable, green … call it what you will, it is the central issue both within the academy and without. Yet the term ecological means different things in different contexts, and the proliferation of uses and abuses has created a kind of meaning smog. For us, ecology means the relation of elements or organisms to their larger context, where actions have consequences throughout a system or environment.

This renewed focus on ecological design has created a cultural condition complete with manifestos, regulations, manuals, products and markets. There are green design gurus and practitioners. There are accreditations, awards and certifications. There are green design standards and improvement standards. And, as with any movement, there is a coordinated market for green building products. Much of the discussion about green design centres on energy use, energy conservation. Energy efficiency and energy optimisation are key terms for an ecological design practice. This ecology of meanings and metrics prompted the 2009 issue of *Harvard Design Magazine* to ask if sustainability and pleasure were irreconcilable. Does being sustainable, using less energy, necessitate doing less or having fewer choices? Does ecological design rely on austerity?

Höweler + Yoon Architecture,
LLP, *Windscreen*, Cambridge,
Massachusetts, USA, 2012. Shifting
gusts of wind spun 220 individual
micro wind turbines to light
up LEDs across the screen.
© Höweler + Yoon Architecture, LLP.

Höweler + Yoon Architecture, LLP, *Windscreen*, Cambridge, Massachusetts, USA, 2012. The installation harnessed wind power beneath MIT's Green Building to create a dynamic pattern of light across an array of micro wind turbines. © Höweler + Yoon Architecture, LLP.

Eco-Literacy

Our own experience with post-Katrina New Orleans was instructive: the city was desperate to rebuild itself, and to learn from the past. Reconstruction took multiple forms. Some designs sought sustainability through LEED certifications and recycled materials. Our *Hover* project did not intend to save energy, or supply energy to the grid. It did not propose a utility for the energy that it produced. *Hover* sought to make energy visible. It sought to locate the site of energy production in the city centre, making energy not an abstract, remote and invisible process, but rather a tangible condition in the centre of the city. By making energy manifest itself in the form of a luminous canopy, it sought not to do any pro-active environmental good, but rather it sought to create an environmental awareness – an Eco-literacy. It creates the capacity for individuals to visualise energy, to understand the sources, methods of capture, products and by-products of energy. And in so doing, concretely alter their energy behaviours in other aspects of their lives.

The technology that has the greatest impact on energy consumption in architecture is not the argon-filled insulated glass units, or the geothermal heat pumps, but rather the human agency of the person who left the lights on, AC running and the windows open. A high performance window left open by a careless user is a high-tech, but useless, solution.

The Eco-literacy movement seeks to educate users about the way in which their actions affect the larger environment; those human actions — not technology — have the highest impact on energy use. The simple mechanism of visualising the effects of human action on energy has the greatest chance of affecting future behaviour. Making the connection between behavioural patterns and energy consumption requires a feedback loop. The energy efficiency displays of the first hybrid cars were revolutionary in that they allowed the driver to get immediate feedback on the relationship between their driving and energy consumption. Drivers presented with real-time feedback adjusted their driving patterns to drive more efficiently. This was dubbed the 'Prius Effect': an effective feedback loop of energy consumption as a consequence of actions in real time, capable of drastically altering user behaviour simply by showing the user the measurable effects of their actions.

Architecture can be understood as part of an information system, a low-definition broadcast medium capable of delivering information to users through its tectonic encoding. The Gothic cathedral, through its dematerialisation of the wall into an attenuated stone screen, was able to communicate a message through its implicit and explicit use of material, light, colour and ornament. More recent understandings of architecture as a semiotic system were popularised by postmodern and post-structuralist readings of architecture that made explicit use of signage, ornament and motifs to create a 'legible' architecture. Our claim for architecture of Eco-literacy builds on these theories of architectural communication to argue for architecture that is expressive of its own patterns of energy consumption and production, and is constructive of a broader energy consciousness. Architecture of Eco-literacy provides feedback to its users, informs their overall understanding of energy systems and their impact on the environment so that their energy behaviour can be productively altered.

Eco-Bling

Amidst calls for verifiable metrics for sustainable design and quantifiable evidences of green credentials, the rhetoric of sustainability compels us to use less energy, optimise systems and increase the functional performance of buildings. Its mantra replaces 'Less is More' with 'Less or Else'. Austerity and restraint are the implicit mechanisms of sustainable practices. Yet the goals of sustainable design are to convince as much as they are to reduce. The communication of energy practices is essential to the project of sustainability. As we have seen, the feedback loop of behavioural patterns and energy use is one of the most effective tools for improving energy efficiency. In fact, changing energy behaviour is more important than any energy technology. Sustainable design is not equivalent to austerity design. Sustainable design can mean doing more, or better, rather than simply less.

NLÉ, Makoko Floating School, Makoko, Lagos, Nigeria, 2013. The school is a prototype floating structure, built for the historic water community of Makoko and located on the lagoon, at the heart of Nigeria's largest city, Lagos. As a pilot project, it has taken an innovative approach to address the community's social and physical needs in view of the impact of climate change and a rapidly urbanising African context. Its main aims are to generate a sustainable, ecological, alternative building system and urban water culture for the teeming population of Africa's coastal regions. © Iwan Baan.

Circling Research with Design
NLÉ's African Water Cities Project and
Prototype Floating School for Makoko

Kunlé Adeyemi

NLÉ, the Amsterdam and Lagos-based studio founded by Nigerian-born architect Kunlé Adeyemi, developed the Makoko Floating School as a prototype structure for their proposed 'Lagos Water Communities Project', following on from their 'African Water Cities' research project. African regions have little or no permanent infrastructure thanks to unpredictable water levels that cause regular flooding. Makoko epitomises the most critical challenges posed by urbanisation and climate change in coastal Africa. At the same time, it also inspires possible solutions and alternatives to the invasive culture of land reclamation. The ecology of floating systems at first glance seems ad hoc, but on closer inspection the water village revels in a highly sophisticated growing organism of ambitious networks.

The impact of rapid urbanisation and economic growth on cities in Africa is now common knowledge and widely discussed, whereas the implications of climate change (a day-to-day reality) are often a neglected factor in urban analysis. An understanding of climatic changes is of particular interest in coastal African cities that are now experiencing a significant rise in sea levels and increases in rainfall.

It has been noted that '[a]lthough Africa is the continent least responsible for climate change, it is particularly vulnerable to the effects, including reduced agricultural production, worsening food security, the increased incidence of flooding and drought'.[1] Coastal towns are by far the most developed of Africa's urban areas and, by implication, have a high concentration of residential, industrial, commercial, educational and military facilities.[2] The Intergovernmental Panel on Climate Change (IPCC) projects that the African coastal population will rise rapidly from 1.2 billion in 1990 to 5.2 billion by 2080.[3] In particular it recognises the Nigerian coast as one of the low-lying areas in West Africa that is likely to experience severe effects from flooding as a result of rising sea levels and climate change, especially at high tides and during the rainy season.[4]

Almost 30 per cent of Lagos, the smallest state of Nigeria, is covered by water and wetlands, and with the increase in flooding this area is likely to expand. At the same time, Lagos is challenged with a shortage of over 5 million housing units to accommodate its growing population. The exorbitant costs of building and the legal acquisition of land are far beyond the means of most people to meet their basic physical and social need – a home.

Makoko, one of the state's so-called squatter settlements, has grown informally in the waters of Lagos over the last 100 years. The community thrives on fishing and logging, providing more than a third of Lagos's fish supply and most of its timber. Here, nearly 100,000 people are living in wooden houses built on stilts in water; the cheapest dwelling units available. In essence, though Makoko has challenges, its inhabitants have found solutions to the problems of overpriced land, housing shortage and frequent flooding, creating opportunities for agriculture, industry and trade. It is one of many global examples of local innovation. Makoko shows maximum urbanisation with minimum means, and NLÉ has explored this territory as a contemporary model and catalyst for adapting coastal African cities to the impact of climate change.

NLÉ has identified the top 20 'African Water Cities' as Cairo, Lagos, Kinshasa, Khartoum, Luanda, Alexandria, Abidjan, Dar es Salaam, Cape Town, Dakar, Casablanca, Durban, Algiers, Accra, Douala, Ouagadougou, Bamako, Lomé, Maputo and Rabat. The African Partnership Forum has stressed that urgent action is needed.[5] These are cities that present challenges and opportunities to cultivate new ways of living in African coastal areas. Other cities will soon join the list. Ganvié, a growing 'water city' situated on Lake Nokoué in southern Benin, north of the city of Cotonou, has been described as 'the Venice of Africa'. Similar to Makoko, it has thousands of wooden houses built on stilts and a population of approximately 30,000 who all live off fishing. The lake is more populous than any other place on Benin's mainland and continues to grow. While water and rising sea levels are often rightly perceived as threats to urban settlements, in Ganvié the lake becomes the new urban terrain, developing its own rules, identities and ingenuities.

Makoko and Ganvié are contemporary models of African water cities. With the support of the Makoko community as well as international organisations and collaborators, NLÉ is learning from models such as these to develop improved prototypes and catalysts for future African coastal cities. Its 'floating school', for example, though its potential economic viability in the longer term is recognised, it is a social contribution/development not intended for commercial gains. Instead, it will generate a viable and ecologically sustainable alternative construction system for the teeming population of Africa's coastal regions.

The School as Prototype

Makoko Floating School is a prototype floating structure for Makoko. Until now Makoko was served by one English-speaking primary school, built on uneven reclaimed land, surrounded by constantly changing waters. Like many homes in Makoko, this has rendered the primary school building structurally precarious and susceptible to recurrent flooding. Sadly, the inability of the building to effectively withstand the impact of increased rainfall and flooding has frequently threatened local children's access to their basic need: the opportunity of education.

In response to this and in close collaboration with the Makoko community, NLÉ has developed a prototype floating structure that will serve primarily as a school, while being scalable and adaptable for other uses, such as a community hub, health clinic, market, entertainment centre or housing. The prototype's versatile structure is a safe and economical floating triangular frame that allows flexibility for customisation and completion, based on specific needs and capacities.

NLÉ, Makoko Floating
School, Makoko,
Lagos, Nigeria, 2013.
© Iwan Baan.

NLÉ, Makoko Floating
School, Makoko,
Lagos, Nigeria, 2013.
School Classroom.
© Iwan Baan.

The triangular A-frame or pyramid is 33 feet (10 metres) high with a 33-feet × 33-feet (10-metre × 10-metre) base. It is an ideal shape for a floating object on water due to its relatively low centre of gravity, which provides stability and balance even in heavy winds. It also has a total capacity to safely support 100 adults, even in extreme weather conditions.

The building has three levels. The first level is an open play area for school breaks and assembly, which also serves as a community space after school. The second level is an enclosed space for two to four classrooms, providing enough space for 60 to 100 pupils. A staircase on one side connects the open play area, the classrooms and a semi-enclosed workshop space on the third level.

The simple yet innovative structure adheres to ideal standards of sustainable development with its inclusive technologies for renewable energy, waste reduction, water and sewage treatment as well as the promotion of low-carbon transport. Furthermore a team of eight Makoko-based builders constructed it using eco-friendly, locally sourced bamboo and wood procured from a local sawmill.

Construction began in September 2012 with flotation mock-ups and testing. Recycled empty plastic barrels, found abundantly in Lagos, were used for the building's buoyancy system, which consists of 16 wooden modules, each containing 16 barrels. The modules were assembled on the water, creating the platform that provides buoyancy for the building and its users. Once this was assembled, construction of the A-frame followed and was completed by March 2013. Makoko Floating School is now in regular use by the community.

The project was initiated, designed and built by NLÉ in collaboration with the Makoko Waterfront Community in Lagos State. The project was initially self-funded by NLÉ and later received research funds from the Heinrich Böll Foundation as well as funds for its construction from the United Nations Development Programme/Federal Ministry of Environment Africa Adaptation Programme (AAP).

Notes
1   Andrew Steer, World Bank Special Envoy for Climate Change, 15 November 2011. The link for this website page is no longer available, but was live on publication of the original article in 2012.
2   Ibidun O Adelekan, 'Vulnerability of Poor Urban Coastal Communities to Climate Change in Lagos, Nigeria', Fifth Urban Research Symposium, 2009. Published in *Environment & Urbanization* (Institute for Environment and Development), Sage Journals, vol 22, no 2, October 2010, pp 433–50, http://eau.sagepub.com/content/22/2/433.full.pdf+html (accessed 10 January 2015).
3   Intergovernmental Panel on Climate Change, 2007, www.ipcc.ch (accessed 10 January 2015).
4   Adelekan, 'Vulnerability of Poor Urban Coastal Communities', p 2.
5   Document prepared by APF support unit and the NEPAD Secretariat for the 8th Meeting of the African Partnership Forum Berlin, 22–23 May 2007, www.oecd.org/officialdocuments/publicdispl aydocumentpdf/?cote=APF/MEETING(2007)2&docLanguage=En (accessed 10 January 2015).

First part of the text, pp 143–4, 'Africa Water Cities' © Kunlé Adeyemi. First published in *City Catalyst: Architecture in the Age of Extreme Urbanisation*, *Architectural Design (AD)*, Wiley, vol 82, no 5, September/October, 2012, pp 98–101. Second part of text, pp 144–7 © 2015 John Wiley & Sons Ltd.

A small step innovating how we make, versus what we make, can render a critical difference at local and global scales, by rethinking the method of how to build efficiently owing to merciless conditions of cost, abundance of waste, climate and terrain. For example, one of the world's great designs for emergent countries was developed during the last 50 years: a brick-making machine. This simple device creates a Compressed Earth Block (CEB), a brick made from earth. Mud or earth is packed into a brick-shaped receptacle, a large lever is pulled down and a perfect rammed earth brick is produced. This system allows people to 'manufacture bricks at their own speed – 8,000 a day or 800,000 in a week – depending on the model. With these bricks schools, homes and hospitals have been built all over South America and the third world. While visiting the University of Lagos in Nigeria, a professor of architecture spoke highly of the use of this local material for a project that required a road to be built to the construction site. Resourcefulness and a holistic strategy allowed reciprocity within the system in three impactful ways. First the building material came directly from the land excavated for the road, so no earth had to be transported away from the construction: no material waste was created. Second, the machine allowed construction to take place without degradation to the land by heavy trucks and machinery, since the CEB machine was adaptable

Local Materials and Local Skills

6

to virtually any terrain. Third, local labour created local training and jobs for future construction. By rethinking how to produce architecture using local operations there is a potential opportunity to catalyse the economic market for developing regions. MASS Design Group has designed some exemplary buildings that utilise local materials, such as brick and bamboo. Local economic development always follows the construction process through the integration of social economic development in an organic system of benefits for the local community. Umubano Primary School in Kigali, Rwanda, has been a testament to these brilliant systemic networks of design of communal structures. Across the world in Ireland, there is a reminder of economic degradation in the historic city of Limerick, yet in this city there are grounds for resilient design. As political and academic institutions tried collaboration to regenerate the city, students from the local school of architecture took the opportunity to engage with local communities to form radical new support networks. These networks and new hybrid programmes have created an organic unity between all institutions and the communities that are carrying forward the city's regeneration. Universities and local governments are creating economic change through the interface between education, politics and urban reform.

left: MASS Design Group, Umubano Primary School, Kigali, Rwanda, 2011. This building uses local materials, such as brick and bamboo. The process of training local people in construction skills creates jobs and is almost more important than the actual building. This acts as a humanitarian design strategy for the long-term resilience of the local community. © Iwan Baan.

right: Peter Rich Architects, Mapungubwe Interpretation Centre, Mapungubwe National Park, Limpopo, South Africa, 2008–10. Local materials and indigenous plants are used in the construction of buildings using traditional methods. Mapungubwe is located on South Africa's northern border with Botswana and Zimbabwe. The society living in what is today a UNESCO World Heritage Site, is thought to have been the most complex in the region, implementing the first class-based social system in southern Africa. © Iwan Baan.

Intelligent Materials and Technology

Alice Min Soo Chun

Materiality, social space, water management, waste management, energy production and consumption, need to be designed and coordinated so that the economic, social and environmental objectives are achieved in the most effective way. Global emissions, energy consumption and material waste necessitate a systematic approach to sustainable scales, large and small.

Industries are moving away from petrol-based materials and moving towards a condition of hybridisation between natural materials, reuse and new technology. What science and technology are finding is that we can no longer separate the choices that we make in materials from their impact on the environment, the economy and the preservation of culture. The dynamic intelligence of natural materials has historically been sustainable and the choices we make will play a critical factor in the future remediation of our global climate. Intelligent choices for materials should be raised to adhere to levels of performance on multiple levels. For instance, upcycling and recycling can reduce and remediate waste production; with this, local communities can create new economies and generate diverse localised opportunities for economic and ecological resilience. New technology is also changing how those materials can perform. Performance in sustainability requires an integrative approach that includes various disciplines in the fields of design, construction and urban infrastructure. Technology and systems are becoming further hybridised as well; what used to be a separate mechanical system can now be compressed within the space of a surface, and what used to be a limit is now an opportunity for redefining architectural discourse, uniting social intent with architectural production.

Materiality, as it is linked to ecology and economy, has been a growing and critical development in design thinking. For instance, the material wood in a country where there is extreme poverty has a direct link to the state of the ecology of that region. In an interview with Nader Tehrani, Professor of Architecture at the Massachusetts Institute of Technology, he explained:

> In Peter Buchanan's exhibit *Ten Shades of Green*, Buchanan says: "Wood is the material with least embodied energy if it is from sustainably managed forests." And it's clear that when you think of all the resources and the attitude to resources, the big advantage of wood is that, of course, you can give the opportunity for reforestation.[1]

In order to feed a population, cooking with wood is culturally relevant. In a country such as Haiti, where the unemployment rate is 98 per cent, and wood charcoal is the primary cooking fuel, over 95 per cent of land is deforested as a result. No jobs in the agricultural sector means no money for alternative fuel to cook, so the wood from the trees in the

Banana fibres are extremely strong and naturally antimicrobial. This woven pattern integrates leftover suede strands and banana fibre into a floor covering. © Alice Min Soo Chun.

local land is the only viable option. The lack of jobs becomes a critical measure of levels affecting education, health and ecology in any region. Can this problem have a material solution? Material choices become critical where in Haiti a population of over 10 million people use charcoal for cooking. If a material could replace the use of charcoal for cooking in a country such as Haiti, it would transform the state of ecological degradation, alleviate the continuance of mudslide disasters, as well as provide jobs for the local economy. There are a number of burgeoning companies with the ambition of alleviating ecological duress. These companies are innovating the way we use agricultural waste. Materials such as banana leaves become perfect material for floor coverings. Local materials along with a binding agent can burn cleaner and longer than the conventional charcoal made from wood. A southern farmer and activist, Joe Duplon, has founded a business, which is a local grass-roots organisation that is creating and selling an alternative charcoal made with coconut shells, bamboo and almond shells, combined with a bio-plastic binder.

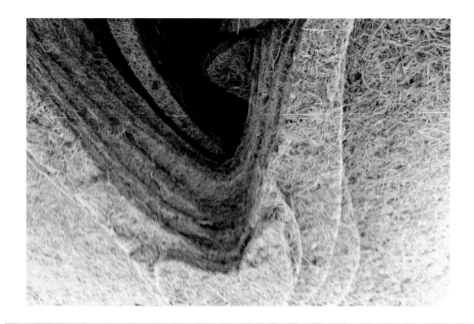

Wood then becomes relevant politically as it relates to building materials. When natural disasters strike a developing country the rebuilding process should include the use of local materials, local skills and progressive relationships with local politicians. The past reliance on imported materials for building has proven to be a debilitating strategy that only works in the short term. The use of imported materials has provided a crippling reliance on outside foreign aid instead of revitalising local labour forces and indigenous resources.

The hillsides in Port-au-Prince are a speckled collage of plywood dwellings that have been painted in an array of colours. Seen on the cover of this book, the colours are in fact a code for the various nongovernmental organisations (NGOs) that are building plywood shed dwellings. They are coloured according to the various NGOs, for example, Christian Relief Services (CRS) are painted blue, the United Nations' (UN) sheds are greenish turquoise and the pink ones belong to another NGO. Each shed is built with ¾-inch thick (approximately two-centimetre thick) plywood with a concrete slab on grade base. These sheds are labelled 'transition housing', yet the timeline of transition may be as long as five years or longer. Using the term 'transition' in these instances somehow justifies the lack of bathroom, kitchen or electricity.

The ambition to reduce extreme poverty needs a series of planning strategies that employ local talents and practices for housing. Most attempts have not succeeded in the recent past, especially in reference to the rampant growth of informal cities developing in Africa. The mistake that governments and NGOs made, which contributed to the failure of housing development, was a lack of integration of local sourcing, innovative design practices and technologies.[2]

opposite: Coconut fibre is plentiful in sub-Saharan Africa. Its many uses range from mattresses to landslide mitigation on barren hillsides. This is an agricultural waste product that is already found locally in the markets of Lagos, Nigeria, for skin exfoliation. © Alice Min Soo Chun.

below: Wood Mills, Makoko, Lagos, Nigeria, 2011. Wood is the common material for building the houses on stilts in Makoko. Wood logs are brought in by waterways from other regions. In the background is a sea of floating logs. © Alice Min Soo Chun.

Peter Rich Architects, Mapungubwe Interpretation Centre, Mapungubwe National Park, Limpopo, South Africa, 2008–10. Mapungubwe is located on South Africa's northern border with Botswana and Zimbabwe. These exhibition and learning spaces take the form of 10 free-form vaults, the largest of which spans 47½ feet (14.5 metres), and a number of regular barrel vaults and domes, which are arranged in a triangular layout linked together by ramped walkways. The vaulting method used relies on fast-setting gypsum mortar and earth tiles. Low environmental impact is achieved by employing local labour and materials. © Iwan Baan.

This section shows the rhizome root system of the bamboo plant, which is extremely useful for deterring soil erosion. This root system combined with vetiver, shown on the right side of the section, combines both vertical and horizontal root systems similar to a biaxial weave, to create a strong natural root textile. © Alice Min Soo Chun.

In an interview with Cameron Sinclair, cofounder of Architecture for Humanity, he stated:

Not only do we have the power (as architects), we have the responsibility in our role within a community. Our role is not only to come up with solutions but to fight and say: "Guys, you cannot do this. You're shipping in wood, you're undermining the local construction economy, and you're coming up with a prefabricated system that doesn't generate long-term jobs. Let's be clear about the intentions of why you're helping."[3]

The sustainable goal is to alleviate the expense on shipping and foreign labour in order to increase local profit from agriculture and local labour. This design strategy is a multifaceted and a regenerative solution, where ingenuity and adaptation create a new materiality for cultural resilience.

Natural Materials

Materiality lies at the heart of contemporary design, yet ancient materials are frequently overlooked as high performance materials with varied structural capabilities. One of the best examples of an intelligent natural material is bamboo. First originating in Africa, bamboo has been used for centuries as a building material, as well as a nutrient for food and a versatile raw material. It has approximately 10 times the tensile strength of steel and is naturally water resistant. It can be harvested and grown sustainably in places with the right environment; in some instances it can grow 39 inches (1 metre) within 24 hours. Bamboo is one of the fastest-growing plants in the world, due to a unique rhizome-dependent root.[4]

Developing regions experiencing exponential population growth are riddled with growing communities that have a vast need for increased housing. A disproportionate number of these communities are found in the belt around the equator. This is where bamboo is found growing in abundance, it is affordable, and is, or could be, a locally grown cultivated resource. The applications for bamboo are endless and its properties are currently being mined for cosmetics, textiles, resonance instruments, water filtration and air purification and other agricultural and economic possibilities. Its fibres are naturally resistant to bed bugs; it can be used along with coconut shell charcoal for an alternative to wood charcoal and can be hybridised into structural concrete. In areas where there is extreme deforestation, mudslides threaten communities every time it rains. Bamboo has immense soil stabilising ability and historically has been used for land remediation because of the interlocking growth of its rhizomatic root system.

Hybridisation of Bamboo and Concrete

In 1950, after the Second World War, Professor HE Glenn, an engineer at Clemson Agricultural College of South Carolina, performed extensive research and tests on the tensile strength of bamboo as an alternative to steel reinforcing in concrete.[5] The first test proved that bamboo could be used as reinforcement in concrete. There were drawbacks to the use of natural bamboo, however, owing to the coefficient of thermal expansion, fungi and insect attacks. It was not until 1995, in Rio de Janeiro, Brazil, that Professor K

Ghavami at the Pontifícia Universidade Católica, did several mechanical tests on bamboo-reinforced lightweight concrete beams. These were built with specific bamboo species that concluded positive under stress testing. There was an increase in strength under applied load as compared to steel reinforced concrete beams. Further research at the Future Cities Laboratory in Singapore, by Chair Dirk E Hebel, found that new composite bamboo fibre material from China allowed for the retention of increased tensile and compressive strength as well as the flexural properties of natural bamboo fibre. The bamboo composite demonstrated a unique ability in compression and bending, which allowed it to absorb more energy than steel before failure. There are extensive plans for testing the control of physical and mechanical properties found in the composite bamboo as it reacts to accelerators, retarders and chemical binders. In the context of a concrete-reinforced matrix, hybridising bamboo composite with concrete may be a carbon neutral alternative to the use of steel components in concrete. On a theoretical level, these innovative strategies propose the possibility of a 'reverse' or 'alternative modernism', where knowledge and technological invention can be learned from the developing global south by the more developed countries of the global north.[6]

Natural Products and Zero Waste

Agriculture employs 65 per cent of Africa's labour force and accounts for 32 per cent of gross domestic product. Agricultural performance has improved since 2000 but growth is not yet fast enough; agricultural GDP growth in sub-Saharan Africa has accelerated from 2.3 per cent per year in the 1980s to 3.8 per cent per year from 2000 to 2005.[7] Africa's food production must increase in order to yield enough food to feed its emerging populations. In tandem with this, industries could take advantage of agro-waste and transform these by-products into new products that can drive new businesses. Some multifaceted agricultural crops that have this potential are beginning to pervade the building market in the area of finishes for interior products.

Coconut fibre and banana fibre are examples of such crops. Both the food product yield of the crop and its waste can be utilised. While it is well known that coconut flesh and milk are incredibly nutritious, less publicised is that coconut fibre can be used as a material in diverse applications from soil remediation, such as brownfield management, or top surface stabilisation to prevent mudslides, to luxury mattresses. It is naturally water repellant and fire resistant. Meanwhile the shells can be used for charcoal and can be an excellent water filter. Companies like Brita are using coconut charcoal as the primary material in their water filters. In some countries, like Jamaica, there are companies that are producing amazing bathroom tiles from coconut shells that rival porcelain or glass tile.

Along similar lines, the banana crop is incredibly resilient and can be used for both food and manufactured products. Banana fibre can be blended with silk to make an incredibly soft textile. Other natural fibres can be combined with a variety of agricultural wastes with new strides in bio-plastic binders allowing for innovative composites, such as cotton and milk protein or flax with bio resin. The strength of the composite strand is found to retain the mechanical and physical properties of the original natural material.

left: Coconut shell bathroom tiles are extremely hard and naturally waterproof. This material looks and feels like stone. © Alice Min Soo Chun.

below: This material, ECOVATIVE, is made from fungal mycelium and agricultural waste. This is a completely natural alternative to polystyrene or Styrofoam. Styrofoam is one of the least sustainable materials, it emits toxic fumes during manufacture, will never decompose and cannot be recycled. © Alice Min Soo Chun.

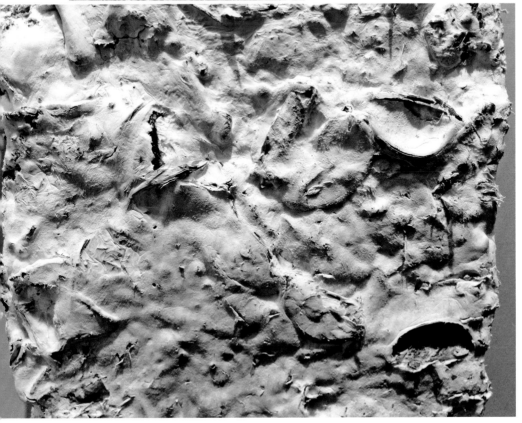

below: The pattern for a stone wall demonstrates culturally significant building skills, where no mortar is used. A system of miniature stone chips fills the in-between spaces where mortar would have been. A local skill and material replaces cement for the interstitial binder. © Alice Min Soo Chun.

opposite top: Paper brick sections. New non toxic bio-plastic binders enable paper to be moulded into strong durable bricks, interlocking connections make mortar obsolete. © Alice Min Soo Chun.

opposite bottom: Recycled bike tyre inner tubes, repurposed to be floor- or wallcovering material. © Alice Min Soo Chun.

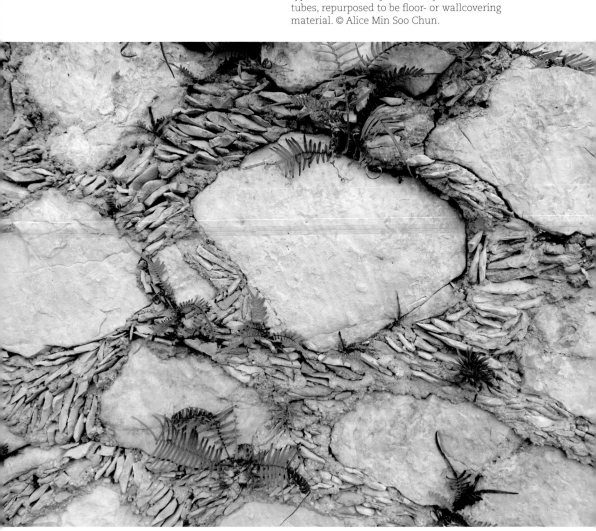

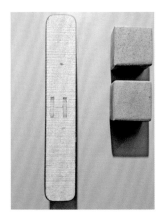

Agricultural Waste to Alternative Energy

Climate change and the reduction in oil reserves internationally have led to the development of carbon-neutral forms of energy to replace fossil fuels and reduce the emission of greenhouse gases into the atmosphere. For countries with an agrarian base, residual waste or biomass created from agricultural waste products – seeds, shells, cores, stalks and animal manure – are readily available, plentiful and almost free. Biomass can be processed into fuel and be used to create renewable energy. A process utilising bio-digesters can turn waste into ethanol fuel for running transport and heating homes. The United Nations estimate that approximately 140 billion metric tons of biomass is generated from agriculture, globally. This is the equivalent of 50 billion metric tons of oil. These waste products have the potential to eradicate the dependence on oil and gas and eliminate carbon emissions. In addition, biomass is just as applicable as a source of energy for large-scale industries as it is for micro businesses.[8]

Among the world's most impoverished countries, the production of sugar cane yields one of the greatest opportunities for waste management and the manufacture of an alternative biofuel, known as cellulosic ethanol. The biofuel is created from bagasse, the fibrous matter or cellulose that remains in sugar production after the cane's stalks are crushed to extract their juice. According to Nationmaster's figures, drawn from United Nations' statistics: Brazil produces over 106 million tons of bagasse per year; Vietnam produces over 62 million tons; India almost 50 million tons; China almost 30 million tons and South Africa produces over 8 million tons.[9] Over the next decade Brazil is expected to continue to be the main global exporter of ethanol, with production almost tripling. Though currently there are challenges attached to the fermentation of sugars from cellulose, in time a balance between yield, operational and capital costs will be achieved for this bioenergy, which should help to promote the economic viability of this fuel source. The choice of ethanol as a fuel could dramatically reduce the high cost of transporting fossil fuels to land-locked countries in Africa or remote island nations. Bio-innovation suggests that in the near future fuels may be created from other crop residues at a reasonable cost. Today, though, sugar cane bagasse remains one of the most promising sources of bio-energy with the best positive net energy balance of cellulosic feedstocks.[10]

Recycling

Plastic and Economic Resilience by Thread

The amount of materials that are disposed of as waste is overwhelming. According to the Environmental Protection Agency (EPA), the United States alone is responsible for generating 250 million tons of waste every year.[11] From this, 55 per cent, or 137.5 million tons of waste is sent to landfills.[12] While statistics concerning the world's waste generation do not exist, it is safe to assume that the quantity is huge, considering that the United States accounts for just over 4 per cent of the world's population. New for-profit companies, such as Thread are taking advantage of this problem and creating a

Makoko, Lagos, Nigeria, 2011.
A boy walks the streets, as
waste and sewage overflow in
a sea of littered piles of plastic
waste. © Alice Min Soo Chun.

solution. Thread's vision is to shift the perception of waste from being an environmental and public health threat, to being regarded as a resource. A disposable mentality exists in the majority of the world, and most view waste as a problem that needs to be buried, when in reality, we are literally throwing away money.

Waste is currently the largest export from the United States,[13] most of which is exported to China. China then utilises that scrap in production, and sells those products around the world. Although a product may be made out of recycled content, that content was most likely shipped around the world to be used, thus negating the positive environmental impact of recycled content, due to the extensive use of fossil fuels for transport.

One of the largest problems developing nations face is waste management. It is common for 30–60 per cent of all urban solid waste in developing countries to remain uncollected, with less than 50 per cent of the population served.[14] With little functioning infrastructure, governments lacking resources and capital, and little to no culture of recycling among the general population, waste management is a nonexistent amenity in the developing world.

Without a way to efficiently collect and dispose of waste, it is left in the streets, thrown down ravines or burned. Little to no separation occurs and hazardous materials, infectious materials and plastics are often burned together. Waste poses serious environmental and public health threats: spreading disease, or pumping toxic fumes into the air from incineration.[15] Household waste creates further problems because of its unsightly appearance. The amount of waste in public places contributes to the slum mentality of people living in poor neighbourhoods.

Recycling offers economic opportunity that impacts on micro and macro scales. By offering money per pound of plastic collected and brought to recycling centres, individuals can generate enough money to feed their families, or pay for school fees. A few cents or dollars for an average Haitian family living on less than US$2 each day[16] can make an immense impact on the quality of life for that family.

Waste is not simply a developing world problem. While developed countries have the ability to collect, bury or incinerate waste, these are not sustainable strategies for the environment. Recycling and upcycling are as yet not fully utilised, and it is estimated that the United States only recycles about 34 per cent of waste generated.[17]

Paper

The estimated 2.6 billion holiday cards sold each year in the United States could fill a football field 10 storeys high.[18] The United States is one of the biggest consumers of paper in the world. Between 1990 and 2002, paper consumption in the United States increased from 84.9 million tons to 97.3 million tons.[19] Environmental awareness due to lobbying by environmental organisations and increased government regulation, has shifted the trend towards environmental and economic sustainability in the pulp and paper industry. According to United Nations statistics, pulp and paper is the third largest industrial polluter of the air, water and land in both Canada and the United States, and releases well over 110,231 tons of toxic pollution each year. Worldwide, the pulp and paper industry is the fifth largest consumer of energy, accounting for 4 per cent of all the world's energy use.[20] The pulp and paper industry uses more water to produce a ton of product than any other industry.

Pioneering companies are now developing hybridised strategies that combine, upcycling and recycling paper. *Paperwood*, a proprietary product, is an innovative new product, which utilises paper to create solid surfacing material that is almost identical at a first glance to wood, although with closer inspection the wood grain is actually made of layers of newspaper. More examples of innovative products using paper are enhancing physical metrics of what paper can be. Technologies combining bio-plastic binders and heat compression can increase the durability and strength of paper composite materials to make paper bricks and solid surfacing for exterior applications.

Textiles

The clothing industry in the United States created an estimated 14.3 million tons of textiles in 2012. The EPA estimates this as 5.7 per cent of total municipal solid waste (MSW) generation. New industries in textile recycling are profiting from and shifting waste into sustainable new materials for building.[21] To date, the Blue Jeans Go Green™ denim recycling programme has collected more than one million pieces of denim. These efforts have diverted over 600 tons of waste out of landfills and will generate approximately 2 million square feet (185,806 square metres) of UltraTouch™ Denim Insulation for use in buildings.[22] Other innovative ways are being created to reuse textile products within wall panelling. In Brazil and other areas of Latin America, artisans and locals are creating wall panels with textiles that are purposefully identifying the origins of the cloth. Many of these panels carry an artisan's touch, where the compositions are one of a kind. These panels can be created with a bio-plastic binder, which makes them nontoxic and durable.

The visibility of waste is an economic differentiator. Waste management is a service that is paid for and dealt with by companies and municipalities. The incredible volume and physical mass of waste is never really seen. This contributes to a 'throwaway' culture, as consumers are not responsible for the waste they create. The minute waste is thrown in the rubbish or recycling bin, our subconscious tends to mitigate our responsibility.

In creating more sustainable systems it is important to provide consumers with the information they need to make responsible, sustainably driven purchasing decisions. If we focus on recognising what goes into the products, and what those products can become, we could reduce some of the needless excess of recyclable material sitting in landfills.

It is crucial that we begin to increase recycling and reuse rates throughout the world, but beyond that we need to truly close the loop on product manufacturing. Once a product is disposed of there should already be a plan for the product to be turned into something else. Terracycle, an organisation in New Jersey, does an exemplary job of this: selling toothbrushes upcycled from yoghurt pots. Customers can return the discarded toothbrushes to be reused in the manufacture of park benches.[23]

To truly impact the shift towards sustainability and reusing waste products as raw materials, it is crucial that this understanding occurs at every step of the supply chain.

Design principles that focus on the reuse of existing products as their supply source are imperative to creating a true demand for recycled materials.

Designers and manufacturers will play a critical role in increasing the amount of recycled materials utilised in production. Manufacturers can invest time and capital into technology capable of creating products from a recycled supply, as an alternative to virgin material. Similarly, designers should design with the idea that their product will be recycled into a supply source at the end of its lifecycle. Manufacturers and designers will need to collaborate to ensure that products can be recycled effectively. By truly understanding product design in the context of a close-looped cycle, allowing for participants along the supply chain to ensure that they are sourcing, designing and manufacturing in a way that enables materials to be used again and again, we can lower our dependence on nonrenewable resources.

Wall panels made from recycled blue jeans.
Artisans craft and press layers of partial blue
jeans together to make a patchwork topography
of blue jean details. © Alice Min Soo Chun.

Notes

1 Nader Terrani, interview by the author, New York, New York, 17 March 2012.
2 Dirk Hebel, 'Appropriateness is a Moving Target: The Re-invention of Local Construction Technologies and Materials in Ethiopia', *ATDF Journal*, vol 7, issue 1/2, 2010, p 40.
3 Cameron Sinclair, interview by the author, New York, New York, July 2012.
4 David Farrelly, *The Book of Bamboo*, Sierra Club Books, San Francisco, 1984, p 25.
5 HG Glenn, 'Bamboo Reinforcement in Portland Concrete', *Engineering Experimental Station Bulletin* no 4, Clemson Agricultural College, Clemson, South Carolina, 1950.
6 Dirk E Hebel, 'Bamboo: the future of vernacular building material', *BFT International*, vol 79, March 2013, pp 30–5.
7 World Bank, http://web.worldbank.org/WBSITE/EXTERNAL/COUNTRIES/AFRICAEXT/0,,contentMDK:21935583~pagePK:146736~piPK:146830~theSitePK:258644,00.html (accessed 10 January 2015).
8 United Nations Environment Programme, 'Converting Waste Agricultural Biomass into a Resource', United Nations Environmental Programme Division of Technology, Industry and Economics International Environmental Technology Centre Osaka/Shiga, Japan, www.unep.org/ietc/Portals/136/Publications/Waste%20Management/WasteAgriculturalBiomassEST_Compendium.pdf (accessed 10 January 2015).
9 Countries Compared by Energy > Bagasse > Production, www.nationmaster.com/graph/ene_bag_pro-energy-bagasse-production (accessed 10 January 2015).
10 Cynthia Bryant and William Y Yassumoto, 'Bagasse-based Ethanol from Brazil Gearing up for Export Market', www.bioenergy.novozymes.com/en/learn-more/publications/documents/biogasse.pdf (accessed 10 January 2015).
11 United States Environmental Protection Agency, 'Municipal Solid Waste', www.epa.gov/epawaste/nonhaz/municipal/index.htm (accessed 10 January 2015).
12 Amanda Wills, 'The Lowdown on Landfills', Earth911, http://earth911.com/news/2009/03/30/the-lowdown-on-landfills (accessed 10 January 2015).
13 Kerry A Dolan, 'Garbage: A Costly American Addiction', Forbes.com, 13 April 2012, www.forbes.com/sites/kerryadolan/2012/04/13/garbage-a-costly-american-addiction (accessed 10 January 2015).
14 World Bank, 'Urban Solid Waste Management', http://web.worldbank.org/WBSITE/EXTERNAL/TOPICS/EXTURBANDEVELOPMENT/EXTUSWM/0,,menuPK:463847~pagePK:149018~piPK:149093~theSitePK:463841,00.html (accessed 10 January 2015).
15 *Collection of Municipal Solid Waste in Developing Countries*, UN-Habitat – United Nations Human Settlements Programme, 2010.
16 Project 81, http://project81haiti.org/?page_id=69 (accessed 10 January 2015).
17 www.epa.gov/epawaste/nonhaz/municipal/index.htm (accessed 10 January 2015).
18 California Department of Resources Recycling and Recovery, '"Give Green" by Decking the Halls with Less Waste This Year!', 4 December 2014, www.calrecycle.ca.gov/PublicEd/Holidays (accessed 10 January 2015).
19 Municipal Solid Waste in the United States: Facts and Figures, www.epa.gov/solidwaste/nonhaz/municipal/msw99.htm (accessed 10 January 2015).
20 United Nations Environment Programme, 'Converting Waste Agricultural Biomass into a Resource'. See note 8.
21 www.epa.gov/osw/nonhaz/municipal/msw99.htm (accessed 10 January 2015).
22 Blue Jeans Go Green Denim Recycling, www.bluejeansgogreen.org/Our-Impact (accessed 10 January 2015).
23 Terracycle, www.terracycle.com/en-US (accessed 10 January 2015).

One City

Merritt Bulcholz

Across the globe there have been devastating cases of economic crisis from Enron to Occupy Wall Street (OWS). Increased unemployment became rampant and reached devastating levels throughout Europe and the United States. The collaboration of local and marginal communities, local academic institutions and political engagement has seen promising results from an unlikely place: Limerick, Ireland. Networks of rich history, education and community engagement have developed design strategies for economic remediation. After the 'One City' case study the typical policy headings of local authority government administration were renamed and their definitions redesigned. Policy is not the best instrument of change, rather it is a logical place to start: without rethinking local policy, actions lack a political urgency.

The island of Ireland is relatively evenly inhabited; houses spread across the landscape like confetti, connected by a dense web of roads and land devolved into small fields. Each morning commuters in their cars take to this network in their thousands, moving in all directions to work, to school. The suburbanisation of rural Ireland is a simple fact rendered clearly visible against a complex and frequently beautiful landscape. Cities have a challenging relationship with this landscape; generally people prefer not to live in the Irish city centres. This strong desire to live in rural places has produced a landscape structure that resists modernisation. This new landscape requires critical examination, thus far avoided in the no-man's land between political rhetoric and policy-based legislation.

Over the past 40 years, Ireland has gone through a social restructuring, becoming a regulated secular state, economically tethered to the global economy. Governance, and in particular local government (municipal government), is at the heart of daily life in Ireland and an essential catalyst for development, dealing with all of the contemporary crises at once: rising sea levels and flooding, water quality, social housing, waste, future planning and economic development, heritage, to name just a few of the things a local authority must deal with. Over the post-boom economic cycle, however, contemporary local government has been functionally reduced to a procurement instrument that is lacking in latitude, short on new thinking and with little political direction due to the weak hand of elected local representatives (administrators rule the land and most funding is distributed via the central government purse in Dublin). Typically it falls to consultants (hired help) to solve the many problems that local government faces, and leads to the common practice of seeking the advice of a third party when a new idea is needed. Driven by the market, and without the intrinsic civic orientation of the local authority, consultants work at arms length from the community's thought processes and reporting, and reports replace action. Moving from commission to commission, disconnected from action on the ground, consultancy seems able only to repeat with slight improvements what was most recently done. Frustration mounts, as a highly educated and wired public demands a complete rethink. How should architectural education act in these circumstances? What is our responsibility as educators of architects? This is a very important question for the School of Architecture at the University of Limerick (SAUL).

Limerick has at its doorstep Shannon Airport, with direct flights to New York, Boston, Orlando, Berlin, Paris, London and a host of other places on either side of the Atlantic, from which companies such as Dell and Johnson and Johnson transit their business (and from where we have attracted faculty members). Our students come mostly from the province and are deeply concerned about the future of their place.

Limerick City suffers from an extraordinarily high proportion of social housing (nearly 40 per cent of total inhabitants), meaning the city has a very low level of social capital. This fact has been well documented in research by University of Limerick sociologists. The development by the neighbouring local authorities, Limerick County and Clare County, of edge-of-city shopping malls and vast housing estates, has ensured that whatever economic activity existing in Limerick exists outside of the city centre. This phenomenon has been compared to the doughnut effect experienced by American cities – except for the fact that Limerick is tiny, a city of around 55,000 inhabitants who are within easy walking distance of their neighbours in the surrounding counties. To try and solve the problem, the national government created an agency to 'regenerate' Limerick City's poorer districts into vibrant sustainable communities. Called the 'Regeneration Agency', it sat politically outside of the system of local governance and struggled to get any sort of foothold as a vehicle of local administration, confined to 'procurement without any political representation'. Given money but no power, the agency was discovered to have neither, largely because the ideas underpinning its existence were irrelevant in Limerick, and the funding had dried up with the disappearance of the 'Celtic tiger'. At the same time the local authorities, and in particular Limerick City Council, found it difficult to work with the Regeneration Agency. SAUL organised a seminar called 'Civitas' – a civic gathering, to discuss the future of the city. The Civitas seminar brought together the local authorities (there were at that time four that had an influence on the region, Limerick City by far the smallest, Limerick County, Clare County and County Tipperary), the university, officials from the Department of the Environment, business leaders and citizens. Civitas revealed a deeply dysfunctional situation, where people working with the best of intentions in local government in Limerick were utterly unable to come together and chart a different path to the future – it was as if a collective future was not even on the table.

In this context, a new school of architecture could act to establish a platform within the university where differing points of view could be aired and fresh ideas and intelligence could be brought to processes of governance. Further, we at SAUL see it as our mission to establish a new relationship between academia and governance, to use the bird's eye view that architecture easily brings, to create space between inevitable change and the contemporary political apparatus. The structural inefficiencies within local government do not enhance the ability to imagine a completely different kind of future achieved in a completely new way, by thinking about it as a process and an outcome in terms of the locale. If the mechanics of governance did not function well due to a lack of trust and mutual respect, and 'the future' as a political question had slipped out of the hands of the citizens, it was clear that a new voice in the form of a new school of architecture could say things equally unpalatable to all sides of the debate without compromising itself. To establish the new idea that the future of the region could be discussed and acted upon collectively, the context for that debate should be based on a high level of intelligence and a firm knowledge base supplied by research conducted by the School of Architecture.

Limerick City is a beautiful medieval city, enlarged by a Georgian quarter set along the Shannon River at the edge of the Shannon Estuary, surrounded by some of Ireland's most fertile and productive farmland, and a short drive from much of Ireland's most beautiful scenery. On paper, Limerick would not appear to be suffering. Limerick County was, up until very recently, a separate administrative district, which actively and successfully competed against the city. The logical merging of the city and county into a single political and administrative entity have unlocked potentials that neither the city nor the county had previously available to them. The split between the rigid geometry of Limerick's Georgian streets, and the many small fields and holdings that shape the geometry of the county is difficult to perceive; the city and the county, rural and urban zones simply mesh and merge seamlessly — the county has urban roads, factories and farms, while the city has farms and offices. Both have houses. The definition and potential of urban life, the city and the region as a connected urbanised zone is both a comprehensive condition and a new set of relations — relations between things that are seldom aware of their coexistence, such as 'the city' and 'the university'. A large part of our mission is to *suggest transformations of the definition and potential of rural life and the city together as one place*; 'One City'. This was the title for our first research project on Limerick.

A geographic information system (GIS) and other mapping tools have brought to light in a very rapid and even manner all kinds of information about the landscape. In Irish local authorities GIS resides within the information technology departments and, as is globally the case, for organising geographic information about a place GIS has become the most powerful tool. This information is very strongly contrasted by local knowledge and the span of human memory, by political processes, and by the enormity of time, such that evidence on a single map, for example, uncritically spans across several millennia.

Our initial project involved the careful disassembly of the layers of the GIS information in order to reveal new structural aspects about the nature of the landscape. These aspects, when contrasted with each other, would reveal new relationships, suggest new ways and manners of working, and discover a close identification between the political landscape and its physical and structural reality. One important discovery of this initial project was that the data held the key for powerful new graphical and visual information about the relationship of the county and the city to each other. Carefully editing the GIS layers, new information about the city-suburb-rural landscape is brought to light. A series of maps chart this landscape, a landscape that is both very old and very new, and above all graphically compelling.

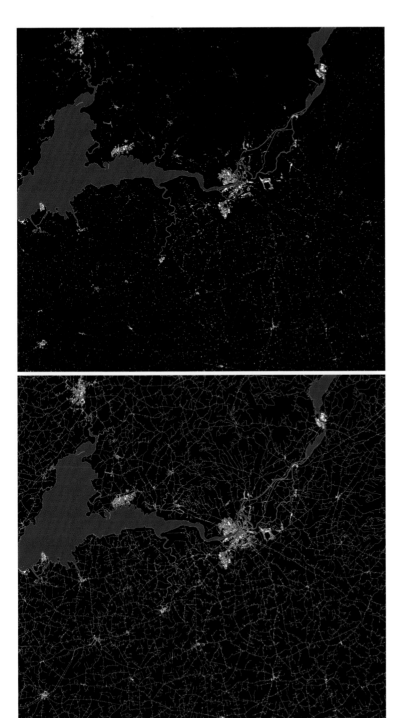

top: Map of
all homes
in County
Limerick, 2009.
© Merritt
Bucholz.

bottom: Map
of the road
network
in County
Limerick, 2009.
© Merritt
Bucholz.

The Intelligence Unit (IU)

We have created several vehicles through which to address the problems emerging from Limerick's situation. It is clear to us that Limerick's problems are not globally unique, as it is our mission to connect with the network of people thinking about the same problems in places similar to Limerick, and to share our research and experience with others. Action is important and imperative to our approach: the framework of action we have designed has already transformed the current economic and political landscape locally as Limerick's two counties have been merged to create a single county, a single government and a single administration. Our project is an important pilot for incubating locally what is grown locally, while at the same time focusing on designing completely new long-term structures that will generate what the city needs: new ideas, new creativity, new conception of now and new actions. Fluidity, flexibility and opportunity with the economic and spatial strategy rely on methods of stimulating easy dialogues between contingent yet tentative strands of Limerick. We aim to demonstrate that within a limited period of time, concrete and realistic projects can be formulated, proposed, structured and run.

An Example of Our Research: 'One City'

From the One City study the typical policy headings of local authority government administration were renamed and their definitions redesigned. Additionally, a policy is not the best instrument of change, rather it is a logical place to start: without rethinking policy, actions lack a political urgency.

A Policy for the Development of Neighbourhoods
(previously Housing Policy)

The term 'housing' focuses on the single house – the idea of neighbourhood embraces all of society living in an area. As a basic conceptual framework, the neighbourhood precedes and outlives the house, and should therefore become the focus of policy.

The problems of isolation, homogeneity, spatial and social segregation in Limerick will be solved through understanding and strengthening neighbourhood structures.

Neighbourhoods need strong identities – the particular character and value citizens attach to the community in which they live, which in turn defines the relationship of the individual to the neighbourhood.

Housing forms the backbone and the infill of neighbourhoods. The connectivity between inhabitants and the establishment of a community works at a neighbourhood scale. The sense of sharing the city works at a neighbourhood scale.

A Policy for the Continuity of the Urban Fabric – Including Nature
(previously Retail and Commercial Policies)

The continuity of the city fabric is related to its durability – a fabric that is more durable than its uses, especially retail, a use particularly susceptible to economic shifts. Nature establishes continuity through its resilience and persistence. What are currently defined as many categories of natural space (private gardens, special areas of conservation, public parks, playing fields, brownfield sites, hedgerows, agricultural field patterns, residual space, semi-natural open space and so on), are actually the fabric of the city and the county. These natural spaces, residual spaces, are those that have the potential to link the city with the counties. As a consequence of their durability, all infrastructure projects have the capacity to strengthen social connections, ecological connections, sport connections, leisure connections and agricultural connections.

Retail has become in recent years a ubiquitous form of development in the county and in the city; as such, it has established new peripheral 'centres', and this has created a polycentric urban form without a clear function, as retail uses grow economically unfeasible. These now need to be considered within their natural setting, the urban landscape of green, and connected in new ways to areas of natural amenity.

The value of the existing fabric of Limerick City beyond its immediate use means that it must possess characteristics that give it value over a long time period. It is important to understand the existing qualities and characteristics of the city fabric and reinforce them, and to allow qualitative development to appreciate over time — over 25-, 50- or 100-year cycles. All will not be solved in a single project, generation or idea.

There is power in the shared identity of the common (collective) places (streets, lanes and greens, country roads and villages). These collective spaces have taken on a variety of forms, from suburban shopping centres to the traditional city centre. There is power in the scale and distance travelled to shop in streets rather than suburbs, and in suburbs rather than streets. There is a continuity of city fabric when it is allowed to develop and persist beyond the needs of any one market.

The history of the city and of the county demonstrates that they are places of continuous change. This ability to transform needs to be understood symbiotically with other factors in Limerick, for example, the commercial 'needs' of flagship icons need to be tested against values of durability, nature and quality. Re-evaluating what exists, understanding what exists, is a critical aspect of understanding the present and the potential of the future; it involves the re-evaluation of existing fabric, reuse and recycling. Limerick, the place, will persist as the market ebbs and flows.

A Policy of Collectivity and Shared Identity
(previously Recreation Sport and Culture)

Limerick City is a single artefact. There are powerful moments, for example, when the inhabitants take over the streets for rugby matches. These are real civic moments; moments when both its citizens, and the outside world, can read the value of Limerick City as a centre. While undoubtedly there are opportunities to promote these moments of pride as part of the 'brand' of Limerick, or part of its tourist strategy, the effect needs to spread into daily life.

The public realm of Limerick City is already of outstanding quality and already reinforces the value of the region. Culture is a ubiquitous urban experience. It is everywhere, and is read in this way by visitors to the city and its inhabitants alike. It ranges from the scale of neighbourhood shops and streets to access to the Shannon waterway. It might be seen in city playgrounds, or adversely measured in traffic nuisance. City culture is not confined to cultural quarters – the city as a ubiquitous cultural realm helps to establish its value.

Culture and sport should be used to strengthen in an everyday way, the identity and self image of the city and to work against the ghetto-isation of the city and its isolation from the counties. It is possible to capitalise on the relatively small scale of the city so that a common cultural platform is established across the city.

The great themes of Limerick, sport and education, should be strengthened and extended within the easy relationship the city-region has with the natural landscape.

A Policy for Natural Infrastructure
(previously Environment, Transportation, Flows (in and out), Water and Energy)
Infrastructure typically puts the needs of man ahead of achieving a balance with nature. However, infrastructure could be imagined as a balance with nature, where man's needs and nature's persistence are measured against each other. Seeking to achieve that balance would become critical to achieving the sustainability of the city and the county.

The city is the flow of water: the river and the flow of the river is a powerful current and source of energy. Water is also captured within the city on its pavements and buildings; this water can be recycled within the city for use, for amenity, for life.

The city is the flow of energy: of consumption, production and management of energy, and is linked to its region through its energy demand. The city needs to be able to act on sustainable principles to reduce energy demand.

The city is the flow of people, movement, and can be defined in terms of mobility in its many forms. The way in which people move through the city and to the region, by trains, with bicycles, by foot or with an automobile must all be given a space, a time and a value within the city's control. The city must be able to develop a permeable movement network that encourages the most energy-efficient forms of mobility: walking, cycling and using public transportation.

Through its infrastructure the city is linked to its region; the various local authorities, and the regional authority must work together to establish common initiatives to ensure the permanence of the city and to define the utility of the city. A culture of natural infrastructure, that promotes stacking of uses and interfaces with the fabric of the city should be developed.

A Policy to Create a Region of Health
(previously part of the National Health Services Executive,
not currently included within Local Authority remit)
Modern health problems, as in any era, as the Institute of Public Health(IPH) has highlighted in its report on public health and the environment, are directly connected to the way the environment is constructed. The IPH report points out, for example, that obesity, diabetes, heart disease, emotional wellness, depression, stress and so forth, are all intimately connected to the choices we make about the built environment and our lifestyle within it.

The city and the county can address health issues directly through promoting and creating their built environment around the idea of creating a healthy society.

A city and county of healthy eating: the county produces healthy food through its farmers and its markets. The city produces food through its markets and butchers. Limerick is a city of good locally produced food, a city of healthy eating.

A city and county of intergenerational living: the city welcomes generations of people living next to each other, within easy access to a wide range of services and facilities, where young and old people meet each other through its spaces, streets and gardens.

A region of health is a place where sport is important. Limerick people use the landscape for a very wide range of sporting activities – kayaking and sculling on the Shannon, running and walking along the Shannon, rugby, the Gaelic Athletics Association (GAA) and soccer pitches permeate the city.

A city of health is a city where people are mobile, able to get around on foot, with easy access to good public transportation, the mobility of its citizens reducing the need to visit hospitals and doctors.

A city of health is directly connected to green spaces that are used for recreation, are safe and well-lit, and comfortable for all generations.

A Policy to Harness Intelligence and Creativity
(economic development and education, part of the National Education system, currently not within Local Authority remit)

The city is a ubiquitous realm of education that establishes its value. There is a very high density and quality of primary, secondary and third-level education in Limerick. These institutions, currently under a single national Education Department, must be restructured in order that they answer to the local area directly. Responsibility for the education of its citizens must be the shared responsibility of the city.

Keeping our graduates in Limerick by creating opportunities for them to thrive here. Pulling ourselves up by our own bootstraps should be an imperative of education in order that it serves the competitiveness and attractiveness of the city as a place to live and work.

The city's vibrant creative community must be leveraged to maximum effect by strengthening, coordinating and connecting existing institutions and bodies.

The fine arts: encouraging the development of a creative community by making it easy for art to thrive, creativity follows low rents and a high concentration of artists: Limerick has both.

We are interested in the long-term viability of such a project. Ultimately creating an institution that generates new ideas and knowledge about the city and its future to interact with the institution of local governance in new and innovative ways. It is our belief that change comes through an informed political position, which is informed with knowledge and equipped with people on the ground enacting the future.

Shelter and Housing

7

Social housing cannot be talked about without mentioning that even Le Corbusier's Unité d'Habitation in Marseilles (1946–52), conceived with great intentions as a democratic machine for living, with integrated landscape, community parks, medical facilities, gardens and schools, in the end failed owing to the lack of deciphering community networks, cultural tensions and political confluence. Le Corbusier designed his own home, ironically inspired by peasant housing, in 45 minutes and had it built by traditional carpenters in the manner of a fisherman's hut. It contained the bare minimum needed for survival: a bed, a desk, a basin, bookshelves. These mundane accessories for living are arguably the most significant for providing humane conditions. This 'ideal house' is relatively the same size and scale as the huts and shelters, called 'transitional housing', which are built and given in tens of thousands to underserved people by the most powerful humanitarian aid organisations. Yet the humane elements are remarkably absent.

The demand for decent, affordable shelter is a daunting challenge in developed and developing countries. The many examples of failed social housing have necessitated further long-term planning. The evolution of housing settlements and the need for innovation has directed the process into a multifaceted matrix of cultural, political and economic factors. These next essays reflect and propose promising alternatives that work in-situ with the environment.

Ronda, Spain. Housing settlements dating from the Middle Ages perch on cliff faces. The diversity of solutions to shelter and housing developed by people around the world is at least equal to the diversity of landscapes encountered, formed by constraints of space, geology, economics and politics. © Irene E Brisson.

above: Stanton Court, Brooklyn, New
York City, New York, USA. © Gans studio.

overleaf: Area Map: the courts along Sheepshead
Bay, identified in red, have bungalows along
internal pedestrian mews without access to the
street except through passages at each end.
© Gans studio.

Missing Scales

Deborah Gans

The resonance of natural disasters, such as hurricanes, floods or earthquakes, has become part of the global occurrence in the 21st century. The challenges of rebuilding housing and infrastructure after these events have compelled designers and planners to create strategies for reducing vulnerability, preparing and withstanding in anticipation of the onslaught of more to come. Communities require strategic responses from different levels of government, in partnership with the private sector and in congruence with public motivation. While minimising exposure is important for reducing vulnerability, recent academic analysis and debate has focused on the ability to cope with, and adapt to, hazard impacts – in many cases rendered synonymous with the concept of resilience. The word 'resilience' is intuitively associated with the capacity to withstand and 'bounce back' from a disturbance. More specifically, 'ecosystem resilience' is concerned with a system's ability to maintain structure/function in the face of disturbance. It focuses on attributes such as persistence, adaptability, variability and unpredictability – all of which are at the heart of evolution and development.[1] After the assault of Hurricane Sandy, the issues of mitigation have also created opportunities for repairing conditions that were in dire need of repair long before the assaults of nature.

Originally developed in the 1920s as bungalow settlements for seasonal usage on marshy infill, the Courts of Sheepshead Bay, Brooklyn are a variation on an old coastal New York City typology. Throughout South Brooklyn, Brighton Beach and Breezy Point are delicate wood frame cottages on pedestrian mews swept with sand, many of which have been winterised, expanded, aggrandised and made more vulnerable to climate change in the process.

Adding to the Sheepshead courts' charm but also to their devastation by Hurricane Sandy is their lowered street elevation. The mews and the bungalows along them stand from 3 to 7 feet (1 to 2 metres) below street level. This sunken court structure is a consequence of the construction of the Coney Island Sewage Treatment Plant in the 1970s that entailed installing new pipes and raising the streets but not the interior of the blocks and their mews. During Sandy, water from the surge and the supercharged sewer filled the lowered courts like bathtubs; but even during everyday storms, rainfall exceeds the capacity of the old pipes and sump pumps so that flooding is a common occurrence.

The legally mandated approach to reconstructing the property of the courts addresses only the 100-year-flood event, not the day-to-day water issues, and requires raising the severely damaged houses to at least the insurable Design Flood Elevation (DFE) or as much as 13 feet (4 metres) above the mews. Post-storm funding for elevating the houses to the DFE comes from the federal government to the City via a programme called 'Build it

Back'. Build it Back pays to repair damaged homes in place, raising only those homes that are more than 85 per cent destroyed. While they are called Community Block Development Grants, in fact, Build it Back programmes are thus far available only to the individual homeowner. This scattershot approach will produce houses at various heights in the neighbourhood and floodplain without a cohesive approach to either water management or urban fabric. Given the ever-increasing risk of flooding in an era of climate change, it is a stopgap approach that transforms the community into interim housing with little chance of long-term survival.

The residents of the six courts, who live with water on a daily basis, have begun to embrace the need for a more holistic approach on a grander scale of time and space than the City currently makes possible. As aficionados of storms and sand, they understand that raising one house will increase the exposure of a neighbour to scour. They want flood insurance for all their homes and a neighbourhood that is sustainable for another 50 years at least, which will require new forms of water management and infrastructure. The mews' population understand the effectiveness of action at the scale of the court in ways that city funders do not yet recognise. While unusual in our political climate of governmental distrust, in this case, it is the individual calling for large cooperative governmental and collective action.

To accomplish this court makeover, the first infrastructure problem to be addressed is the social infrastructure for collective action. Many of the homes have been continually occupied by multiple generations of the same family for almost 75 years, giving the neighbourhood a robust network of social relationships; but there is a dearth of community development corporations, housing organising groups and established social service providers to coordinate the rebuilding process and represent many of the most devastated local residents. The shifting state of building codes, zoning, the new flood maps and the complexity of the funding programme have challenged the ability of individual residents here, and throughout the city, to take full advantage of rebuilding funding and assert their interests. The noble role of the *court captains* was revived during the storm emergency, but they concerned themselves primarily with immediate needs and physical safety. It was at our open-call meeting at the bar of the Sheepshead Bay Yacht Club, and among other non-profit meetings, our subsequent *visioning* sessions for each court at the Sheepshead Nursing and Rehabilitation Facility that neighbours discussed not just the agendas we presented but their larger future, including the basic question of would they stay or would they go. Our greatest accomplishment so far has been to help catalyse the formation of a more organised, more proactive and more politicised court collective.

At this moment, two of the courts have concentrations of homeowners ready to act collectively to both raise their homes and implement new resilient infrastructures as finances allow. These two courts are also significant pilot sites due to their locations, size and potential for replicability. Webers Court, situated directly on the waterfront, south of Emmons Avenue, presents a common coastal design challenge, while Stanton Court presents an upland site vulnerable to rainfall and the uniform typology of bungalows found throughout South Brooklyn.

On Stanton Court, the bungalows were not robustly built to begin with so raising them will most likely involve reinforcing or rebuilding much of their structure. To make them not only insurable but also structurally sound, truly weathertight and systemically efficient by current performance standards means replacing them. The residents have rallied around a scheme that would replace many homes with prefabricated 'green' bungalows, raise all the houses to the same level, even though the DFE varies along the mews, and implement a series of new hard and soft infrastructures. At 13 feet (4 metres) above the mews, individual stair access to each house would become onerous, especially for the aging population, and unwieldy given the small area and footprint of each bungalow. Consequently, we have proposed a shared boardwalk that would gradually ramp up from the street level. Besides meeting America with Disability Act (ADA) standards, this shared boardwalk provides the opportunity for other collective elements, including a patio, stepped seating and an emergency solar array.

The area beneath the boardwalk is used as a continuous water-management landscape. Working with Jason Loiselle of Sherwood Design Engineering, we have developed a scheme to replace and upgrade the current subterranean piped infrastructure and sump pump, which are inadequate, and to remove the extensive paving currently at mews level and replace it with plantings, swales and gravel.

The community had previously organised itself to petition the city, not over their daily flooding, but over zoning. Confronted by development where several small lots were replaced with a five-storey apartment house, they feared the demise of the bungalow neighbourhood and succeeded in having the area of the courts down-zoned to preserve its character. Now, given the low elevation of Sheepshead, when the mews is raised, the houses will still need to be lifted further off the ground and beyond the height limitation. The Department of City Planning will accommodate this infringement, which will occur in many neighbourhoods affected by the storm; but it is concerned that classic New York City streetscapes will be disrupted. In this case the boardwalk will allow the scale and feel of the original community to persist in a new form.

A more radical proposal would change the property of the court in order to capture land for both development and conservation trust. Currently, the property lines of each lot run under the centre of the mews, which is governed by an informal covenant. Court residents all chip in to pay Roto-Rooter when the combined sewer beneath the mews path stops up … frequently. The residents want the city to take responsibility for this sewerage and water as if it were a public street, which would mean changing the property lines, raising the mews to street level on top of large amounts of fill, submitting to both a Uniform Land Use Review Procedure (ULURP) and a Department of Environmental Protection Capital Project process, which takes 10 years. While the timeframe and uncertain outcome were unappealing, this scenario suggested another potential approach to the land. If the residents were willing to treat their mews as a shared property, why not collectivise the entire court? Currently the bungalows have narrow side yards – as narrow as 1 foot (30 centimetres) – that do little to provide light or amenity. If the residents united their properties and constructed their new bungalows

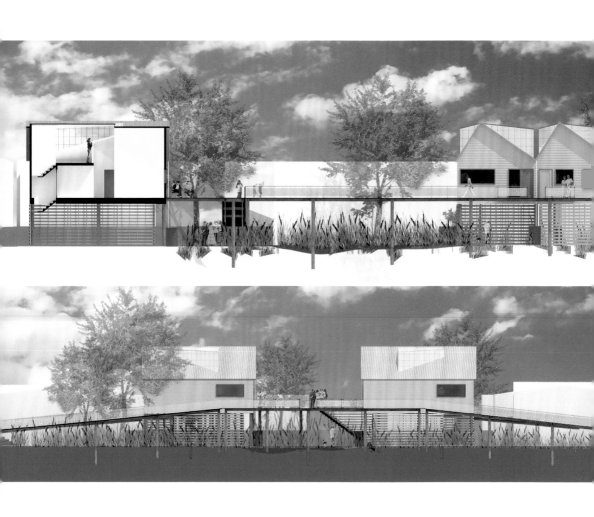

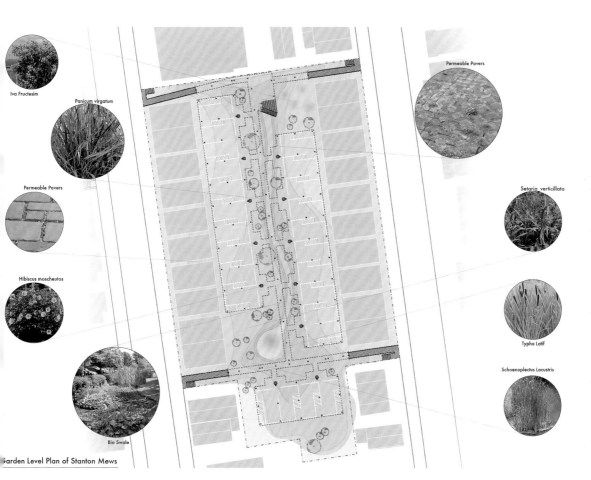

Iva Fructesim

Panicum virgatum

Permeable Pavers

Hibiscus moscheutos

Bio Swale

Permeable Pavers

Setaria_verticillata

Typha Latif

Schoenoplectus Lacustris

Garden Level Plan of Stanton Mews

opposite: Section through Stanton Court. Raised bungalows edge the new boardwalk that runs along the mews and connects to the street. (Drawing by Sean Gold.) © Gans studio.

above: Rendering of Stanton Court where the entire site beneath the raised houses and boardwalk becomes a water management landscape. (Drawing by Cristina Zubillaga.) © Gans studio.

above: View of Attached Bungalows. By eliminating narrow side yards, the court gains property for shared water gardens, shown here, accessed by a stair leading from the boardwalk. (Drawing by Sean Gold.) © Gans studio.

overleaf: Master Plan. Greenways along each mews and new water gardens on court lots are either acquired by the City or assembled by residents to improve water management. All subsurface drainage leads to the larger landscape at the coastal edge, which also serves as a storm buffer. © Gans studio.

as attached row houses, they would create, from those side yards four new properties to be either developed and sold by their cooperative or reserved for wetland.

To truly manage the quantity of rainfall in an age of climate change, the additional space for green infrastructure suggested by the cooperative scheme will be required. An alternative land resource for these water gardens, which would not demand the restructuring of court property lines, would be the vacant and severely storm-damaged properties. A year-and-a-half after the storm, with no monies yet distributed by Build it Back, new abandoned properties, in addition to those destroyed by the storm, have come to exist in every court. This suggests a potential city or state strategy to purchase these lots for wetlands that together can create both a pedestrian green way and a water management system at the neighbourhood scale. In each of the 'upland courts', north of Emmons Avenue, there could be opportunistic infill gardens that would provide sufficient water uptake to eliminate daily flooding. At Emmons Avenue, subterranean drainage and a culvert could divert the water further downhill to the bay, where a different set of ecological approaches would be employed.

The second exemplary court, Webers Court, is situated at the bay. Our work there has revealed the deep understanding that residents have of the challenges of water, even at the larger scale of their coastline.

The residents understand the strengths and vulnerabilities of the city's beach replenishment practices along the coast, which move sand rapidly into their harbour, and the potential of a proposed levy system to exacerbate rather than halt flooding if a drainage system is not built behind it. All the residents of south Sheepshead want the city to explore the feasibility of monumental, muscular flood barriers, extending from the adjoining community of Gerritsen Beach to the Rockaway Peninsula, as outlined in the city's Special Initiative for Rebuilding and Resiliency (SIRR) report, *Stronger More Resilient New York*, issued in spring 2013. They also want to address the coastline at the scale under their control. At the residents' suggestion, we have developed a plan for their spit of land in relation to the coast including, for example, an additional quirkily shaped groin towards Gerritsen Beach to help keep the Plum Beach replenishment where it is. Working once again with Jason Loiselle and additionally, Rosamund Palmer, we have developed a fortified bulkhead to break up the force of a surge, and small wetland inlets to absorb those vectors. The bulkhead would culminate in a stepped seawall to absorb wave action and protect its primary structure. As for the houses themselves, which are larger than bungalows as commensurate with the value of their beachfront property, there too, we are following the lead of the residents who have begun to pile up dormers in anticipation of abandoning the ground floors. In lieu of lifting the houses, we have proposed adding a floor at the top, underpinning piles for a new foundation, and then deconstructing the ground floor into a lattice-sheathed porch.

These projects in Sheepshead are actually our second effort to work with communities directly after a storm; the first was Plum Orchard in New Orleans East after Hurricane Katrina. Much to our astonishment, despite the different ecologies and local cultures, the two communities have organically produced urban thinking at a similar scale, which is a

above: Webers Court, Brooklyn,
New York City, New York, USA.
© Gans studio.

opposite: Section through Webers
Court from the street to the
coastline with a habitat skirt storm
buffer. (Drawing by Rosamund
Palmer.) © Gans studio.

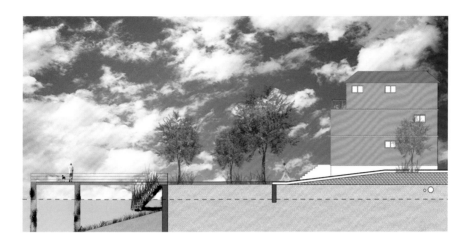

missing scale in urban thinking, between the individual property and the larger district. In New Orleans, this missing scale was a sub-neighbourhood of approximately 12 blocks within natural and man-made boundaries. In Sheepshead it is the totality of the six courts. As in New Orleans, the storm served as a catalyst first for the development of a community, and then for the invention of missing scales of design action in relation to it. Much that is difficult to accomplish at the scale of the individual property is easier to accomplish at a scale like a court, ranging from ADA access to houses raised 13 feet (4 metres) in the air to drywells for water management. Much that is difficult to implement from above is easier to effect from within the neighbourhood, from shared backyard landscapes to property easements. These intermediate scales leverage small individual acts of design to incrementally produce self-sustaining neighbourhoods and create, as an invaluable by-product, organised and informed citizens who are agents in the further planning of their own sustainable futures.

Note

1   CS Holling and B Walker, 'Resilience Defined', *Internet Encyclopedia of Ecological Economics*, 2003. http://isecoeco.org/pdf/resilience.pdf, (accessed 10 January 2015).

reCOVER
Emergency Shelter Interventions

Anselmo G Canfora

Popular themes in mid- to long-term disaster recovery housing include prefabrication and modular designs, partnerships between the academy and governmental, nongovernmental and commercial entities, rapid response and flexibility in size and complexity. All issues that Anselmo Canfora of the architecture faculty at the University of Virginia, and director of reCOVER, discusses in this essay. Using the work of reCOVER as a case study, he reflects on the major challenges facing the integration of the humanitarian shelter design with the pedagogical requirements for a professional architecture programme. Such initiatives have seen a rise in academic settings in the last decade, reflecting both the lack of adequate transitional housing and a burgeoning interest in young designers to engage early, and deeply, in public service-oriented design.

In 2005, the most active Atlantic hurricane season in recorded history resulted in a series of natural disasters devastating to human life, the built environment and the United States economy. Newspapers described the dire living conditions victims of natural disasters were enduring at every post-disaster stage. The focus of the media on this plight was topical, but ebbed and flowed, largely influenced by a 24-hour news cycle. The mediocre, even harmful, types of temporary housing prevalent in the form of travel trailers, became a recurring headline suggestive of a deeper systemic problem. There was clear evidence of genuine support and grass-roots effort to address this terrible situation, but it often resulted in scattered, ad hoc housing solutions. For a problem of this magnitude and complexity, a more flexible delivery strategy was required; a process based on a design/build project delivery system would allow for an iterative and more responsive prototyping and testing cycle, focused on the production and delivery of safer and more accommodating forms of transitional disaster recovery housing.

A closer look into the history of camps established to house internally displaced persons and refugees from natural disasters and conflict revealed a chronic housing problem. The housing type intended for finite emergency or relief periods immediately following a disaster had become the long-term standard; the temporary tents and trailers, by default, became permanent solutions. It was perplexing to learn that domestic and international government agencies did not have a viable strategy in place to address protracted housing crises. Ad hoc, quick fix responses to large-scale events further jeopardise the health and wellbeing of vulnerable populations when regulatory inspections fail to ensure that the structures meet basic building safety standards. Compounding this complex problem is the classification of natural disasters as low-probability, high-impact events that have historically influenced a reactionary mindset extending from months to years after a disastrous event.

Building on the activism and hands-on teaching of the late Samuel Mockbee and the accomplishments of Rural Studio, a number of architecture schools have modelled their design/build programmes to assist marginalised communities in rebuilding houses, schools, churches, and community facilities post-disaster or as part of an effort of renewal from economic hardship. These efforts have continued to grow in number and have clearly indicated an impassioned response to domestic and international catastrophic events on the part of students, faculty, nongovernmental organisations and advocacy groups, such as the former Architecture for Humanity.

The initiative reCOVER was founded in 2007 at the University of Virginia (UVA), in part, as a response to the need for improved post-disaster recovery housing. Over the last seven years, students, staff and faculty at the School of Architecture have engaged a variety of research and design-build projects, based on the principal effort to assist marginalised communities in building a capacity for sustainable and supportive housing, educational and manufacturing facilities. Currently, reCOVER has completed or is developing a series of projects in Haiti, Nicaragua, South Africa, Uganda and the United States. To begin with the reCOVER framework has four important objectives that define its overall mission:

- The advancement of translational research in the area of building materials, methods and techniques, defines the primary objective of reCOVER. Each building project is focused on producing two outcomes: first, a viable building solution, which meets or exceeds the expectations of the beneficiary community and second, the prototypical development of new buildings that combine conventional construction with innovative methods.

- The second goal, one that relates directly to the role of the architecture academy, is to balance the educational purpose of design research projects with the demands and challenges that come with projects involving actual clients and nongovernmental organisation intermediaries. A key factor is to frame specific research questions about local conditions, building materials, technologies and construction, which students can engage with as a part of their own emerging design methodologies. Simultaneously, students work collectively on the overall project development and share the responsibility in executing the deliverables. Full-scale mock-ups and prototypes work as instructional tools to demonstrate workable connections between students' design ideas and building techniques. This allows for an ongoing feasibility assessment of a proposal to be implemented in collaboration with the partner organisation and beneficiary community. The goal is to synthesise a set of classroom lessons and field experiences towards a comprehensive architectural design education and applied research in the area of building construction.

- From the inception of each project, a third goal is to establish a mutually beneficial partnership with a humanitarian, community-based organisation, which

Rendering, reCOVER,
house exterior courtyard.
© Anselmo G Canfora.

demonstrates a commitment to building sustainably for marginalised communities. It is important that the organisation has a well-established and trusted presence in the community. The organisation's philosophy, history, leadership, structure and financial resources are studied prior to making commitments. Whether the organisation operates domestically or internationally, it is important that its personnel are familiar with, and responds appropriately to, the cultural, social and political characteristics of the community; an important qualification is a thorough knowledge of the community's history and access to local building resources.

- The fourth goal, in the area of large-scale manufacturing of the reCOVER transitional disaster recovery housing system, is the development of commercialisation strategies to bring the product to market. Through federally and state-funded grants, we have been working with modular and panellised housing manufacturers in Southside, Virginia, to prefabricate and test a series of prototypes for environmental, structural, material, packaging and deployment performance specifications. These prototypes are being field-tested to demonstrate the efficacy of the reCOVER housing system in relation to industry competitors. Market analysis and business plan development are equally important aspects of this process, and collaborators in private commercial and public governmental sectors are critical in identifying viable market entry points through United States and foreign governmental agencies and nongovernmental organisations. These efforts are also driven by the necessity to generate funding for ongoing reCOVER research and development, student scholarships and programme support.

reCOVER Coursework

reCOVER studios' courses and research and development seminars are offered to undergraduate and graduate architecture and engineering students with the primary focus on how issues of social equity, environmental justice and advanced technologies of construction and manufacturing can have a direct impact on the quality of the built environment. Students are asked to act through design and engage project stakeholders in an open-ended dialogue. Design is discussed in relation to building and as an iterative, nonlinear, lateral and vertical activity. Students are encouraged to engage in rigorous research along with speculative thinking as an ongoing 'checks and balances' in a dialogue that occurs across drawings and full-scale mock-ups.

The studios have specifically dealt with transitional disaster recovery housing, primary school buildings and factory facilities in developing countries. Comprehensive design problems require the application of technical knowledge from previous undergraduate coursework in building systems, structures and construction. From conceptual development to construction documentation, the studio structure emphasises interdependence between individual and group iterative processes integrated as part of an interdisciplinary approach. The use of indigenous materials and local construction practices to inform the design process is underscored at the earliest stages of each

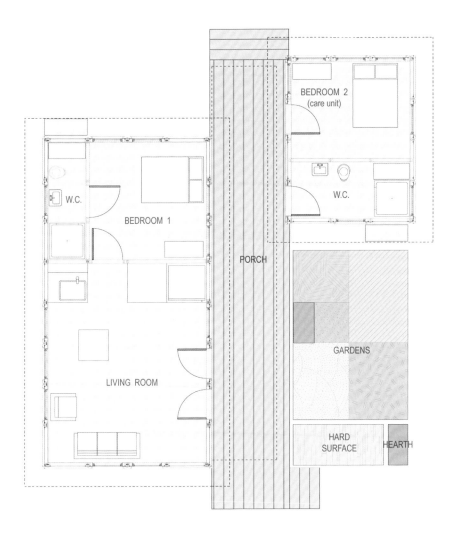

BEDROOM 2
(care unit)

W.C.

BEDROOM 1

W.C.

PORCH

LIVING ROOM

GARDENS

HARD
SURFACE

HEARTH

Breathe House floor plan.
© Anselmo G Canfora.

project. The building's performance, aesthetics, construction and budgetary parameters are developed and maintained in direct collaboration with the non-profit organisation partner and the representatives of the beneficiary community. The priority is to involve students in an exploratory design problem that balances equally a set of lessons learned from academic exercises in the studio, with those to be learned in the field as part of collaborative efforts with builders and volunteers. The reCOVER pedagogical approach prepares architecture and engineering students for diverse career trajectories by imparting sound, foundational knowledge and skills in the area of building design, construction and technology, while raising social consciousness.

The overall studio framework integrates academic, civic and professional goals, and prioritises the beneficiary community's needs. The improvement of construction techniques and details, environmental performance and integration into existing context, are design criteria reinforced at all phases of the project. Interdisciplinary collaboration is an essential component of the studio for the realisation of domestic and international, public-interest projects. A significant educational experience is achieved through the daily, direct involvement of architecture and engineering students. From preparatory planning and conceptual work, to design development and construction documentation, to actual on-site volunteer construction and community engagement, architecture and engineering students work together to help realise projects.

Specific site conditions and building criteria challenge the students and directly influence the design of the building. For example, the accepted general parameter for the use of hand tools and safe lifting distances without mechanical assistance by small groups of construction workers and volunteers, drives a general design strategy of modest spans and heights and the lightweight construction of reasonably small, repetitive modular building components. The location and orientation of the building on the site is influenced by optimal orientation to the sun and prevailing winds, but also carefully considers the minimisation of the amount of cut and fill, which is usually completed with manual labour in remote sites without access to large equipment. Students learn that the design of the building needs to positively affect the building sequence as a set of 'smaller projects' with hourly, daily or weekly goals that prove to be an effective on-site constructional strategy towards overall building quality. These smaller and more manageable tasks prove to be helpful to community volunteers' morale as they ensure means to accomplishing discrete goals on a more frequent basis.

Students study site strategies for potential agricultural and recreational uses by the local community. In the case of a school in Gita, Uganda, the studio developed a productive landscape strategy that took advantage of the terraced land around the school building slated for cultivation. The tropical climate of the region, two annual harvest cycles, rich soil and access to water made this component of the overall design possible. During studio discussions, the partnering non-profit organisation communicated that the local community would benefit from extracurricular agriculture classes on the terraced, three-acre site. The purpose of these classes would be two-fold. First, to provide new skills and techniques that could be useful for students whose families were subsistence farmers

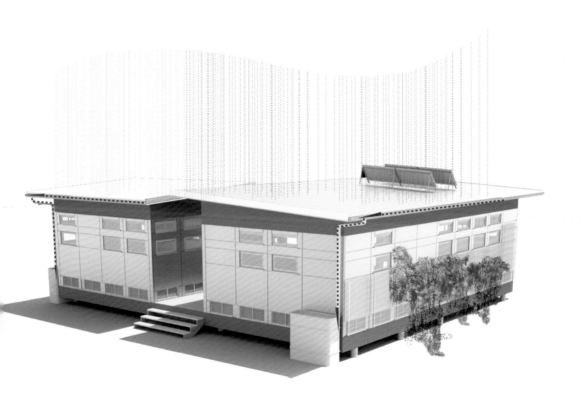

Water collection: roof
rain-harvesting system.
© Anselmo G Canfora.

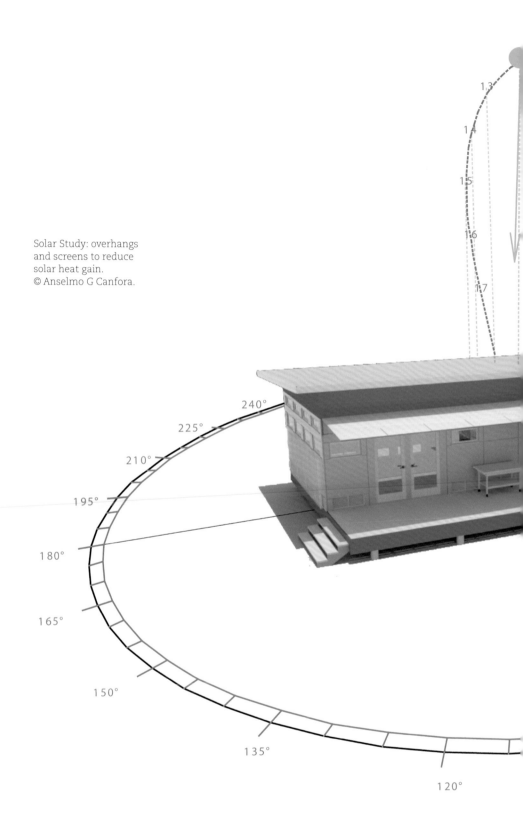

Solar Study: overhangs
and screens to reduce
solar heat gain.
© Anselmo G Canfora.

13

14

15

16

17

240°

225°

210°

195°

180°

165°

150°

135°

120°

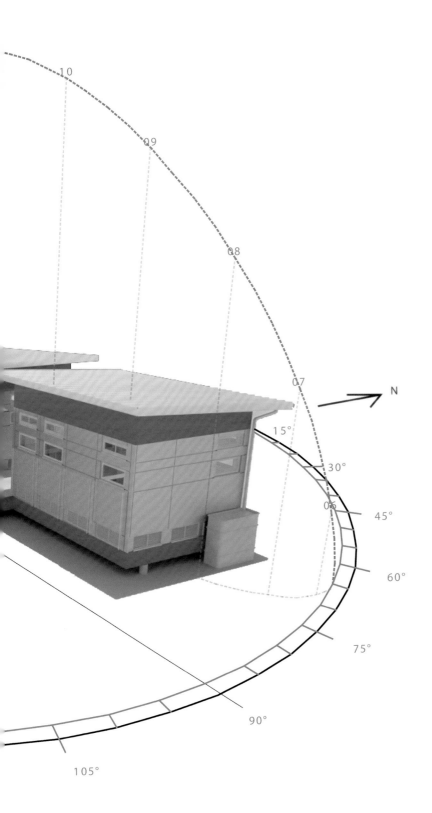

1.0

0.9

0.8

0.7

15°

30°

0.6

45°

60°

N

75°

90°

105°

and, second, to help form a vocational training programme for students who may not pursue continued education. The productive landscape component of the primary school was carefully considered throughout the design process and influenced the placement and orientation of the building, most importantly the classrooms, relative to the future agricultural plots.

In structuring the design studio content, a careful balance is maintained between discipline-specific instruction and development of students with the needs and desires of the community stakeholders; one is always valued relative to the other. The studio design problem is based on the specific goals of the project to ensure students have the necessary time and space to develop their own design ideas and contextualise them in collaborative group work. The goal of the studio is not simply to deliver a practical solution for the organisation to build but, more importantly, to give students direct opportunities to shape the process that best serves their education and also meets the expectations of the beneficiary community.

reCOVER: Applied Design Research

The reCOVER Transitional Disaster Recovery Housing (TDRH) system is currently in the prototyping phase. The approach to disaster recovery housing begins with the assertion that safe, healthy and resilient housing serves a basic human right. This is especially true for victims in devastated communities recovering from the physical and psychological tolls of natural disasters. Interdisciplinary teams of architecture, engineering, medicine, business and commerce faculty, students and professionals are involved at coordinated stages of the project. Equally important to this activity are the teams of builders, fabricators, manufacturers and modular industry consultants with whom we work closely to refine and test prefabricated building components, staging and deployment scenarios. The management and interaction between these teams is a very challenging and important part of implementing this design research. The day-to-day collaborative problem-solving aspect of the work with faculty, students, manufacturers or consultancy groups has an invaluable influence on the way in which we adapt to changes and adjust the trajectory of the work. Given the complex phases and numerous stakeholders involved in the TDRH project, from schematic design to what has most recently emerged in the form of commercialisation interests, we remain focused on its primary purpose to improve the quality of housing for disenfranchised communities who find themselves in deplorable conditions. We are resolved to uphold a process that exemplifies an ethical mode of practice and is engaged in the world to effectively address the challenges we face as a society. This is especially critical as the research and design work models effective behaviour for students, members of a younger generation who are committed to the new roles and responsibilities they will have as architects and members of communities entrusted with the common wellbeing.

An important element of the reCOVER TDRH system design to consider when adapting it to different cultures and climatic conditions is a well-planned spatial organisation that supports a family and community's daily life, indoors and outdoors. The housing

St Marc, Haiti, 2012.
Volunteers, students and
community members
work on the assembly of
the Breathe House.
© Anselmo G Canfora.

proposal for the recovery in Haiti responds to the strong relationship between indoor and outdoor living customs of the Haitian culture; by incorporating a large porch, removable awning and living walls for vertical gardens, the modest square footage of the house takes on an expansive quality. Daily activities flow freely between interior and exterior spaces and the building's design supports communal interactions. Close attention was given to the outward orientation of the interior spaces towards windows placed at an appropriate height to ensure direct views to the gardens while maintaining the privacy of the occupants. It is vital to the project's cultural and social sustainability that it carefully takes into consideration the organisation and aesthetic adaptability of each house to work well in a clustered, communal setting. Accessibility for the physically disabled is integrated with the outdoor living porch. These spatial relationships ensure an effective use of indoor and outdoor functions related to safety and convenience of communal activities. While protected from the elements, high visibility is an important aspect of the clustered communal organisation of a single unit as well as multiple housing units. The reCOVER TDRH system considers the relationship the building has to the ground to be of great importance in terms of ventilation and effectively negotiating uneven terrain.

In a subsequent prototype (currently sited at the UVA Milton Fabrication facility), the building envelope is comprised of fully prefabricated panels. The integration of a mechanical connection at the vertical seams between panels and the horizontal seams

opposite: Charlottesville,
Virginia, USA. reCOVER
prototype monitored for
energy performance.
© Anselmo G Canfora.

above: Charlottesville, Virginia,
USA. Student-assembled
reCOVER prototype house on
north terrace of Campbell
Hall. © Anselmo G Canfora.

between the wall panels and floor and roof panel system makes the on-site assembly user-friendly and structurally dependable. This locking mechanism, which requires only the use of hand tools, ensures a tight seal between panels and a strong structural integrity of the entire building envelope assembly. The adaptability of the panel cladding allows for a variety of aesthetic options without sacrificing the weatherproof performance of the building envelope. Comprised of efficient prefabricated building components, the design is based on a simple, safe, on-site assembly process. The entire structure can be assembled by a group of six to eight inexperienced volunteers with the supervision of one to two experienced builders. The system is described as a 'plug-and-play' strategy of prefabricated, panellised components and limits the number of individual building parts necessary to complete the house. This timesaving strategy has a substantial economic impact in terms of reducing overall costs associated with supporting volunteer groups during construction with little to no building experience. This approach is designed to directly involve the local community affected by a natural disaster during the rebuilding process and contributes to a sense of empowerment during the recovery phase. The design of the prefabricated system also takes into consideration the reduction of material and hardware costs as part of the structural and weatherproofing detailing of the panels. The modular design allows for an overall increase or reduction of square footage per unit to provide a range of sizes. As part of the interior fit-out, a variety of storage and amenities provide different design and organisational options.

The structural system is designed in collaboration with the architecture and engineering firm Ove Arup in the United Kingdom. The firm's Arup Cause programme, initiated in 2006, has a clear mission to raise awareness and understanding of humanitarian relief projects and is strongly committed to projects with a clear focus on the sustainable design and construction of communities in developing countries. The Arup Cause programme has established a remarkable record of working with domestic and international nongovernmental organisations and academic institutions to conduct important design and engineering research and development projects. It provides a range of in-kind services from specialised technical analysis and simulation, project management, communications support to financial assistance. Since 2008, we have been working with civil and infrastructural engineers with Arup's London and Cardiff offices. Additionally, the design of the TDRH system benefits from current engineering research and development conducted in collaboration with colleagues in the School of Engineering Computer Science Department. The reCOVER TDRH prototype is one of four test-beds funded as part of a 2010 National Science Foundation, Emerging Frontiers in Research and Innovation (EFRI) Science in Energy and Environmental Design: Engineering Sustainable Buildings (SEED) grant. Most recently, the reCOVER TDRH is one of two featured projects funded in a one-year, Tobacco Indemnification and Community Revitalisation Commission grant. The grant, titled 'Partnership for Design and Manufacture of Affordable, Energy-efficient Housing Systems', funds three full-scale reCOVER TDRH prototypes. This aspect of the research is linked to economic development in Virginia and focuses on the technological modernisation of the modular and panellised manufacturing industry

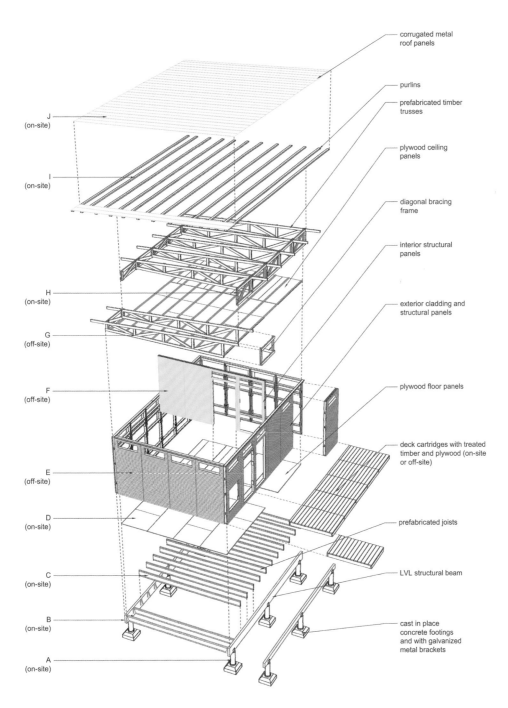

corrugated metal
roof panels

purlins

prefabricated timber
trusses

plywood ceiling
panels

diagonal bracing
frame

interior structural
panels

exterior cladding and
structural panels

plywood floor panels

deck cartridges with treated
timber and plywood (on-site
or off-site)

prefabricated joists

LVL structural beam

cast in place
concrete footings
and with galvanized
metal brackets

J
(on-site)

I
(on-site)

H
(on-site)

G
(off-site)

F
(off-site)

E
(off-site)

D
(on-site)

C
(on-site)

B
(on-site)

A
(on-site)

Building elements and
construction order.
© Anselmo G Canfora.

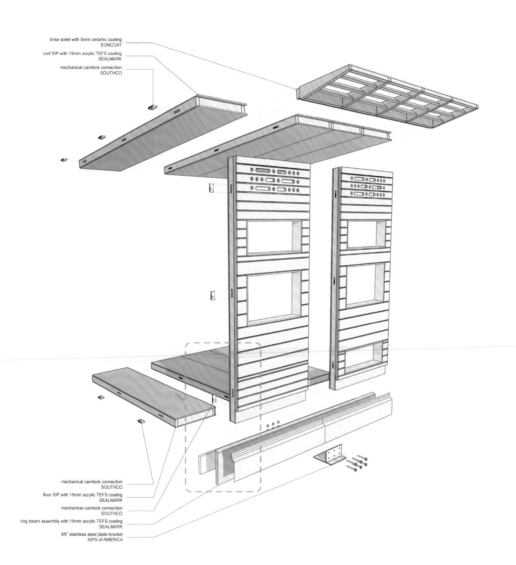

brise soleil with 5mm ceramic coating
EONCOAT

roof SIP with 15mm acrylic TEFS coating
SEALMARK

mechanical camlock connection
SOUTHCO

mechanical camlock connection
SOUTHCO

floor SIP with 15mm acrylic TEFS coating
SEALMARK

mechanical camlock connection
SOUTHCO

ring beam assembly with 15mm acrylic TEFS coating
SEALMARK

3/8" stainless steel plate bracket
SIPS of AMERICA

Composite wall panel
components and assembly.
© Anselmo G Canfora.

in Southside, Virginia. In addition to creating new jobs in the region, the existing labour force will acquire new skills in computer-aided design and computer-aided manufacturing (CAD/CAM) technologies and processes, while building on their extensive manufacturing experience and know-how. New computer numerically controlled (CNC) fabrication technologies are integrated in the way we teach, design and build as part of a measured and deliberate process. These new technologies are most effective when their added value can be assessed early on in the prototyping phases of a project. Working with manufacturing partners on the development of the 'Breathe House' prototype, we have affected how automated manufacturing and manual fabrication can be synthesised to improve the overall construction quality, affordability and transportability of transitional housing for disaster recovery. A primary objective of the Tobacco Commission grant is to, 'develop the industrial design and manufacturing base to produce highly energy-efficient, comfortable housing systems'. We are currently working on the minimisation of material waste and increasing production efficiencies to meet future potential demands for the reCOVER TDRH system domestically and internationally.

As we gain more field experience working with humanitarian organisations assisting marginalised communities, domestically and internationally, the reCOVER educational and design research goals are to focus more sharply on the responsibility the architectural academy will have when preparing students to enter a profession serving a rapidly expanding client base. How to balance these growing demands with the delivery of an effective architectural education will continue to be a central pedagogical question at UVA's School of Architecture and other academies in North America and internationally. Collectively the teaching and research of architecture schools will continue to centre on two essential and recurring themes in the architecture discipline: the tools and craft of building and the people for whom buildings are made. The critical synthesis of these themes is necessary to address the complex challenges we face as a discipline and a society in the 21st century.

Education
and Practice

8

In the last decade there has been a seemingly exponential rise in attention to humanitarian design in architectural education – be it public interest, disaster-response, community-based and so forth – reflecting the enthusiasm of students and educators to effect a change in the built environment and access to design. It has raised any number of issues, including the conflict between pedagogical aims and the needs of a given target group. Then there are the ethical questions about students providing free design services or design being provided to underserved populations by trainees rather than fully qualified professionals.

Sam Mockbee's Rural Studio serves as a historical root for many programmes desiring to engage in community service-oriented design within the academic studio. It is a comprehensible decision to engage with service design as the funding for design in such projects, solicited or unsolicited, is minimal or nonexistent. If no design services were available, are students not an improvement? The man hours poured into speculative design proposals in a studio are staggering, typically 14 students spending three to four months of effort on ideas, projects, concepts and space planning for projects that may never have existed or will never come to be. Is it any wonder that students and professors alike jump at the chance to apply that effort to the daunting unmet needs and unsolved problems of our contemporary society?

Jacmel, Haiti, 2013. Architecture students from Bowling Green State University, Ohio, meet with the community school board for a design workshop. © Irene E Brisson.

Humanitarian Architecture Is Hip. Now What?

Eric Cesal

> Working as a volunteer, project manager and executive director of Architecture for Humanity, Eric Cesal's wealth of on-the-ground experience and upper-level organising is both propelled by and informs the point of this essay, a call to designers to stabilise and make responsible in the long term this current surge in the attention given to humanitarian architecture. Cesal argues that the decisions architects make can have a profound impact on the communities and economies they work in − and it is a choice whether to attempt to make a positive or otherwise effect.

In May 2013, Cameron Sinclair, cofounder of the former Architecture for Humanity, took the stage as a keynote speaker of the 2013 American Institute of Architects Convention. For those within the field of humanitarian design, it had implications. It signalled a shift. Humanitarian design was no longer fringe. It was not something renegade − it was not something that skittered around the periphery of architectural dialogue. It was, literally and figuratively, at centre stage. More remarkable was the fact that at this particular convention, humanitarian design was also at stage left, right, in the orchestra pit and the rafters. A tide had rolled in, and I counted dozens of lectures, seminars and presentations focused on different models of humanitarian design, an issue that had been struggling for years to find an adequate voice.

In full disclosure, Cameron Sinclair happened to be my boss. And many of the other speakers happened to be close friends. But none of that changed the implications of the moment. Humanitarian architecture was once again in vogue.

To anyone with a sense of history, it was also a bit unsettling. Architecture had tried before to balm the world and had failed rather fantastically. The resurgent popularity of humanitarian architecture might be more properly understood as a full revolution of an ongoing cycle. A cycle that will see the profession, within 20 or 30 years, again turn a blind eye to the ills of the world. A discussion was held in several circles: how to make humanitarian principles a lasting component of practice itself. How would you ensure that basic humanitarian concern for one's fellow human beings would be a part of practice, regardless of future evolutions of style, form and technology?

A few weeks prior I had been standing at the window of my spartan apartment in the Tenderloin neighbourhood of San Francisco, as far from humanitarian disaster as my life gets, and I spied a man, obviously affluent, walking a chunky brown dog. The dog stopped, and crouched on its haunches, intending to defecate. The affluent man looked around, as if to make sure no one was looking, let the dog do its business on the pavement, and then carried on hurriedly. Humanity, at its finest.

A few minutes later a building maintenance man emerged from one of the adjacent buildings, dragging a long hose, and started working his way down the pavement. This was not in response to the recent defecation, this is just what he did every day. He directed his high-pressure stream of water back and forth across the path in a lazy motion, ambling down the street in no particular rush. As he did, the water forced away the cigarette butts, condom wrappers and, after a while, the same large pile of dog poop that had recently captured my attention.

The affluent man's single act of not picking up his dog's poop commanded a chain of causality. The building then had to waste hundreds of gallons of fresh water to clear away the dog's poop. To me, it was a narrative exposing the differences between those who create a problem, those who respond to it, and those who prevent it.

And so goes the story of humanitarian design in the developing world. Laurels are passed around for responding to conditions that shouldn't have existed in the first place. The design profession has, by and large, abdicated its responsibility over day-to-day problems while visibly seeking glory in fixing the gargantuan problems spun out of our own neglect.

I myself have been a part of this problem. I have collected my share of accolades for work done specifically in the aftermath of disaster. I have played the white knight — deliberately and accidently — by swooping in and rebuilding that which never should have fallen. I don't seek absolution because the work was necessary. But I have learned the error of my ways and hope to shed light on an essential contradiction of humanitarian practice.

The contradiction arises from the mechanics of fame within the profession of architecture itself.

Designers find success in creation, not restoration or remediation. Our moments of success are defined by our ability to create something *new* that transcends or eclipses whatever paradigm the world was used to. Moreover, to do so in a way that's visible and for which we can claim credit. Through that process we establish a tick mark in the continuum of designers and architects. We become *known*. It is not wrong to expect an architect to do this. But we must acknowledge how such a construction biases architects to *responding* to conditions rather than preventing them.

Nobody ever became famous responding to a theoretical disaster in a place no one has ever heard of.

Poor communities and the developing world are no stranger to our good intentions. For over a century, the first world has tried with maddeningly erratic success to cure the problems plaguing the bottom billion. More maddening is the fact that so many of these problems can find their roots in colonial and Cold War policies imposed on these populations but absent of their consent.

While these policies — motivated by economic, political and military concerns — are implemented, a great silence erupts from the profession of architecture. And when the policies bear terrible fruit, the architectural profession stands ready and willing to lend a hand. It's great to wash away the dog poop, but why not just curb the dog in the first place?

An obvious question might be: *where does the responsibility of an architect end?* Isn't it naive to believe that an architect can be an all-powerful social engineer? Didn't we try that before? The answer is certainly yes. Why try again? Because that's the only way that anything ever gets done. Those that try again define the march of human progress through history.

Following the Nuremberg trials, the United Nations General Assembly recognised the need for a permanent, international court to deal with issues of genocide and other crimes against humanity. However, the International Criminal Court was not convened until 2003. During the two-generation delay, the world endured the Ethiopian Red Terror, the Khmer Rouge, the Iraqi Kurd massacres and the Rwandan genocide. Would it have been appropriate to give up?

In 1863, the United States signed into law the emancipation proclamation abolishing slavery in the United States. And yet it still persists. There are believed to be about 10,000 forced labourers in the United States at this time.[1] Should society abandon the fight? Are 10,000 a satisfactorily low number? At what point does it become acceptable to retreat to the sidelines while injustice persists?

In 1964, the United States declared war on poverty. And yet, poverty still exists. Any reader needs travel for only 15 minutes in his or her own community to see it.

Gratefully, the professions of law, sociology, politics, diplomacy and international relations have never abandoned the fight against genocide, slavery or poverty. Because progress is entitled to only the stubborn.

One could still argue that such broad questions of social justice are the province of the aforementioned professions. And that architecture, even if it does maintain a level of social concern, can rightfully abstain from such pursuits. The trouble is buildings. Buildings touch *everyone*. And are relevant everywhere.

The design and construction of buildings forms the nexus between the profession of architecture and global society. Buildings are either a source of benefit or detriment to every single living person on the planet. Judging by the tenor of the 2013 American Institute of Architects Convention, architects now believe they could be of benefit.

If they intend to be of benefit, they must adopt the naïve and unreasonable optimism that is the hallmark of all crusaders. To fight injustice is to believe that every inch matters, even while acknowledging that the goal is unattainable. The argument, therefore, about whether humanitarian design is effective becomes a red herring. We should try and save the world because it needs saving. And to do less smacks of apathy and cynicism.

Where to begin? How might architecture even begin to wrap its collective head around such gargantuan problems? We begin by understanding where those problems come from.

In a word: poverty.

Genocide and civil war are the symptoms of an economic illness. By some estimates, the probability of conflict increases threefold when inequality among ethnic groups is at the 95th percentile.[2] Religious, ethnic and political groupings often have ancient reasons to hate each other, but economic inequalities regularly provide the spark to ignite pogroms the world over.

Modern slavery also seems to be an expression of an underlying economic condition. Rapid urbanisation and a wide conversion to mechanised agriculture and away from subsistence farming have created an economic vulnerability that allows millions to easily fall victim to debt bondage – modern slavery.[3] There are now more people in bondage worldwide than all of those that lived and died in the multicentury transatlantic slave trade.

Similarly, with disaster. A recent surge in the frequency and severity of global disasters has spawned a catchphrase for those in the trade: *there's no such thing as a natural disaster*. A bit kitschy, but true nonetheless. And a reality that I have experienced repeatedly first hand. Earthquakes, hurricanes, tsunamis and tornados are unavoidable aspects of our natural world. But the principal cause of death in any disaster is the built environment – or lack of one. In every modern disaster, we've found that poorly built structures, and poorly planned communities, lack the fortitude to withstand even those disasters that the developed world might consider minor. Without basic structural and community stability, much of the world's population is at risk. The developing world has inferior buildings for the same reason it has inferior healthcare and inferior nutrition. When your day is about survival, you cut every corner that you can. Frequently, that results in constructing buildings with the critical bits missing. Leaving out a little bit of rebar here, and a little bit of cement there, you rapidly erect a building that can't support itself under stress. Buildings fall down. Falling buildings kill people.

By now, the mastermind behind all these crimes should be self-evident; disaster, genocide and slavery all have a common root: poverty and inequality. And a state of poverty is most easily recognised by the absence of homes, and the absence of jobs. Architects have the power to create both. Architects can wait until those things are destroyed, and then try to restore them. Or they can acknowledge the immense responsibility that comes with this power and create these things in their daily work.

What would an architect do if he or she wanted to mitigate poverty through design?

First, we must dispense with the Victorian notion that space itself can reduce poverty. It was in vogue for several centuries – this idea that if spaces were light and airy and clean, they would naturally solve social problems. It must have made sense, at some point. 'Our' spaces – the spaces of the wealthy, the successful and the privileged – were nice. And we didn't have the crime and public health problems in our neighbourhoods. Therefore, we merely needed to make 'their' neighbourhoods more like 'our' neighbourhoods and all the problems would abate. A mutation of this idea was a central theme in Modernism. We no longer sought to reinvent the poor places of the world in our own image, but rather to reinvent them along scientific principles, as if straight lines and right angles could cure things like poverty and its attendant effects.

The humanitarian architect of today must realise that the process is at least as important as the product. As an architect, it is his or her opportunity and responsibility to design both. We can, through our design decisions influence the wide community of builders, buyers, sellers and transporters that participate in the execution of a design. A humanitarian designer cannot consign him or herself to a passive role, and believe that the process of building, or the product of a building, is outside of his purview. He or she must believe that progress lies in his or her hands. The tactics are the easy part:

Create Jobs

Through material decisions, an architect can greatly influence the jobs created by a project. In our contemporary first-world practice, we are trained to embrace the efficiency of mass production. To increase cost-effectiveness and value in a building, we look for components that are standardised and familiar. For many clients, it's a programme requirement: you must use standardised components to ease in the operations and maintenance of a building. But if your objective is to create jobs, this logic may be inverted. By emphasising materials that are handcrafted and locally sourced, you can create jobs that promote local pride and economic wellness. The decision of whether to use metal studs or wood studs is one that could be driven by code, climatic decisions or local tradition and so on. Another way to consider such a choice is to ask oneself: *which economy do I want to stimulate?* The decision to use metal studs will positively impact all industries associated with the manufacture, transport and installation of metal studs. This might include ore extraction, foundries, fitters, companies that make rivets, companies that make rivet guns, companies that make metal screws (as opposed to those that make nails) and so on. A decision to use wood studs would likely benefit forestry industries, nurserymen, long-haul trucking and many others. Depending on where each material is sourced, it is wholly possible that the benefits would differ by whole countries or continents. It should be part of the designer's process to consider the full economic value chain during the design process.

Stimulate Local Economies

Every product is part of a value chain. It takes materials and labour to source, assemble, transport and install. Every step, in each value chain, for every product, creates an opportunity to stimulate a local economy. Considerations of sustainability, such as the green building certification programme Leadership in Energy and Environmental Design (LEED), have prompted us to ask more questions about where our building components come from. The next step is to ask what they do while they're there? Do they create jobs, in sourcing, assembly, transport or installation? Are the jobs dignified and sustainable? Were they produced by an extraction economy (eg mining) or an investment economy (eg forestry)? Asking these questions affords designers an opportunity to positively engineer a local economy by making deliberate design decisions in favour of the local economy. This is not unrelated to our previous discussion on job creation. However, it has broader implications. If we choose products, technologies or processes that have secondary and tertiary economic effects, we amplify our impact. For example, suppose you chose a product that had significant transportation requirements. This would stimulate economies related to trucking, truck sales, shipping, packing, auto parts, road repair and other things. This would be of substantially more benefit in a country that had a well-developed auto industry and no alternative means of transportation (eg rail transport). If you make this design decision in a country with no auto industry, much of the economic stimulus is likely to be transferred outside the country — to the country with the most available imports.

Leverage Local Capacities, Don't Overshadow Them.

Patrimony is perhaps the most difficult obstacle to overcome when trying to practice humanitarian design. Vanity is a perfectly human tendency. What is an overeducated first-world designer to do when confronted with an illiterate third-world builder? After a decade of education and training, is it possible that the first-world designer still has something to learn? Yes, naturally. Every country, no matter how poor, has its building professionals. They may not bear the name 'architect', 'engineer' or 'builder', but they practice the same trade as we do. If we were to assume the capacities and skills, would we be putting that local professional out of work? To do so would perpetuate the worst aspects of all humanitarian work: the creation and maintenance of a dependent aid state.

These tenants can be woven into any design, any practice, anywhere in the world. They do not require one to leave one's community, one's job or one's task. They merely require a consciousness of the world that exists outside the modelling table or the design studio, and an awareness of the inherent power of choice and design.

Humanitarian architecture is enjoying a bit of a renaissance. It's fashionable again. The question before us is whether we allow this goodwill to become a part of another chapter in the history of architecture, or weave it into the grammar of the text itself. Whether we take steps to address the inhuman conditions created by others, or take steps to prevent those conditions from ever coming into existence.

Over a billion people worldwide are currently living in substandard conditions. The United Nations estimate that climate change will generate over 50 million refugees in the next 25 years. The majority of the world's population lives with threats to water security. Architects possess the technical skill to solve these problems. And to prevent new ones. Do they have the will?

Notes

1   National Human Rights Center at the University of California at Berkeley.
2   G Østby, 'Inequalities, the Political Environment and Civil Conflict: Evidence from 55 Countries', in F Stewart (ed) *Horizontal Inequalities and Conflict: Understanding Group Violence in Multi-ethnic Societies*, Palgrave MacMillan (Basingstoke), 2010, p 213.
3   Kevin Bales, 'Expendable People: Slavery in the Age of Globalization', *Journal of International Affairs*, vol 53, no 2, Spring 2000, pp 461–84.

Reading Codes Is a Whole New World

Grainne Hassett

Grainne Hassett is a practising architect and senior lecturer at the new School of Architecture, University of Limerick, Ireland (SAUL). Hassett Ducatez Architects, working with buildings and urban design and involved in both teaching and research, was established in Dublin by Grainne Hassett in 1995, with Sarah Jolley joining in 2003. Since inception, the practice has received several architectural awards, both in Ireland and internationally, and the practice has lectured, published and exhibited, built and carried out research work. In 2010 Grainne Hassett published *A Necessary Contract*, a reflection on two architects and two artists and how their practice impacted on the advancement of their work.

Since 2011, under the initiative of Maxim Laroussi (SAUL) and with the enormous assistance of Abdelghani Tayyibi of *les Ecoles Nationales d'Architecture de Fès et Marrakech* (*l'ENA de Fès* and *l'ENA de Marrakech*), Grainne Hassett has led a third-year field trip from SAUL to Fez and Marrakesh in Morocco, joining forces with student and tutor groups in successive years from the ENA Fez and ENA Marrakesh schools to work together. The field trip typically encompasses urban and building restoration techniques used on the UNESCO sites of Fez and Marrakesh.

I am the person wearing a pink sweater in this photograph, taken in 2011. In the photograph we are sitting on the stone floor of an empty, beautiful 11th-century madrasa, an Islamic school, in the city of Fez, Morocco. The building is held in trust by an American college. The man sitting on the ground with the MacBook is our colleague, Irenee, an architect and a wonderful writer about architecture and other things. Based in London, he occasionally teaches at a number of prominent locations. The audience is a mixed group of Irish and Moroccan students of architecture on a teaching field trip. The photograph was taken as Irenee tried to give a lecture, without a projector, in a building without electricity or toilets.

Irenee's lecture was about *bricolage*. Shortly after, he published the piece in a European architecture magazine. That day in Fez — perhaps the group had been sitting on the stone floor too long — I felt the subject was not understood. This was an early indication that cultural values in architectural theory are not shared between the Western and the Arab worlds.

And geography, it seems, is destiny. In the photograph, the woman sitting behind me, to my right, is responsible for many urban refurbishment projects in this UNESCO World City. At our meetings in Fez, we were grateful for her insights but struck by how we shared few contemporary references. She rarely visits Europe or the United States, possibly because of the Schengen Agreement. We encountered this over and over again

Medersa Cherratine, Fez,
Morocco, February 2011.
A student and tutor group
from l'Ecole Nationale
d'Architecture de Fès and
the School of Architecture,
University of Limerick (SAUL),
Ireland, listening to a lecture
in the Medersa Cherratine, an
11th-century *madrasa* in the
centre of Fez's old city.
© Abdelghani Tayyibi.

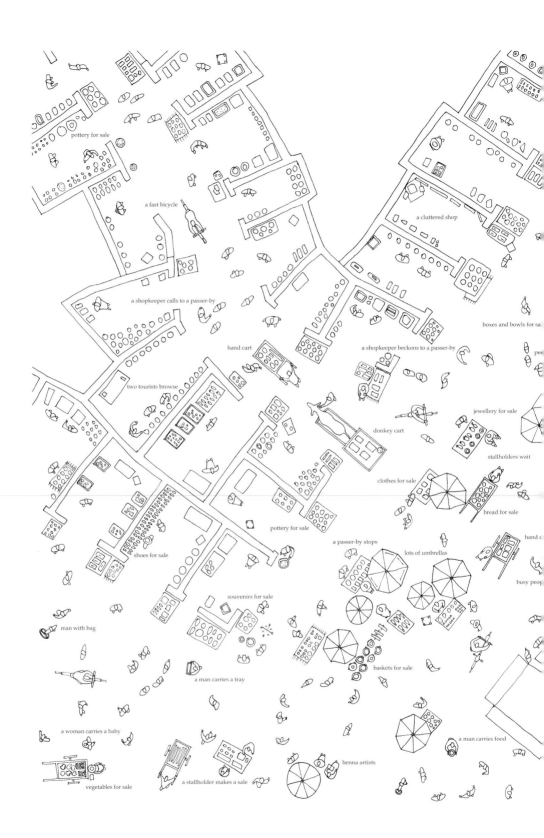

pottery for sale

a fast bicycle

a cluttered shop

a shopkeeper calls to a passer-by

boxes and bowls for sa...

hand cart

a shopkeeper beckons to a passer-by

pe...

two tourists browse

jewellery for sale

donkey cart

stallholders wait

clothes for sale

bread for sale

pottery for sale

a passer-by stops

lots of umbrellas

hand c...

shoes for sale

busy peop...

souvenirs for sale

man with bag

a man carries a tray

baskets for sale

a woman carries a baby

a man carries food

vegetables for sale

a stallholder makes a sale

henna artists

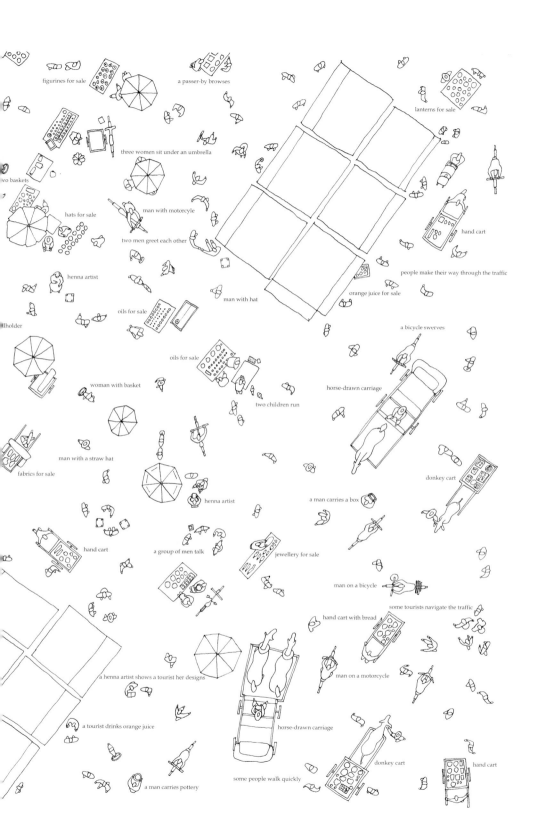

figurines for sale

a passer-by browses

lanterns for sale

three women sit under an umbrella

two baskets

hats for sale

man with motorcycle

hand cart

two men greet each other

people make their way through the traffic

henna artist

man with hat

orange juice for sale

oils for sale

llholder

a bicycle swerves

oils for sale

woman with basket

horse-drawn carriage

two children run

man with a straw hat

donkey cart

fabrics for sale

a man carries a box

hand cart

a group of men talk

jewellery for sale

man on a bicycle

some tourists navigate the traffic

hand cart with bread

a henna artist shows a tourist her designs

man on a motorcycle

a tourist drinks orange juice

horse-drawn carriage

donkey cart

hand cart

some people walk quickly

a man carries pottery

henna artist

during our trip. None of the architects, and few of the students we met really knew of Rem Koolhaas and it did not seem entirely relevant.

The fact that we lacked a shared cultural edifice for our architectural projections poses questions for architectural theory building. The Irish architecture students were there to study as much of the context as they could in one week, and return to the University of Limerick to develop their architectural projects. We have done this taught field trip for three years and joined forces with students from Fez and Marrakesh schools of architecture. Part of the week takes in urban conservation techniques on sites.

Across the Arab world, the older parts of cities, towns and settlements are a built accretion of rooms, organic and seemingly haphazard. The streets, leftover ribbons in the honeycomb, are labyrinthine. Mostly consisting of high blank walls, with few orienting features, they can be terrifying to the westerner. They cannot be understood in terms of the well-established principles of defensibility, visibility, orientation or *genius loci* as described in Western architectural theory. Most likely, they are self-governing places, with precisely their own principles of defensibility, visibility, orientation and *genius loci*; clannish but easily understood if you know the code.

But knowing the code is the thing. This is an urban typology that is under described in Western architectural theory. It is not absorbed into our central architectural culture. It is not encoded or encapsulated within our repertoire of architectural understanding. When we reach into our architectural minds, we find no models to help us think about this type conceptually anew, save those of repair and restoration, a subset of mainstream architectural thinking.

Reading codes is always a whole new world. In any city you need to know the code to read it. For instance, the blank walls of the classic Arab typology contrast with the large windows of the Jewish typology in other quarters of the same city. So there is a difference within the urban fabric, signifying ethnicity and religious value.

If we have not absorbed this typology into mainstream architectural theory, then when teaching in Morocco we are faced with a dilemma. For a start, teaching architectural design is often about proposing something new. Arguably, models of anything, from education to farming, must succumb to periodic analysis and renewal. Yet the older Arab urban archetype seems almost timelessly compelling. It is hard to see how or why to improve on the model.

The buildings are handmade, as is almost everything in Morocco. They are not unsanitary, irrigation and sewage systems developed early in the dry world. They are fireproof. They are climatically smart and culturally embedded. The benefits of departing from the model do not spring to mind. The climate, especially the heat, is an overwhelming fact in Morocco. This is a zero-energy system for shelter, which makes the heat and the cold nights bearable. What is left to design?

There is a consistency in the arrangement of this Arab building archetype across the Middle East and North Africa. The indispensable *Traditional Domestic Architecture of the Arab Region* by Friedrich Ragette (Editions Axel Menges, 2003), full of useful drawings, shows page after page of a single repeated building plan. It is the same from Algeria to Iraq.

In it, the generic building plan is a central courtyard with a necklace of rooms around it. If this is the plan of a house, the house next door is the same. The two houses and the next house are all stuck together any which way. In this environmentally savvy system the courtyard brings in light, air, cooling and organises circulation. Because of it, openings in external walls are obsolete. Adjoining units simply adhere to one another, wherever they fit together. The courtyard is always a regular shape — a square or a rectangle — the rest is an agglomeration of rooms around it. In a large palace, the overall plan is formed from the repetition of many such courtyard and room units. Buildings for businesses, schools and markets follow the same pattern.

The system is a honeycomb and the unit is the room and courtyard typology. Streets are just a leftover by-product, a major break with Western architectural typologies. In this world they are not primary elements; within the figure-ground equation, they are neither. Again, breaking with standard architectural theory, the semi-private courtyard is figure, and the private rooms are ground. The North African street, with no arranged public facades and no symmetry, is neither figure nor ground.

At best, they can become intensely public in the *souk* but without a centre, beginning or end. There they seem to turn inside out and the edges of streets are lined with lock-up bazaar shops, again blank walls, all dead-ends piled high with millions of small objects; an overwhelming river of colour.

With no need for windows to admit unwanted heat, the high walls are mostly blank with occasional openings for entrances into homes. These are always through a *chicane*, to maintain privacy. The street-necklaces wind and twist without discernable orienting features to join up parts of the city, which have become too big, or to delineate clan areas.

So the concept of public life in the Arab world is not the same as it is in the Western world. It is definitely not the same as the concept of public life that developed in modern

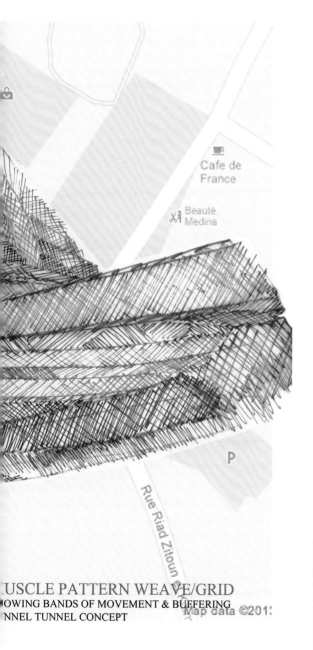

USCLE PATTERN WEAVE/GRID
OWING BANDS OF MOVEMENT & BUFFERING
NNEL TUNNEL CONCEPT

Place Jemaa el-Fna,
Marrakesh, March
2013. A plan drawing
showing the pattern
of movement of
people, cars and
animals through the
Place Jemaa el-Fna.
© Georgy Daly.

Western cultural theory. That theory of public life, developed from the Enlightenment onwards, gives the Western architect a set of tropes to work with. Public, private, piazza, basilica, figure and ground, form and field, network and dispersion – architectural theory we use as a springboard, concepts we use to compose plans, ideas we use to teach. These tropes draw almost solely on Western models, with a brief foray into *Japonisme*, fashionable as the 'Other' in the 19th century.

But in Morocco this is of no use. There are no piazza, basilica, form, figure and field tropes; there is only a honeycomb. Inserted into it are public typologies; mosque, library, school, guild workers' arcades. But these are embellished repetitions of the courtyard and room type. They are embedded into the honeycomb, they are never set apart.

So as architecture teachers, each time we return from Ireland to Morocco to teach, the more puzzling it becomes. It can be hard to figure out if things are different or if they are the same. I return to my point at the outset – your audience needs to be complicit in your culture; your students need to share the edifice upon which your judgement is founded.

Some values are universal, so it is easy to move through early teaching steps working with the students – becoming aware of the urban context, deciding on a good brief, a sympathetic scale of operation, maybe even an appropriate construction. Why not repeat the classic building unit over and over, accreting one unit onto another? How big could the honeycomb be? What is its natural scale?

And, left alone, the architectural project in Morocco would build itself. Traditional Arab architecture makes a lot of sense in its context. The plan and section arrangement, the thick walls, narrow and high rooms, the wind funnels, the cool glazed surfaces, the tiny windows with thick wooden shutters, huge doors to close when it gets cold, all strung around a leafy, watery courtyard; this works very well, even without hippie nostalgia. In the overwhelming climate, it seems contrary to try anything else, as the bad modernist imports attest.

You start to feel it should all be like this, since it just works. To introduce a large-span space might be interesting, but harder to cool, and would require an investment in industry, transportation and new logistics, which seem to bring no benefit. So you wonder how to invent something new. You wonder what to do with the type you have found. And then you wonder why we need to invent something new. You wonder about the benefit of introducing large-span technologies; steel beams or engineered wood technologies made in factories, transported in trucks and erected by crane into this economy. You wonder how the economy works, how labour, capital and materials flow.

The structure of things, the structure of how things are organised in a given society generally reflects the material to hand and the social structures and the technology of that society. This is true of irrigation systems in Yemen, of high-speed trains in Singapore, and it is also true of the organisation of buildings and urban systems.

So we dug deeper and we started to understand the social structure underlying this technology better.

The old building system is handmade, made out of materials using earth. Walls are either made of thin flat bricks or of fat ragged earth 'adobe' blocks or of rammed earth,

Place Jemaa el-Fna,
Marrakesh, March 2013. A
model collage drawing by
year three (2013) student
Sarah Mannion proposing
a shelter around the
edges of the market area
of the Place Jemaa el-Fna.
© Sarah Mannion.

Building Site, Fez, Morocco,
February 2011. Young man
carving a geometric pattern
by hand on door panelling
for a UNESCO restoration
project urban site.
© Grainne Hassett.

plastered over with mud. Floor structures are spanned by cedar beams and planks; ceilings are filled in first with stripped branches and then covered with boards; flat roofs are made waterproof with polished earth. Master craftsmen carve repeating geometrical and intricate patterns in plaster and wood, drawing the templates by hand. The relief patterns, cut outs, fractals and repetitions feel the same, in grain and type, as those being constructed digitally by graduates of fine art, architecture and fashion at the London degree shows held each summer. Back in Morocco, glazed tile panels are made up back to front on the floor in a jigsaw first, then raised slowly into place. It looks like a model of sustainability. It seems to match the pattern of local labour economies, cheap and plentiful and available material, ditto.

But the local labour economy is precarious also, and we are unsure how it is connected to our Western economies. In 2013 we set the Moroccan and Irish students to work together, interviewing Berber women about their lives in Tafza, a village an hour's bus ride from Marrakesh. We asked half of the group to survey the soft infrastructure of the Berber village. They needed to find out where the school was, how often the clinic opened, what sport was played, by whom and where; they were asked to unearth the stories and map this spatially. We set another group to topographically survey the entire terrain of this never-before-mapped village, using their wits, logbooks and pencils. No modern-day conquerors, they were hugely relieved to discover it reappearing on Google maps a week later.

We learnt that the clinics never opened. We were told doctors would be loath to move to a village with few good educational prospects for their own children. The empty new clinics contained no equipment; no nurses, no midwives came. Nobody had a car. We learnt that in the free public health system hospital in Marrakesh, an hour away by car, you would need to pay several people before accessing various services, including the emergency room. It was explained to us that this was a good system, this *baksheesh*. It allowed, we were told, for flexibility in arranging things. With money everything could ultimately be arranged, much better than our northern European inflexibility.

In the village, women told the students that few could afford to send their children to the free school, because they could not earn enough at work to pay for after-school care. Miniature herdsmen, the children led a few sheep around. The women worked selling Argan oil, making carpets, collecting firewood, cooking and minding children. Men stood around, some made pottery and traded. The street was rough dirt.

Some houses were more elaborate, others basic. In places, people and animals lived together in small rooms. Women squatted in the dirt, cooking in very effective fire pots made by scooping together clay; in a nearby lane people made tourist trinkets, models of the Eiffel Tower, in the same clay. Rubbish is thrown down the slopes of the village, and not collected, though plastic and paper waste is noticeably scant in Morocco. There is little packaging.

The water supply of the village was recently installed. Four families share part ownership of one olive tree, with an ingenious irrigation system. Mortality is a matter of chance. All of this is in a city an hour's flight from Europe and a little over two hours to London, or Madrid. Unless it is to pave the street of Tafza, what is the use of an architecture school here?

Tafza, a Berber village south of Marrakesh,
March 2013. Students from l'Ecole Nationale
d'Architecture De Rabat and the School
of Architecture, University of Limerick
(SAUL), Ireland, talking with village women,
mapping stories of the soft infrastructure of
the village. © Grainne Hassett.

So it seems life in parts of Morocco, depending on where you are born and whether you survive, is pure subsistence at a meagre level, despite the public health, transportation, education and governance systems. The inordinately vast quantities of handmade things for sale; all of the tin plates, cloths, necklaces, leather bags and clay pots bear witness to a low-paid labour force. We wondered if, after all, it made sense to say that the construction system based on this vast worker force is sustainability at its most perfect.

It was clear that our terribly bright Moroccan architecture students did not come from this milieu. Mostly female, they will graduate and work largely in the policy or urban repair projects of UNESCO sites, in itself a vast project, with difficult tourism demands. But they will work a little on new projects too, on hotels, hospitals and villas.

In Morocco, we found the architecture students quickly drew problem-solving solutions, perhaps with some decoration. I understand this response and where it comes from. When we worked in the field together, we were collectively more comfortable making drawings from old restoration techniques and learning about existing, arguably sustainable practices. The irrigation systems, the straightforward construction, the elegance of waterproof plaster in hammams polished with egg yolk, all of the handmade earthy wares of Morocco are refreshing and compelling. These we could study, these we could discuss. When we moved to *project*, things became difficult again.

We seem to have moved well beyond problem solving and artistry in Western architectural practice. For some time now, in order to imagine and compose an architectural project, in our Western way, abstraction is needed. Abstraction is, among other things, a mode we use for a work process, a method to allow us to organise matter into an architectural project. But abstraction in Morocco and abstraction in Western architectural theory diverge, presenting us with a final dilemma.

We have become adept in architecture studios and schools all over the Western world, Asia and Oceania at the abstract manipulation of matter. Flipping forms, repeating patterns, twisting strips, atomising squares, repeating arrays of points; it does not matter that this is not matter at all; often what matters to us is the elegance of the compositional agility.

When we use multiplication, arrays, geometry or mirroring to arrange bits of the architectural project, we are drawing on recent digital practices. Now, as we are 3D-printing the project, slicing it out in singed layers on a laser cutter, the process is becoming more and more entwined with the method of its production, so entwined we have often forgotten what we are doing. Still, the parts we are arranging, the cubes, ramps, strips, planes, blobs and voids are based on a repertoire, which was developed in Western architecture. This is not a repertoire shared in Morocco for two reasons; first, geometry and visual patterning mean something else in Morocco, and second, modern art did not develop concurrently with Paris, London, Moscow or New York for historical colonial reasons.

Compositional elegance is important in an architectural project. But the gap between the advanced compositional discourse of Western architectural culture and Moroccan architectural culture is too great for it to be a useful tool to pack when we travel there to teach. It does not seem useful to conceptualise the architectural project, using the terms of engagement of our Western architecture school-studio discourse.

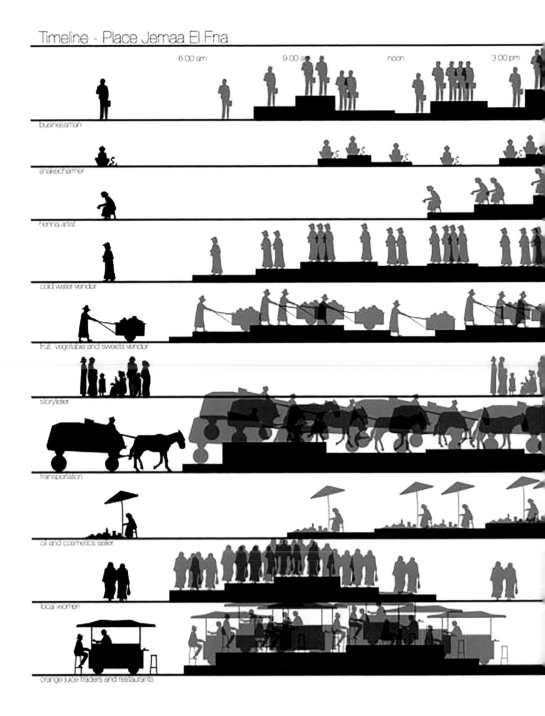

Timeline - Place Jemaa El Fna

6.00 am   9.00 am   noon   3.00 pm

businessman

snakecharmer

henna artist

cold water vendor

fruit, vegetable and sweets vendor

storyteller

transportation

oil and cosmetics seller

local women

orange juice traders and restaurants

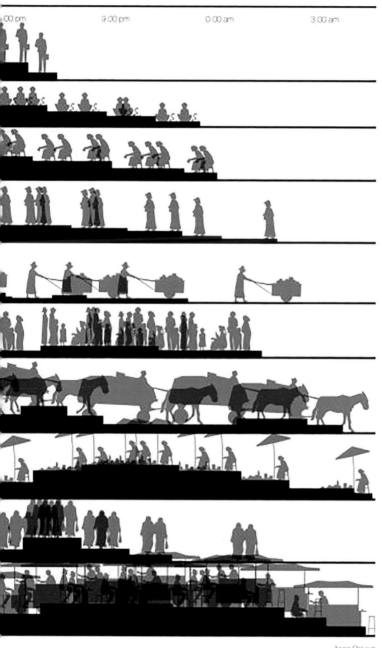

Place Jemaa el-Fna, Marrakesh, March 2013. A timeline drawing by year three (2013) Erasmus student Anna Bokodi shows the time lapse occupation of the Place Jemaa el-Fna by different peoples. © Anna Bokodi.

In Islamic architecture, abstraction is used in the ornamentation of surfaces. The ornamentation, also using multiplication, arrays, geometry and mirroring is always a referent. It signifies something, like Allah or Unity. The decoration is not abstract as westerners understand abstraction; in Islam the shapes and patterns are meaning carriers. They belong to a world of symbols and the stories they tell. This layer of code embedded into the surfaces of buildings can be read if you know how.

So decoration, shape, pattern and representation have definite roles in Islam. These are perfectly good roles, but they are not those shared by Western art theory. For us, abstraction has myriad roles now. Often it is also a symbol, a representational device, not really *abstract* at all. A white cube might signify purity, clarity, maybe even hygiene or progress. Nowadays, it probably also signifies old modernity. So some abstract shapes and patterns have become, through cultural association, recognisable meaning carriers, almost globally. On this we agree with an extensive chunk of the world. But for us, abstract manipulations are compositional devices. When we moved to use abstraction as a compositional tool for architectural projects with our Moroccan students, things became thornier. It was difficult to explain why we would use abstraction, bearing in mind the role of abstraction in Islam. Though nobody objected to our strange method, it seemed as if we were attempting to teach *modernisme*-light, or some sort of French-style. The idea was not embedded and shared.

Finally, we found our way, with some relief, when we started working on the inimitable Place Jemaa el-Fna in Marrakesh. Given the choice, five of our pluckiest students elected to try to work with it. We allowed them to develop their own brief, and suggested total immersion, though there was hardly any other choice. Jemaa el-Fna is Africa's largest, and to my mind scariest, urban square. It has no precedent in Western architectural culture.

The students had to develop their own drawings, drawings they had not seen before in architectural publications, to try to describe the spatiality of the square. It is a temporal spatiality, defined only by its human occupation. Early in the morning the washed square is an empty surface, only defined by a wall of juice sellers' carts, piled up with pyramids of oranges. The huge surface of indeterminate shape is gradually crisscrossed with people and donkeys as the trade of the day gathers pace. Cars weave on the edge of the flow in a sort of naturally regulated river of motors and pathetic beasts. Snake charmers and monkey-on-a-chain merchants appear next, springing and whirling to catch tourists. Over the day, rags will be spread on the ground and the trading of trinkets, prayers, remedies and pigeons begins on the flat surface. Boys with brass cups slung around their necks, traditional thirst quenchers, walk across the space. There is no shade, no enclosure. Horse and carriage ensembles for tourists wait patiently, the horses in good condition. No walls, no awnings define the spaces; just seeming understandings, the ground gradually filling up more and more. As night falls the square is crowded and dark, but it intensifies again, turning into an outdoor restaurant as food carts, kitchens, tables and canopies are laid out, steam and smoke rise and lanterns light faces. In the darkness, on the edges, the Arab story-tellers sit cross-legged on the ground, surrounded by a rapt and very large audience. They tell their stories only in Arabic, a last surviving activity not accessible to a Western tourist.

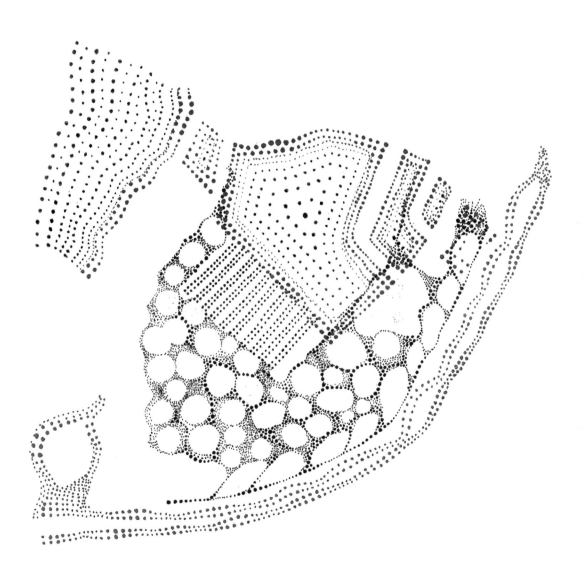

Place Jemaa el-Fna,
Marrakesh, March 2013.
Plan of the occupation of
the ground by people, cars
and animals, showing the
many encampments of the
Place Jemaa el-Fna.
© Georgy Daly.

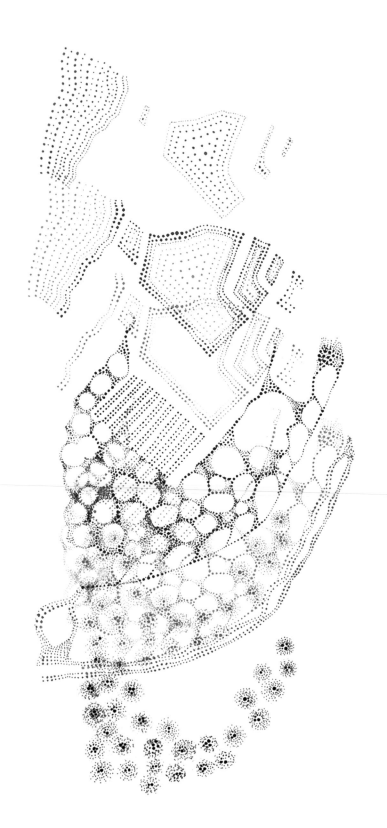

Place Jemaa el-Fna,
Marrakesh, March 2013.
Plan of the occupation of
the ground by people, cars
and animals, showing the
many encampments of the
Place Jemaa el-Fna.
© Georgy Daly.

Taking cues from the artist Kathy Prendergast's *City Drawings*, and Daniel Spoerri's *Forensic Dinner Party* drawings, the Irish students made mappings of the occupation of the space. This was a starting point from which to *project* and was exchanged on Facebook with their Moroccan colleagues. They were adamant that the Place Jemaa el-Fna ought not change and should not be built on. We pushed them hard to propose a new project, explaining that this was the way of the world and that someone else would develop the square if they did not take charge. Their new projects largely dealt with the surface; three proposing an intelligent reworking to give some shade, refrigeration, drainage, clean water and public toilets. We were relieved that their projects were genuinely well observed and visually rich.

With Morocco's late liberation from colonial status and its persistent agrarian structure and given that we have no shared understanding of language, code or symbol, we westerners are the learners in this process, finding our own cultural capital deliciously wanting.

For now, teaching design studio in Morocco to either Moroccan or Irish students poses a challenge. Both teams seem to be missing something, though on either side it is a different thing. In particular, Moroccan students do not necessarily share the same culture of abstraction, or of Western design studio practices as we do. Not a bad thing perhaps, but we are similarly stuck on our side, when we find our mental reservoir of architectural tropes inadequate to deal with North African urbanism, a world not very well described in Western architectural theory. Second, the cultural background: the socioeconomic basis for public buildings, for housing, for schools, and also for industrialisation and labour is quite different to that in Europe. So a building-type, such as a clinic, that European architectural culture presumes to be good, might never become occupied in Morocco. A construction technique we presume to be the epitome of sustainability may have labour conditions underpinning it we do not fully grasp yet. And finally, the older Arab urban archetypes seem almost preposterously compelling in contemporary environmental terms. It is hard to see why or how to improve the model yet I doubt if that is the truth. It is a great position to be in.

Architecture, Planning and Politics

9

A variety of points of view have been discussed in the preceding sections; the impact of building decisions is far-reaching, touching the most intimate and personal moments of people's lives and impacting the social and economic situations of entire regions or nations. Presumably all architecture tacitly or explicitly engages in political systems. As we see time and again, humanitarian architecture encounters the same issues as all design, but underlying assumptions are revealed by the critical or unstable environments within which it is practised. Decisions about what to design, who to design for, what the design process will be, who the designer will be, where and when building will take place, who the builder will be, and how the design will be built, can all become incredibly sensitive political questions, revealing and challenging – we hope – problematic status quos.

An example of the range of political interpretations in architecture was surveyed in New York's Museum of Modern Art 2012–13 exhibition, *9 + 1 Ways of Being Political*, which presented a range of responses to social and political questions and public space.

A short review of the last two centuries of utopian visions and grand urban plans suggests that the best of intentions can go terribly wrong. Any evangelical advocate of *the* solution to humanitarian design is suspect. In discussing architecture, planning and politics as a single theme, the goal is to shift the focus away from formal design and towards an examination of the processes by which designs are invented and implemented. Finally, the impact of design decisions on end users must be carefully considered and monitored in order to respond better to each subsequent design problem.

Ducis, Haiti, 2012. Local leaders, urban planners and women's association representatives use satellite maps to discuss and locate community development priorities. © Irene E Brisson.

Delmas 32
A Post-Disaster Planning Experience in Haiti

Sabine Malebranche

Where the scale of architecture may not always have to interact with the complexities of political and community dynamics, urban planning by definition does. In this case study of a multifaceted master plan for a neighbourhood that suffered major damage in the 2010 Haitian earthquake, Sabine Malbranche describes in detail the economic, political, social and safety pressures facing a master plan and the in-depth community engagement that the firm **SODADE** includes as a critical facet of their process. As one of the few Haitian-owned and operated planning firms in the country they demonstrate, and here elucidate, the techniques of survey, visioning, workshop and feedback that they use to incorporate the voices of a wide range of stakeholders in the planning process. In each context the forms of participation must be adapted to the particulars of the situation and the people involved. This example serves as a diverse set of tools and modes of inquiry, put to use in an attempt to capture a community's vision.

Introduction and Background

The 2010 earthquake in Haiti, centred west of Port-au-Prince, devastated the Delmas 32 neighbourhood and caused significant loss of human life, assessed at approximately 7,000 people. The urban zone of Delmas 32, located in the township of Delmas, spanned roughly 114 acres (46 hectares) and in 2009 had an estimated population of 76,000 individuals.

An investigation led by the *Bureau de Monétisation des Programmes d'Aide au Développement*/Bureau of Monetisation of Development Aid Programmes (BMPAD), a state organisation, gauged that after the natural disaster, approximately 29 per cent of housing in the neighbourhood was destroyed, 12 per cent had undergone lighter damage that could be repaired and roughly 36 per cent of housing required serious repairs before its reuse by the local population. Therefore housing structures in this zone remained quite unsafe. It also became apparent that the infrastructure and services were not meeting the needs of the population.

Despite the extreme precariousness of the post-disaster situation, the community of Delmas 32 worked with the *Conseil du Project de Développement Participative*/Project Development Council (COPRODEP), a committee representing roughly 60 communitarian associations, which over the past three years has worked on the recovery and raising community awareness of questions related to local development. With COPRODEP the community had a voice to put forward its requirements to the municipality of Delmas and other local authorities, in order to ameliorate living conditions in the medium and long term.

Delmas 32, Haiti, 2011. A post-earthquake view of Delmas 32, a dense neighbourhood situated on either side of a steep ravine in the centre of Port-au-Prince. © Addly Célestin/SODADE.

In the context of these challenging conditions, BMPAD decided to establish in Delmas 32 a Plan of Post-Disaster Urban Recovery and Reconstruction. The plan would facilitate the conceptualisation of the neighbourhood's spatial rehabilitation, based on the pressing needs of the population, in an attempt to improve their living conditions and provide them with basic services.

Post-Disaster Recovery and Reconstruction
Plan Objectives for the Urban Zone of Delmas 32

One of the plan's primary objectives was a model neighbourhood development plan, with a communitarian character, representing a shared redevelopment vision based on consensus and broad participation. This would allow the team of urban planners responsible for the project to channel and give form to the concerns and expectations of the local population, and to spatialise redevelopment decisions. Strategic interventions and urban planning activities stemmed from the proposed directions for development and would constitute the plan's structuring activities for the recovery of Delmas 32.

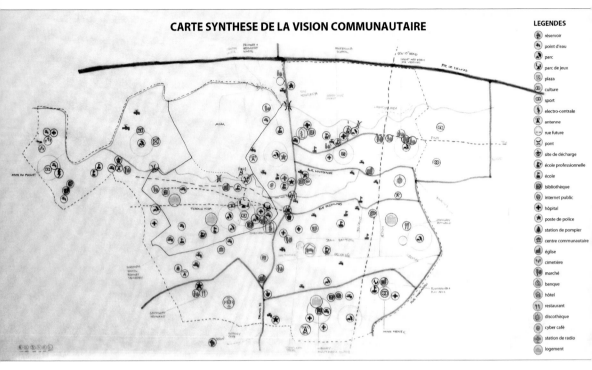

CARTE SYNTHESE DE LA VISION COMMUNAUTAIRE

LEGENDES

- réservoir
- point d'eau
- parc
- parc de jeux
- plaza
- culture
- sport
- electro-centrale
- antenne
- rue future
- pont
- site de décharge
- école professionnelle
- école
- bibliothèque
- internet public
- hôpital
- poste de police
- station de pompier
- centre communautaire
- église
- cimetière
- marché
- banque
- hôtel
- restaurant
- discothèque
- cyber café
- station de radio
- logement

top: View along Rue Delmas 32, primary transportation artery through the neighbourhood. © Addly Célestin/SODADE.

above left: Displaced persons camp along the ravine in Delmas 32. © Addly Célestin/SODADE.

above right: Existing neighbourhood water distribution station. © Addly Célestin/SODADE.

opposite: The first step in the planning process involved the collection and compilation of official cartographic data with community focus group feedback. © Addly Célestin/SODADE.

Methodology for Elaborating the Conceptual
Post-Disaster Recovery and Reconstruction Plan for Delmas 32

The *Société d'Aménagement et de Développement*/Society for Planning and Development (SODADE), was chosen to elaborate the Post-Disaster Recovery and Reconstruction Plan for Delmas 32. It developed a methodology, based on two complementary approaches, which were combined to yield the greatest degree of stakeholder involvement. The first was an objective understanding of facts about the Delmas 32 neighbourhood; the second was a community consensus on the hierarchy of its priorities and its vision for the integrated development of the zone. The two approaches worked as follows:

The technical dimension was centred primarily on fieldwork, encompassing diagnostic tools to capture the state of affairs and characteristics of the area and a literature search for available technical data on the neighbourhood. This process included the following elements: site visits, an analysis of the damage, documentation of spatial and economic practices, housing styles and methods of habitation, the utilisation of space for economic activities, collective amenities, basic services, transportation infrastructures and environmental questions. The analysis also highlighted the assets, wealth and constraints of the zone and required the collection and analysis of cartographical data and synthesis of official data sources.

The human dimension of our approach was based essentially on the integration of the local communities into the diagnostic process, and an understanding of the project and the milestones to be attained. The effective participation of the local population, local authorities and community leaders through the organisation of focus groups or thematic working groups, was key to identifying the strengths of the zone and the challenges to be met.

Community involvement was implemented through site visits led conjointly with members of the community and our field teams, supported by photographic and video documents and GPS readings, which allowed for precise and reliable maps and documentation of the Delmas 32 neighbourhood to be realised. Focus groups were organised with members of the Delmas 32 community to better identify the history, cultural and spatial practices, the potentials, the problems and the requirements of the zone. These focus groups provided an opportunity to listen and engage in discussion with community leadership, diverse professional groups within the area, public health representatives, youth representatives and faith leaders. The theme of 'risk, disaster and environment' was the object of one particular focus group. The results of these thematic focus groups and interviews, initiated with all target groups and players involved in the development of the area, allowed the identification of the development's priorities and constraints.

Based on a representative sample from the zone, a partial investigation was conducted by the community. This investigation produced a quantification of amenities, lodgings, services and the quality of infrastructures and the usage of space by the population of the Delmas neighbourhood. Lastly, a Community Participatory Planning Workshop yielded the first few elements of spatial planning, the community vision that would complete the process.

Community Participatory Planning Workshop with the Community of Delmas 32: Principles, Methods and Results

Municipal Palace of Delmas/29 October 2010

The Community Participatory Planning Workshop brought together 80 participants. This workshop constituted one of the most important steps in the elaboration of the participatory planning process for the plan. Invitations were sent out to associations represented by the Delmas 32 COPRODEP, to the City Council of Delmas, to the Haitian State, to Haitian and international nongovernmental organisations, and to international aid institutions actively intervening in Delmas 32.

This convening, held at the Municipal Palace of Delmas, was a one-day event. Its primary objective was to involve stakeholders in the process of reflection and spatial planning of their community. The Delmas local authorities actively participated in the process and validated the results. This workshop initiated three exercises: first documenting the individual maps that people made of their community, second a reflection on the issues identified in the area by theme and third, the spatialisation of the planning vision for Delmas 32 by the different working groups.

top: Working groups developed maps and lists of current community resources and unmet needs. © Addly Célestin/SODADE.

above: An initial focus group engaged a variety of local stakeholders in a discussion of perceived community needs. © Addly Célestin/SODADE.

Mental Map Spatialised by the Community

The goal of this first exercise was to allow participants to draw a personal and individual map of the neighbourhood or the area in which they lived. This exercise was adapted from, and based on, the theory of American urban planner Kevin Lynch (*The Image of the City*, 1960) who in the 1960s developed the technique of understanding a city and its form based on the living experience and the everyday perceptions of its inhabitants.

Thematic Maps: Opportunities and Constraints

The objective of this exercise was to engage participants in thinking about the themes relevant to the existing conditions in Delmas 32. Divided into groups, participants deliberated over a theme identified within the neighbourhood. The themes given priority and used for the exercise were:

Physical infrastructures
Social infrastructures
Economy
Recreational activities
Environment and risks
Lodging

These themes were also addressed within the community focus groups. Reconvening as a group, each team presented the spatial results of its reflections.

Synthesis Map for the Visions of the Community: the Community Vision

The goal of this final exercise was to synthesise the results obtained in the first two exercises and to reach a development vision for the neighbourhood. The teams formed were tasked with drawing a map that represented and reflected the existing conditions and their desired development opportunities for improving the community's living conditions.

At the end of the exercise, each team presented their development vision to the larger assembly; the concepts were presented by superimposing them one upon the other, thus showing the community's unified and collective vision for the future development of their neighbourhood.

This collective effort presented the basic elements of the conceptual plan, which was then prepared and elaborated on by the urban planners responsible for the project. The superimposition of the six different maps developed by the working groups formed a map, synthesising and translating the visions of the community. The beauty of the exercise was that the different groups envisioned a quality space with amenities and services that overlapped and meshed along the axis of Delmas 32.

The community vision highlighted the need for a higher-quality restructured environment than had preceded the earthquake and integration of identified services. The restructuring proposed by the community began, in part, with the development of social and community facilities, such as libraries, community centres, childcare facilities,

top: Group representative
presenting resultant
community map. © Addly
Célestin/SODADE.

above: Synthesising
neighbourhood maps and
perceived subregions.
© Addly Célestin/SODADE.

SCHEMATISATION DE LA CARTE DE LA VISION COMMUNAUTAIRE

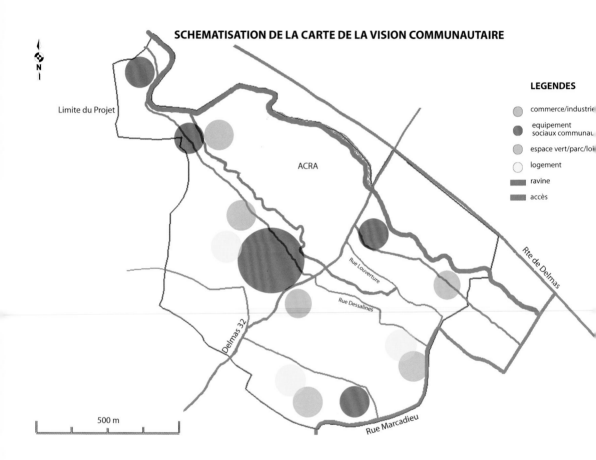

LEGENDES

- commerce/industrie
- equipement sociaux communau
- espace vert/parc/loi
- logement
- ravine
- accès

Limite du Projet

ACRA

Rue Louverture

Rue Dessalines

Rue Marcadieu

Rte de Delmas

Delmas 32

500 m

Schematic Map of the Community
Vision. The map identifies major
development types in relationship
to primary and secondary
transportation routes and
environmental features.
© Addly Célestin/SODADE.

community clinics, churches, police stations, a fire station, national and secondary schools as well as professional schools.

The second category of services was commercial services, to be centrally located along the axis of Delmas 32, the heart of the neighbourhood, to ensure economic development in the zone. Thiotte Market, for example, at the entrance to Delmas 32, needed to be reconstructed to meet building standards. The community also considered mortgage banks, nightclubs, cybercafes and radio stations necessary. The community vision underscored the urgency for rehabilitating existing infrastructures and initiating the construction of new ones adapted to neighbourhood requirements.

Proposed public spaces and community structures were to be distributed throughout the urban zone. Two water reservoirs, the provision of new water fountains to ensure better distribution, neighbourhood parks, playgrounds and sports fields were key elements prioritised by the participants. The need to construct housing to adequate building standards in all residential zones was visible throughout the Delmas 32 neighbourhood.

Within the scope of the community vision, it was proposed that important secondary access roads, such as Rue Dessalines, Rue Louverture, Rue Crepsac and Rue Jean Georges, be developed. Diverse structures and services would be distributed along these routes in such a manner as to make them more centrally located with respect to the different zones. Additionally, a new transversal access road was proposed to extend Rue Dessalines to Delmas 30.

The analysis highlighted the fact that the community's vision was coherent and articulated the idea that a large number of amenities and services could be distributed throughout Delmas 32.

Conclusion

The different steps presented in this methodology were integral components of the Community Participatory Planning process established with the community of Delmas 32. This method of community planning has as its ultimate objective the formal facilitation of community input to address their perception of the space in which they live, their interpretation of the problems identified in the neighbourhood and their future aspirations for the sustainable development of their area.

The combined results of all of these steps will constitute the first basic elements of the Delmas 32 Conceptual Plan, and integrate the deepest aspirations of its beneficiaries.

Building On, Over, With
Postcolonialism and Humanitarian Design

Irene E Brisson

In order to engage with the political ramifications of design, it is imperative to engage with history. The history of many of the marginalised and at risk regions of the world is deeply enmeshed in the colonial past of the last three centuries. This essay discusses the relationship between colonial pasts and current humanitarian aid work. The theoretical lens of postcolonialism provides a critical stance towards a path forward among heterogeneous groupings of professionals and users, nationals and foreigners.

Humanitarian Design – Troubled by Postcolonialism

Time and again people have turned to the forms of their settlements and shelters as mechanisms to express cultural ideals, regulate patterns of behaviour and embody political and social structures. From Ledoux's plans for the utopian saltworkers' town of Chaux[1] to Michael Bloomberg's micro-apartment initiative in New York City[2] to Curitiba's now aging public transportation system, there is as great a range of methods as there are goals, which architects and urban planners, politicians and even religious leaders have pursued tacitly or explicitly via building.

There is an equally long history of the fallout from utopian endeavours to improve the human environment, particularly for the purported benefit of the most marginalised and those with the fewest resources. From speculative examples, such as Le Corbusier's radical proposal for a Paris razed of its historical fabric and replaced with Modernist towers, to implemented projects like the much publicised failure of the Pruitt-Igoe housing project in St Louis, Missouri, whose infamous demolition has been called 'the day Modern architecture died',[3] architects have often, and infamously, come up short in accounting for the complexities of the social context of their work.

This is not cause for despair or resignation, but an invitation to thoughtful reflection on a new wave of idealistic design movements. At the beginning of this book, Christian Hubert and Ioanna Theocharopoulou pose a definition for humanitarian design as a question, 'Can design thinking that typically only responds to crises help provide new models of more equitable and socially responsible living?'.[4] Eric Cesal then expands on this sentiment, exhorting architects to forego the publicity of crisis to attend to its

Georges H Baussan, National Palace, Port-au-Prince, Haiti, 2011. The palace is an example of neoclassical architecture executed by a French-trained Haitian architect in the early 20th century. © Irene E Brisson.

prevention by using the design and construction process to ameliorate root causes of poverty and inequality. These hopeful and challenging visions orient us towards the future, but every humanitarian actor also encounters a past and brings personal and social identities formed by history to bear on the work. These histories, especially in aid contexts, are often rooted in and marked by European colonisation from the 16th to the 20th centuries. This essay opens up a discussion of the influence colonial history has on humanitarian aid and design and the ways in which postcolonial theory can shed light on pitfalls and openings in the design process when this global hierarchy comes into play.

Given the swell of enthusiasm in contemporary society to apply design thinking to major problems facing the world, including but hardly limited to: increasing urbanisation with its attendant poverty; inadequate transportation, sanitation and other infrastructures; and rural poverty especially as linked to environmental degradation and global warming — how can a responsible designer enter the fray with a productive blend of criticality and optimism? It should be clear by now that there is no single design methodology or style that will create a perfect world — history, if not common sense, bears this out. But there is a sense of optimism in this second decade of the 21st century that we as designers can act, we can — must — do better, do more, be accountable for the changes we produce in the world.

This optimism does not negate the very real problems confronting, and underlying, humanitarian architecture and public interest design. First and foremost is the question of why some populations are in such dire straights compared to others? Why is there such polarisation of wealth and resources? The answers are many, of course, and discussed at length in other scholarship. Here we will focus on repercussions of colonisation and the particular challenges facing designers working on humanitarian projects — troubling the work with analysis from a postcolonial perspective. The location of need and crisis in specific places, and histories, prompts us to bring humanitarian design into critical conversation with postcolonial theory, which investigates colonialist discourses and power structures to frame the postcolonial structures of settlement, development and control that endure.

Today the preponderance of international aid flows from economically and politically dominant, developed countries to poorer developing countries. It does not seem to be an unrelated coincidence that many of those nations and regions currently economically and ecologically vulnerable, and therefore the greatest recipients of humanitarian efforts, are formerly colonised lands. The reasons are not exclusively political, for example, colonies in the tropical zone were established because of environmental conditions that favoured cash crops, such as tobacco, tea and sugar. But this zone also has a high risk of extreme weather events like tropical storms, flooding, tsunamis and earthquakes. The lack of wealth, infrastructure and other protections against natural disasters may well be linked back to the zone's postcolonial state. The complex histories and power dynamics between those who typically deliver and those who receive aid, raises the questionable assumption of a binary and, apparently, unidirectional flow of resources from rich to poor, global north to global south, former colonisers to the formerly colonised.

Antonio Gramsci, the Italian scholar whose early 20th-century writings have been instrumental for postcolonial studies, posited the relationship between the politically and economically dominant north of Italy, and the resource-rich south at unification as colonial-like; resource extraction from the south was, monetised in the north, something which is echoed in economic conflicts within and between other regions. While a critique of international aid as a neocolonial project is clearly framed as interactions between former colonial and colonised nations, we would do well to remember that similar dynamics occur within other countries, as Gramsci discussed. There are many distressing examples of urgent need within politically powerful, stable, economically dominant countries; post-Hurricane Katrina New Orleans, southern Appalachia and Detroit, come to the fore as examples of crisis within the United States. Postcolonialist theory points specifically to international forms of domination, but we may see similarities in patterns of engagement in domestic and international aid exchanges.

Aid as Neocolonialism via Authority versus Power or Aid as Authority

Postcolonialism is a mode of thought that interrogates the production of knowledge and power by former colonisers, particularly the West, attempting to dismantle the dominant cultural discourse that persists. Historically, colonialism can be defined as a directional relationship wherein power and knowledge were imposed and imported by a dominant force upon a subject. This inequitable power dynamic is important to remember, especially

Zorange Housing, Port-au-Prince, Haiti, 2013. Housing development from the late 20th century in Zorange exemplifies government design executed outside of existing organic developments. © Irene E Brisson.

left: Katherine Dunham Cultural Center, Port-au-Prince, Haiti, 2014. Recently opened, the cultural centre hybridises vernacular forms reminiscent of thatching styles with contemporary architectural forms. © Irene E Brisson.

below: Hotel Oloffson, Port-au-Prince, Haiti, 2012. The hotel is an example of the French colonial gingerbread style, which was adopted by Haitian architects and builders. © Irene E Brisson.

for designers. Cultural influences flow both ways and the histories and cultures of the formerly colonised are also integral to the former colonisers. The immense production, resource exploitation and technical developments of the colonial era changed the entire world — and arguably created the modern age.

Colonial power was implemented and supported by force, either by military occupation, enslavement or economic dependency. The inequitable and displaced production of power propagates itself through authority regardless of the presence of physical force. Key scholars, such as Edward Said, have stated the establishment of authority was at the heart of colonisation, which endures in the postcolonial era and haunts humanitarian design:

> There is nothing mysterious or natural about authority. It is formed, irradiated, disseminated; it is instrumental, it is persuasive; it has status, it establishes canons of taste and value; it is virtually indistinguishable from certain ideas it dignifies as true, and from traditions, perceptions, and judgments it forms, transmits, reproduces. Above all, authority can, indeed must, be analyzed.[5]

As such, explicit military and political occupations are perhaps the least effective and not the only means of establishing authority. As professionals, the architect's stock-in-trade is to be an authority on the subject matter of building and designing. When noncoercive professional knowledge is not inherently problematic, but when humanitarian design acts with authority it must be interrogated — specifically we must question the legitimacy of authority in an environment of crisis. If disasters are explicitly or implicitly read as failures — though the failure of what or by whom may go unspoken or analysed — then aid can take the form of benevolent paternalism as it imports skills or knowledge perceived as having been lacking. The professional knowledge that the humanitarian designer brings may be very much needed in a given situation, but it is not entering a vacuum and, as stated by Said above, it carries the 'traditions, perceptions, and judgement'[6] of the cultures of its production. Even when unintentional, aid can become a 'humane' conduit for the imposition of foreign systems of thought, reproducing a colonial-like relationship. As Said identifies, postcolonialism and the continued 'othering' of the non-Western world is not marked by explicit violence: 'the influence of ideas, of institutions, and of other persons works not through domination but by what [Antonio] Gramsci calls consent'.[7] The fact that a location in the midst of crisis has urgent and unmet needs sets up a particularly delicate situation wherein consent may be given for or the introduction of foreign methods may be accepted with less criticism than in a more stable situation. The culture of need can support a consensual and problematically one-directional exchange of knowledge and power.

The humanitarian project, as a whole, expands well beyond design, but the participation of architects becomes directly and tangibly written into the urban fabric of nations, so our responsibility is great. For example, Bruce Nussbaum, writing on fastcodesign.com asked: 'Is the new humanitarian design coming out of the US and Europe being perceived through post-colonial eyes as colonialism? Are the American and European designers

Ducis, Haiti, 2012. In this community planning meeting local stakeholders, local professional architects and American design students discuss a master plan strategy from at least three different points of view. © Irene E Brisson.

presuming too much in their attempt to do good?'[8] He answered himself, 'yes – although …', and suggests as a solution that local designers, as available, are better prepared to solve local problems, but his question set off an impassioned argument within the field about the role of foreign designers in developing countries.

It is critical to ask who and where are the local designers and are they being supported, educated and included in development efforts? Given the activity in public interest design within the United States among those with a strong design education, it is unlikely that there will be a cessation of humanitarian design activity by external actors, and arguably it should not cease. To be responsible practitioners we must pose these questions to ourselves time and again, and remember that doing something is not always doing good; first do no harm.

At the initiation of every building project there is a primary decision to create: on previously unbuilt land, to demolish and rebuild on a used site, to reuse in whole or part an existing structure. When working in a post-disaster or development situation the same choices are presented to the architect, or the scaled-up corollaries for planning, but the implications of power and knowledge are shifted. The designer is in a powerful position to consider the implications and relative success of various modes of engagement and physical interventions that build on historical traditions, build over damaged or demolished structures or salvage and build with existing forms and infrastructure. Hybridisation of these basic categories is the most likely outcome of a critical practice.

Self-criticism must not freeze one's ability to act in a complex global culture; the work of architects and planners is literally that of creating places and the work is embedded in particular contexts. For this reason, we must recognise our roles in global power structures and question the assumptions of culture, function and aesthetics underpinning design. The perspective of postcolonialism is not to be used as a continuation of a binary worldview of Western and Other, but rather as a model of a complex and ambiguous world that profoundly challenges the status quo.[9] We are in search of a guide not to utopian but productive relationships. Antonio Gramsci, whose thinking has influenced much of postcolonial discourse posited: 'The starting-point of critical elaboration is the consciousness of what one really is, and is "knowing thyself" as a product of the historical process to date, which has deposited in you an infinity of traces, without leaving an inventory … therefore it is imperative at the outset to compile such an inventory.'[10]

Both a great strength and weakness of design practice is the emphasis on acting with as much information as available, but without excessive delay for answers that have not yet been reached. We must consider each place and time as the unique amalgam of social, cultural, economic, political and other forces that it is. The conception of an 'Other', a 'non-Western world', the 'colonised' has been centuries in the making and postcolonial theory sets as its project to question and reveal the historical and current simplifications of places and peoples to these homogenous categories. Following Gramsci's lead, designers must begin with work on compiling an inventory of their historical traces and social biases, as well as all those forces present at the site of the work. This is likely to uncover great injustices but, rather than freezing with potential culpability, this finer resolution and critical distance will hopefully lead to more sensitive and integrated design work. With this inventory – albeit imperfect – the designer must set to work.

Notes

1   Barry Bergdoll, *European Architecture 1750–1890*, Oxford University Press (Oxford), 2000, p 99.
2   adAPT Request for Proposals (nd) in *NYC Department of Housing Preservation & Development*, www1.nyc.gov/site/hpd/developers/adapt-nyc-rfp.page (accessed 10 January 2015).
3   Charles Jencks, *The Language of Post-Modern Architecture*, Rizzoli (New York), 1984, p 9.
4   Christian Hubert and Ioanna Theocharopoulou, 'Humanitarian Design: Notes for a Definition', *Ground Rules for Humanitarian Design*, (eds) Alice Min Soo Chun and Irene E Brisson, John Wiley & Sons (Chichester), 2015, pp 20–35.
5   Edward W Said, *Orientalism*, Pantheon Books (New York, NY), 1978, pp 19–20.
6   Ibid.
7   Said, *Orientalism*, pp 6–7.
8   Bruce Nussbaum, 'Is Humanitarian Design the New Imperialism?', Fast Company, 6 July 2010, www.fastcodesign.com/1661859/is-humanitarian-design-the-new-imperialism (accessed 10 January 2015).
9   For elaboration see Homi K Bhabha, 'Post-colonialism' *The Dictionary of Human Geography*, (ed) RJ Johnston, Blackwell Publishing (Oxford), 2009, p 561.
10 Antonio Gramsci, *Selections from The Prison Notebooks*, (trans and ed) Quintin Hoare and Geoffrey Nowell Smith, International Publishers (New York), 1971, p 324.

Select Bibliography

- Abrams, Charles. 'Squatter Settlements: The Problem and the Opportunity', *Ideas and Methods Exchange*, no 63, Office of International Affairs, Dept of Housing and Urban Development (Washington DC), 1966

- Appadurai, Arjun. 'Deep Democracy: Urban Governmentality and the Horizon of Politics', *Environment and Urbanization*, vol 13, no 2, International Institute for Environment and Development (London), October 2001

- Aquilino, Marie Jeannine (ed). *Beyond Shelter: Architecture for Crisis*, Thames & Hudson (London), 2011

- Bell, Bryan and Katie Wakeford (eds). *Expanding Architecture: Design As Activism*, Metropolis Books (New York, NY), 2008

- Borden, Gail Peter and Michael Meredith (eds). *Matter: Material Processes In Architectural Production*, Routledge (New York, NY), 2012

- Brenner, Neil. *Cities for People, Not for Profit: Critical Urban Theory and the Right to the City*, Routledge (Abingdon), 2012

- Charlesworth, Esther. *Humanitarian Architecture: 15 Stories of Architects Working After Disaster*, Routledge (Abingdon), 2014

- Dean, Andrea Oppenheimer and Timothy Hursley. *Rural Studio: Samuel Mockbee and an Architecture of Decency*, Princeton Architectural Press (New York, NY), 2002

- Duany, Andres and Jeff Speck with Mike Lydon. *The Smart Growth Manual*, McGraw-Hill (New York, NY), 2010

- Gehl, Jan and Birgitte Svarre. *How to Study Public Life*, Island Press (Washington DC), 2013

- Lai, Jimenez. *Citizens of No Place: an Architectural Graphic Novel*, 1st edition, Princeton Architectural Press (New York, NY), 2012

- Lepik, Andres. *Small Scale, Big Change: New Architectures of Social Engagement*, Museum of Modern Art (New York, NY), 2010

- Lynch, Kevin. *Managing a Sense of Region*, MIT Press (Cambridge, MA), 1976

- Lynch, Kevin. *The Image of the City*, MIT Press (Cambridge, MA), 1960

- McDonough, William and Michael Braungart. *Cradle to Cradle: Remaking the Way We Make Things*, North Point Press (New York, NY), 2002

- Mostavi, Mohsen with Gareth Doherty (eds). *Ecological Urbanism*, Lars Müller Publishers (Baden, Switzerland), 2010

- Neuwirth, Robert. *Shadow Cities: A Billion Squatters, A New Urban World*, Routledge (New York, NY), 2005

- Oliver, Paul. *Dwellings: the Vernacular House World Wide*, Phaidon Press (London), 2003

- Papanek, Victor J. *Design for the Real World: Human Ecology and Social Change*, 2nd edition, Chicago Review Press (Chicago, IL), 2009

- Pred, Allen. *Making Histories and Constructing Human Geographies: The Local Transformation of Practice, Power Relations, and Consciousness*, Westview Press (Boulder, CO), 1990

- Rudofsky, Bernard. *Architecture Without Architects: an Introduction to Non-pedigreed Architecture*, Doubleday (Garden City, NY), 1964

- Said, Edward W. *Orientalism*, Pantheon Books (New York, NY), 1978

- Schumacher, Ernst Friedrich. *Small is Beautiful*, Blond & Briggs (London), 1973

- Smith, Cynthia E. *Design for the Other 90%*, Cooper-Hewitt, National Design Museum, Smithsonian Organization (New York, NY), 2007

- Stohr, Kate and Cameron Sinclair (eds). *Design Like You Give a Damn: Building Change from the Ground Up*, Abrams (New York, NY) 2012

- Tilder, Lisa and Beth Blostein (eds). *Design Ecologies: Essays On the Nature of Design*, Princeton Architectural Press (New York, NY), 2010

Index

Ground Rules for Humanitarian Design is the eighth AD Reader. This reader series from John Wiley & Sons, the publishers of *Architectural Design* (*AD*), invites influential architectural thinkers and educators to compile anthologies on core topics of study for students of architecture and design.

Previous titles in the AD Reader series include:

The Digital Turn in Architecture 1992–2012

Edited by Mario Carpo

978-1-119-95174-2 (pb)
978-1-119-95175-9 (hb)

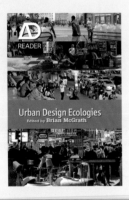

Urban Design Ecologies

Edited by Brian McGrath

978-0-470-97405-6 (pb)
978-0-470-97406-3 (hb)

Manufacturing the Bespoke
Making and Prototyping Architecture

Edited by Bob Sheil

978-0-470-66582-4 (pb)
978-0-470-66583-1 (hb)

Computational Design Thinking

Edited by Achim Menges and Sean Ahlquist

978-0-470-66565-7 (pb)
978-0-470-66570-1 (hb)

The Post-Modern Reader

Edited by Charles Jencks
(Second Edition)

978-0-470-74866-4 (pb)
978-0-470-74867-1 (hb)

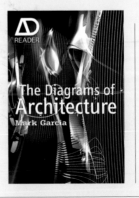

The Diagrams of Architecture

Edited by Mark Garcia

978-0-470-51945-5 (pb)
978-0-470-51944-8 (hb)

Space Reader
Heterogeneous Space in Architecture

Edited by Michael Hensel, Christopher Hight and Achim Menges

978-0-470-51943-1 (pb)
978-0-470-51942-4 (hb)